A Reading Scrapbook

About the author

David Cliffe was born in Macclesfield, Cheshire, in 1946. Early influences included the Church of England, the open countryside, reading the local paper, and the public library. He studied English at Leeds University – the history of the English language, medieval English Literature, folklore, and dialect. After a postgraduate diploma in librarianship, he set about looking for work, and Reading Public Libraries was the first institution to say 'yes'. He was employed in public libraries in Reading and Berkshire for the whole of his career in paid employment in a variety of posts. It was towards the end of this time that he was able to devote time to the local studies collection in Reading Central Library, which made this book possible.

His career in publishing local history began in 1978, with a guide book to Reading, and has gathered momentum following his retirement, with publications about Reading, and about Macclesfield, the town where he grew up. For some years he wrote a weekly local history column for the *Reading Chronicle*, and he now writes monthly for the *Caversham Bridge* newspaper.

For many years now he has been Chairman of the Berkshire Local History Association, and of The History of Reading Society, writing for their newsletters and journals, giving talks, leading walks, and organising visits. In 2024 he was honoured to receive an award from the British Association for Local History, for his 'outstanding individual contribution for his skills in promoting the history of Reading through his work in the Local Studies Library, and support of others in the field of local history'.

Also published by Two Rivers Press

Reading Quaker Meeting: A history by Geoff Sawers and Izzy Brimelow
Over Water, Under Ground by Fahad Sperinck
Reading Gaol: A short history by Peter Stoneley
The Happy Prince by Oscar Wilde, illustrated by Sally Castle
Coley Talking by Margaret Ounsley
When Reading Really Rocked by Adrian Moulton, Mike Warth & Austin Matthews
Bricks & Brickwork in Reading: Patterns & Polychromy by Adam Sowan
Reading's Influential Women by Terry Dixon & Linda Saul
The Art and History of Whiteknights edited by Jenny Halstead
The Art of Peter Hay by John Froy with Martin Andrews
Signs of the Times: Reading's Memorials by Malcolm Summers
Rural Reading by Adrian Lawson & Geoff Sawers
The Constitutionals: A work of fiction by Peter Robinson
Islamic Art Meets British Flowers by Hadil Tamim and Adrian Lawson
Reading Abbey and the Abbey Quarter by Peter Durrant & John Painter
Reading's Bayeux Tapestry by Reading Museum
Silchester: Life on the Dig by Jenny Halstead & Michael Fulford
The Writing on the Wall by Peter Kruschwitz
Allen W. Seaby: Art and Nature by Martin Andrews & Robert Gillmor
Fox Talbot & the Reading Establishment by Martin Andrews
All Change at Reading by Adam Sowan
The Reading Quiz Book by Adam Sowan
Caversham Court Gardens: A Heritage Guide by Friends of Caversham Court Gardens
Down by the River: The Thames and Kennet in Reading by Gillian Clark
The Stranger in Reading by John Man, edited by Adam Sowan

Other books by David Cliffe

The Stranger in Reading: an Unofficial Guide (Reading Libraries, 1978 and 1980)
Roots and Branches: the Centenary History of Battle and Caversham Libraries
    (Two Rivers Press, 2007)
Praise in the Heights: the Centenary History of Caversham Heights Methodist Church
    (Caversham Heights Methodist Church, 2009)
Picture Palace to Penny Plunge: Reading's Cinemas (Two Rivers Press, 2017)
The Street-Names of Macclesfield (Self-published, 2018)
Superstitions of the Macclesfield Area (Self-published, 2020)
Abbot Cook to Zero Degrees: an A–Z of Reading's Pubs and Breweries
    (with John Dearing and Evelyn Williams. The History of Reading Society, 2021)
Treacle Town: Life and Tradition in Macclesfield (Self-published, 2022)

First published in the UK in 2024 by Two Rivers Press
7 Denmark Road, Reading RG1 5PA
www.tworiverspress.com

Copyright © Two Rivers Press 2024
Copyright © in text David Cliffe 2024

The right of the author to be identified as the author of the work has been asserted by him in accordance with the Copyright, Designs and Patents Act of 1988.

All rights reserved. No part of this publication may be reproduced, stored in or introduced into a retrieval system, or transmitted, in any form, or by any means (electronic, mechanical, photocopying, recording or otherwise) without the prior written permission of the publisher.

ISBN 978-1-915048-14-1

1 2 3 4 5 6 7 8 9

Two Rivers Press is represented in the UK by Inpress Ltd
and distributed by BookSource, Glasgow.

Cover design by Nadja Robinson
Text design by Nadja Robinson and typeset in Parisine

Printed and bound in Great Britain by Short Run Press, Exeter

A Reading Scrapbook

A history of the town
through printed ephemera

David Cliffe

Introduction and acknowledgements | 1

I. Markets and auctions | 3
II. Shopping | 12
III. Department stores | 37
IV. Trades and services | 45
V. Manufacturing | 73
VI. Transport | 88
VII. Restaurants, hotels, pubs and breweries | 104
VIII. Churches and religion | 112
IX. Clubs and societies | 118
X. People | 126
XI. Stage, screen and radio | 135
XII. Music and dance | 154
XIII. Sport | 162
XIV. Royalty, festivals and processions | 171
XV. Crime and punishment | 193
XVI. Local government | 198
XVII. War and peace | 218

Reading printers | 243
Sources | 248
Illustrations | 250

Introduction and acknowledgements

This book shows how the people of Reading lived, over the last 300 years and more, using ephemera as the evidence. It looks at how they made a living, what they did for entertainment, and the tribulations which some of them had to endure.

'Ephemera' has been taken to mean pieces of printed paper, cardboard, and in one instance, silk, which were intended to be used for a limited period only. In some cases this was once only, when they were advertisements, receipted bills, tickets to travel or tickets of admission. Some of them were useful for a whole year, such as calendars, and others were valid for an indeterminate period, such as the banknotes issued by local banks. I have not included directories or newspapers, which contain untold riches, even though they were only intended to be kept until the next edition appeared. Nor have I included hand-written letters and postcards. Most of the ephemera included here are items that happen to have survived, and to have found their way into one of two collections.

One of these belongs to the Department of Typography & Graphic Communication at the University of Reading, in Whiteknights Park. It contains many examples of the work of Reading printers, and is an educational resource. The other one is in Reading Central Library. During the last five years or so of my time in paid employment, I was working there as a librarian and was given the time to sort through the large and rich local studies collection which had been amassed over many years. The books, pamphlets and journals were added to the online catalogue, and several thousand items in the illustrations collection were catalogued and scanned and made viewable on the website. But it soon became apparent that the collection also contained many fascinating items which could only be described as ephemera, usually found in old envelopes and boxes because no-one had known what to do with them. There was not the time, alas, for me to catalogue and scan these items of ephemera, but this book will give a good idea of what is contained in the collection. It is housed in a series of boxes, roughly sorted by subject.

I have tried here to illustrate the variety of items and subjects represented in both collections. The items vary in size, from a trading stamp or ticket to a poster, and from a leaflet to a booklet. This inevitably means that it has not always been possible to make the whole of a document legible on the page of a book. I could easily have written the book again using different examples. Goodness knows how many more interesting items have survived, in the collections of other institutions and individuals, and especially in The Royal Berkshire Archives and in Reading Museum.

The final section in the book contains information on the Reading printers whose work is illustrated here. Most of them are 'jobbing' printers, carrying out minor contracts for local firms and individuals, though Reading had one or two firms with a nationwide reputation. The subject of printing in the town is worthy of a book in itself.

It was fortunate that during the early part of 2020 I had managed to photograph or scan many of the documents represented here. It meant that during the restrictions necessitated by the COVID-19 pandemic, I was able to do much of the writing. Access to the online British Newspaper Archive also proved a boon. It answered many of the questions which arose, though not all of them. Once I was free to browse the Central Library's collection, and to visit The Royal Berkshire Archives, I was able to do the final checking.

Thanks are due to Barbara Morris, who is a volunteer at the Centre for Ephemera Studies, and who suggested that I might like to write something along these lines. At Reading Central Library, thanks are due to the Manager, Simon Smith, and to Katie Amos, who now looks after the local studies collection. And at The Royal Berkshire Archives, Lisa Spurrier gave me good advice. Thanks are due to all three of these institutions.

Of the private individuals who have lent material for the book I should mention the late Gerry Westall, the late John Whitehead, the late Norman Wicks, and Alan Bosher and Thomas Macey, who are very much with us.

I don't know of any other book which looks at the history of a particular town through the ephemera it produced. The increasing use of online electronic documents in the twenty-first century probably means that in the future, it will be impossible to produce an updated edition. Putting the book together has shed rays of light on how people lived in the past, and my hope is that it will inform, intrigue and entertain present-day readers, as it has entertained me.

David Cliffe, April 2023

I. Markets and auctions

Towns might be said to be the 'invention' of the Romans, who in occupying much of the island of Great Britain established a series of settlements, with a network of new roads to connect them – occasionally including pre-existing settlements such as that at Silchester. Roman towns were centres of trade, with market places, and Silchester was the nearest of them. The archaeological record suggests that the area which was to become Reading was only lightly settled.

In the historical record the first mention of the name 'Reading' appears in the *Anglo-Saxon Chronicle* for 871. The old centre was around St Mary's Church, with the market place outside its west door – the area now known as St Mary's Butts.

The establishment of Reading Abbey, to the east, in 1121, brought about the expansion of the town, with new roads and bridges. It was the Abbey which now regulated the markets and fairs, and which collected the tolls from the traders. A new market place was laid out, to the north connecting to New Street – which was to become Friar Street. To the south, it connected via a new bridge over the River Kennet, and a new wide street called London Street, with the road towards London. The bridge, on the site of the present-day High Bridge, was the bridge by the hythe – the main wharf for the town, where the Abbey also collected its dues. The new market place, conveniently by the main Abbey gate, remained as the site of Reading's street market until 1974.

Markets were held on fixed days of the week, the main one being on Saturdays, mainly for food, with a secondary one on Wednesdays. Fairs were held on set days of the year, usually around a saint's day, and were occasions when 'foreigners,' who were not citizens of Reading, were allowed to trade in the town. When the Abbey was in control, there were four fairs a year, and in 1834, when John Doran published his history of the town, there were still four, but on different dates – 2 February, 1 May, 25 July, 21 September. Some of them were held over four days. The July fair, St James's, was for livestock, and the fair in September was the cheese fair, and the time for hiring farm servants. By the seventeenth century, these gatherings were so well attended that they had migrated from the streets to The Forbury.

Opposite page:
1. The 'Middle Row' was a row of shops which ran along the middle of Broad Street, which were demolished around 1850.

The year 1539 brought great changes, when the Crown seized the Abbey and its property, executed the Abbot and dispersed the monks. The markets and fairs continued, but with the Crown collecting the tolls, until 1560, when the town obtained a charter, and the corporation could run things. Trading continued in the open, but there would have been a covered area, presumably near the street now called The Butter Market. On warm sunny days this would have been needed to prevent the butter from melting.

The first indoor market for general produce opened in 1800, and John Doran describes the building as it was in 1834. It was a 'long square' covered with a light roof supported by pillars, with entrances in the Market Place and Broad Street. The Broad Street entrance was a handsome stone portico. Half of the building was occupied by butchers' stalls, and the other half was 'allotted for the use of market women, who come here with various articles of produce.' The fishmongers and other traders were outside the building, near to the portico in Broad Street. The Clerk of the Market lived just inside this portico, in a house on pillars. This house was remembered by Pat Smart from a time just before the outbreak of war in 1939 (see Sources, p. 249). Over the years, the building must have proved unsatisfactory, and in 1853 a Reading Corporation Act was obtained, allowing a new covered market and corn exchange to be built. The new market and corn exchange opened on 23 June 1855.

The buying and selling of corn in Reading must have been important long before a building for that purpose was thought necessary. John Doran says that the corn market was conducted on a 'spacious open piece of ground' near the Church of St Laurence, and that the corporation exacted a toll of a pint of corn from each sack that was traded there. The new building would enable the Borough to exercise even tighter control – as stated on the notice over the page, the Reading Corporation Markets Act of 1853 made it illegal to sell corn anywhere in the Borough except for the appointed place or places. The other Berkshire towns in the corn-growing areas were not slow to follow: Wallingford in 1856, Wantage in 1859, Newbury 1862 and Hungerford in 1871.

A competition was held for the design of the corn exchange, and for a new building for the covered market. There were two finalists, one of them being the Borough Surveyor, Francis Hawkes. The Central Library has a copy of his entry. In the end it was decided that both finalists, Mr Hawkes and J. B. Clacy, should carry out the contract jointly.

THE NEW MARKET

FOR

VEGETABLES, FRUIT, POULTRY, FISH, EGGS, BUTTER, FLOWERS, HARDWARE, &c., &c.,

IS NOW

OPEN DAILY

From 6 a.m. to 4 p.m., and on SATURDAYS till 9 p.m.

Entrances from the Market Place & Middle Row.

Application for Stalls, &c., to be made to JAMES KNIGHT, Collector of Tolls.

PRINTED AT THE *READING MERCURY* STEAM PRESS.

BOROUGH OF READING.

CORN MARKET.

The Council of the Borough of Reading, in the County of Berks, having given Notice that the NEW CORN EXCHANGE and MARKETS WILL BE OPENED for public use on the *Twenty-third day of June* next, deem it right to call the attention of persons engaged in buying and selling Corn, and others having business at or frequenting the Corn Market, to the following Section of the "*Reading Corporation Markets Act, 1853.*"

SECTION 12.—"And after such Corn Exchange is open for use, Corn "shall not at any time be pitched for sale within the Borough, except at "such places as the Corporation from time to time in that behalf shall "appoint. And every person who offends in that respect shall, for every "such offence, forfeit a sum not exceeding Forty Shillings. And any "person who, after such Corn Exchange is opened for use, shall, on any "market day or other day, sell or expose for sale by sample any Corn or "Grain in any place within the limits of this Act, except in the Corn "Exchange or such places as the Corporation shall from time to time "appoint, or except in his own dwelling place or shop, shall for every "such offence forfeit a sum not exceeding Forty Shillings."

And Notice is hereby given, that all persons acting contrary to the said Statute will be proceeded against for the Penalties thereby imposed.

Dated this 31st day of May, one thousand eight hundred and fifty-five.

By order of the Council,

J. J. BLANDY, Town Clerk.

Opposite page:
2. The corporation keeps control of the markets and the tolls arising from them.

The corporation decided to build a new corn exchange in the 1930s, which was opened on Caversham Road in 1936 – at what turned out to be the end of the era when corn was traded in this way. The architect of the new exchange was a Reading man, Eric Steward Smith, and it was a remarkable building, framed by lofty elliptical arches of reinforced concrete with large windows, high up, to admit plenty of daylight. There was a glass dome over the entrance. Its days as a corn exchange must have been limited; from 1946 the building was the Majestic Ballroom, and later it was the Top Rank Club, where bingo was played. In the 1980s it reverted to being a dance hall, now called Washington Heights, which in the 1990s changed its name to RG1. After closure in 2002, the building was empty, apart from squatters, until demolition, in 2005. On its site, and that of the neighbouring Duke of Edinburgh public house, there is now a block of flats.

The old corn exchange became a part of the indoor market, until the area was devastated by enemy bombing in 1943. After the war, the area was redeveloped as the Market Way Arcade.

The market hall and corn exchange of 1855 were connected to Friar Street by the Market Arcade promoted by Alderman J. C. Fidler which opened in 1894. After the bombing of the area in 1943, the area was redeveloped, with the Bristol and West Arcade, lined with lock-up shops and cafes running from Friar Street (where the Bristol and West Building Society had its Reading branch) to Broad Street. The imposing portico on Broad Street was unfortunately removed. A passageway, Market Way, joined it from the Market Place, through the old entrance to the Corn Exchange, which still has its clock with a bell-cote above.

These walkways were allowed to become run down, and were eventually closed. A branch of J. Sainsbury was built on the site of the Broad Street entrance, probably meaning that the convenient walk-way will never be reinstated. At the time of writing (2023) various planning applications have been submitted for the redevelopment of the site, but work has yet to begin.

A designated livestock market had been under consideration by the corporation for some time, but the initiative was seized by a private company, who opened the site in Great Knollys Street in 1850, some years before the markets in the town centre.

Since, under a charter granted by Queen Elizabeth I, the corporation had been granted the right to hold markets within the Borough, the Cattle Market

3. The Reading Cattle Market Act received royal assent on 15 July 1850, after the issue of this certificate.

Company had to obtain an Act of Parliament to hold a market, under which it had to pay £5 a year to the corporation for the privilege.

The share certificate illustrated here was issued on 1 May 1850, which makes the numbering of the three shares, Nos. 6–8, puzzling, since the shares had been on offer from July 1849. It is signed by Rupert Clarke, solicitor to the Company, and Alexander Dickson and James Haslam, two of the Provisional Directors – provisional because at the time the certificate was printed, the Act of Parliament had not gone through.

Before the establishment of the Cattle Market, there had been a livestock market at Loddon Bridge, and some animals from the area had been taken directly to the Smithfield Market in London. The market at Reading was built

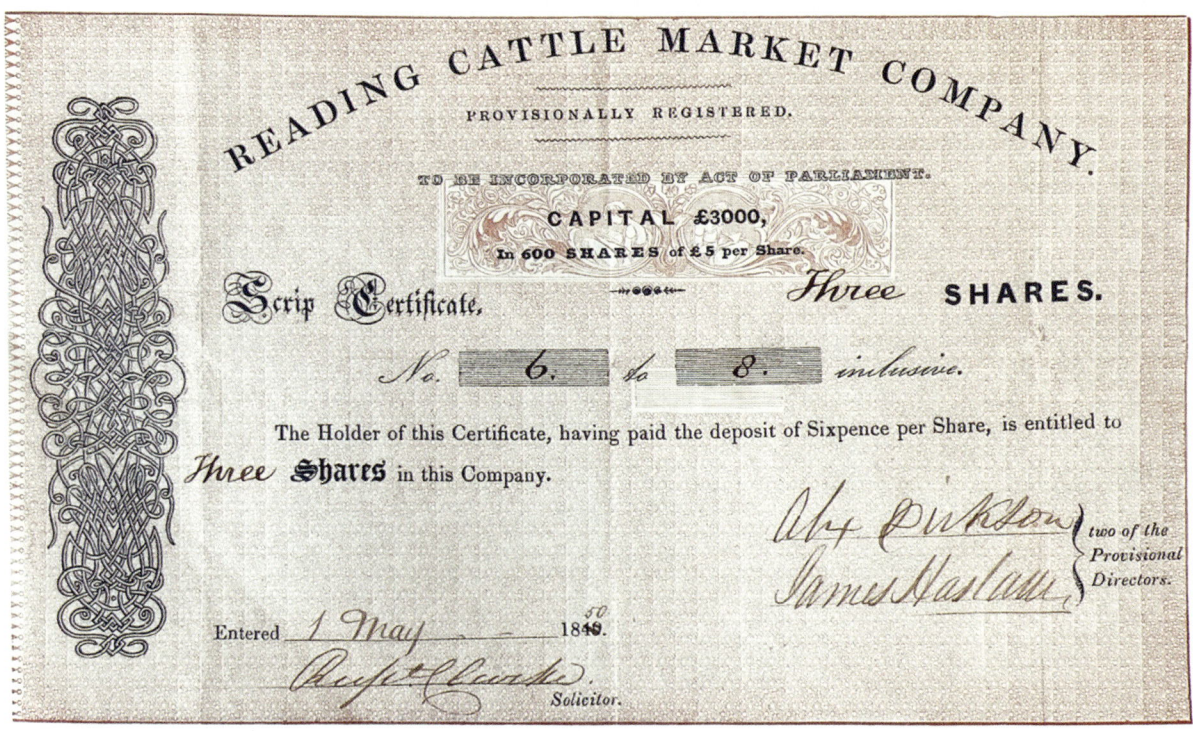

on the Portman Brook Meadow, and a field called The Cricket Field, both of them parts of the Knollys estate. There was some debate over the days on which markets should be held. The decision to hold them on Mondays caused some dismay, and correspondents to the local paper feared that it would cause 'a desecration of the Sabbath Day by those who live at even a moderate distance from Reading, and are disposed to send their cattle there.'

The site chosen for the market was close to the railway, and many older Reading people will remember the two roads running up the slope, on either side of the Caversham Road railway bridge, one labelled 'Abattoirs Road' and the other, 'Cattle Pens.'

Over the next 50 years, the Cattle Market buildings had deteriorated, and by 1903, the corporation was thinking of taking them over. The Company asked for £11,000, but the corporation quibbled. In the end, £8,200 was settled on, and the corporation sought to borrow £9,200 from the central government, the additional £1,000 being for rebuilding and repairs. An inspector was sent to Reading for a Local Government Board of Enquiry, the site was visited, and the loan was agreed. The purchase was completed in 1904.

It is easy to forget that until the mid-twentieth century, Reading was very much a country town. Besides the markets, there was a large firm of seedsmen, a firm making milking machines, and a university with a school of agriculture and its own farms.

From its 1850 opening, the Christmas Fatstock Show was an annual event at the Cattle Market, at which farmers got together, in a spirit of (hopefully) friendly rivalry, for the showing, judging, and the awarding of cups, trophies and cash prizes for the best animals. In 1991, pigs had to be in the show yard by 9.30am, and cattle and sheep by 10, when the judging began.

Some of the names of the awards listed in the booklet overleaf are very much connected with the local farming community – for instance, the Leonard Sutton Cup, which was presented by Colebrook and Company. Mr Sutton was from Sutton and Sons, the seedsmen, and Colebrook's were the butchers and graziers with a shop in Broad Street, Reading, and shops in other nearby towns. The Alf Meade Cup had been donated by Mr Meade MBE, the meat wholesaler, whose motto was: 'You must succeed with meat by Meade.' The

4. The programme of the last of the fatstock shows, after 141 years.

Lumley Thimbleby Perpetual Challenge Cup recalls the firm of Thimbleby and Shorland, who for many years have been the auctioneers at the Cattle Market.

The carcases of the winning entries at the show would doubtless once have been proudly hung in the windows of butchers in the area, decorated with colourful rosettes to denote the prize. In fact, before today's more stringent food hygiene requirements, and the squeamishness of customers, the sides of beef, lamb and pork were often hung outside the shops, as old photographs attest.

On the day after the 1991 show, the Fatstock Show Dinner was held at The Travellers Rest in Henley Road, Caversham, with tickets at £15, including wine.

Livestock sales dwindled in the 1980s, and this show appears to be the last one. The market still holds auctions of furniture, antiques and collectibles, and occasional sales of horse-drawn carriages and contractors' plant and equipment, and twice a month, on a Saturday, a farmers' market is held.

Another kind of market where auctions were held were the 'repositories' for horses, and horse-drawn vehicles, in the days before motor road transport. According to the catalogue, part of which is illustrated here, Robert Tompkins' Royal Horse and Carriage Repository was established in 1856. Presumably Mr Tompkins had received permission to call it the 'Royal' Horse Repository, and to display the royal coat of arms on its advertising.

This kind of establishment must have been in great demand, and besides the Tompkins Repository, eight others appear in Reading directories of the time, including Michael Donovan's (later Oliver Dixon's) in Crescent Road, and Targett's in London Road.

Tompkins had his repository on Friar Street, on the site later occupied, 1921–1999 by the Central Cinema (later the ABC Central, the Cannon and the MGM). The cinema in turn was replaced by the Ibis and Novotel Hotels. But these Saturday sales were held at the Cattle Market in Great Knollys Street.

Another of his enterprises was to build the Queen's Hall in Valpy Street, a large public hall which could seat 750. A section of it still stands, occupied by the Valpy Street Bar and Bistro, which displays his initials on the gable. After his death in 1897, the hall was sold to Petty's the printers (see p. 246).

5. Robert Tompkins was also a keen sportsman who rode to hounds and organised Reading Races when they were held on King's Meadow.

On this particular Saturday in 1889, nine carriages were on offer – wagonettes, buggies, phaetons, carts, and a hansom cab – along with different kinds of harness. There were 27 horses, all with their ages and heights (in hands and inches) given, and with comments such as 'quiet to ride,' 'good trapper,' 'splendid fencer,' 'good hunter,' and 'carries a lady.' The other livestock included five dogs, eleven rabbits, cockerels, hens, bantams, ducks and drakes, turkeys, pheasants – and a talking magpie in a cage, which sold for six shillings.

The Royal Horse and Carriage Repository failed to change with the times, and went out of business in 1912.

II. Shopping

Many invoices and receipts, some of them with attractive headers, have survived from old Reading shops, and a selection is illustrated here. By the nineteenth century the town was the shopping centre for people from miles around, and so it has continued.

Originally, shops were places where goods were made, as well as being sold, and in the Middle Ages there were shoemakers, tailors, drapers, cabinet makers and cutlers, among the tradesmen. Later, shops usually sold things which had been produced elsewhere.

Reading was never a great centre for shopping arcades, where shoppers could stroll and look at the displays, protected from the weather, but the Harris Arcade, of 1929, between Friar Street and Station Road, survives. The Market Arcade of the 1890s was destroyed in a bombing raid in 1943, was rebuilt after the war as the Bristol and West Arcade, but has been closed once more, pending a promised redevelopment.

Leading on from shopping arcades came shopping malls, or shopping centres. The Butts Centre opened in 1972, later re-named the Broad Street Mall though it wasn't in Broad Street. At first, on a lower level, it had a Fountain Court with fountains playing and a restaurant. The short-lived Friars Walk, off Friar Street, opened in 1974, and closed in 2004. Then in 1999, the vast Oracle shopping centre arrived, increasing the town's retail floor space by a third, and putting it into the top ten towns and cities in the country as a place to shop.

By this time, Reading was said to be the country's 'average' town, a place for market research and for testing new products.

Of the nineteenth-century and early twentieth-century shops illustrated here, only Hickie's music shop survives.

We begin our survey with Philip Davies, wholesale and retail grocer and tea dealer, who signed this bill in December 1840. His first appearance in local papers suggests he had started the business in 1831. By 1850, the shop was being run by Davies and Son, but it was not mentioned after 1852. The 'Rev. Mr. Hasker,' who had paid 2s. 6d. for three pints of Patent Imperial Oil, must have been the Rev. William Hasker, Vicar of Baughurst.

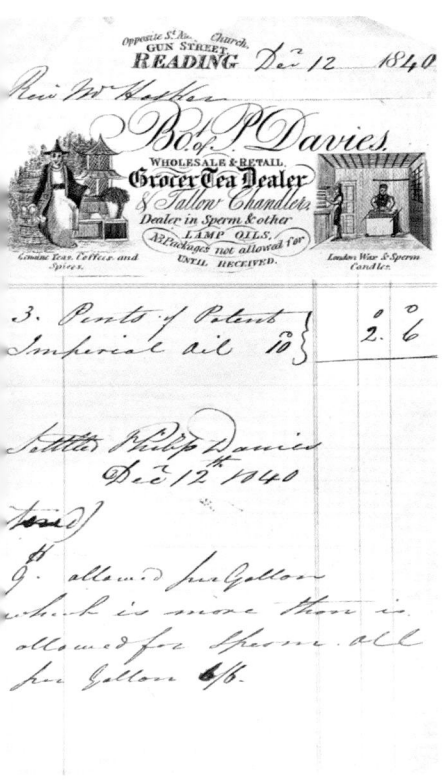

6. The bill for Patent Imperial Oil

On the left of the bill-head, the illustration shows a Chinese person, of indeterminate sex, wearing a pointed hat, which is similar in shape to the roof of the pagoda which stands in the background. This is to advertise the availability of 'Genuine Teas, Coffees and Spices.' In the picture to the right, one man appears to be looking into a series of drawers coming out of the wall, and another man is working, with bare arms, at a bench. He may well be dipping the wicks of candles into a tub of hot wax to make candles, since the picture advertises 'London Wax and Sperm Candles.'

Besides being a grocer, the text tells us that Mr Davies is a tallow chandler, and a dealer in sperm and other lamp oils. Tallow candles, made from the fat of sheep, would have been the cheapest and smokiest kind of candle. It has so far proved impossible to discover what 'London Wax' might have been, but it was probably beeswax. Sperm candles were the best of all, and said to burn four to six times brighter than beeswax candles. Similarly, sperm oil was the best lamp oil, and the most expensive.

Spermaceti was a product of the whaling industry. The business of producing it was rather gruesome. Sperm whales were killed, and the oil was extracted from glands in their heads. Fats, waxes and oils manufactured from whale blubber were not so highly prized.

Gas street lighting had been set up in Reading in the 1820s, but by the 1840s was by no means universal in houses, and the pipes of the two rival gas

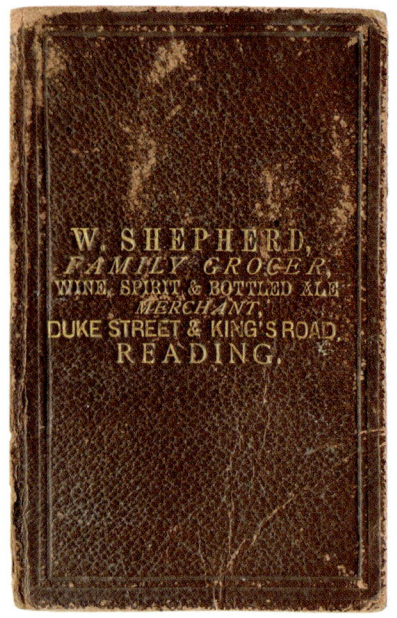
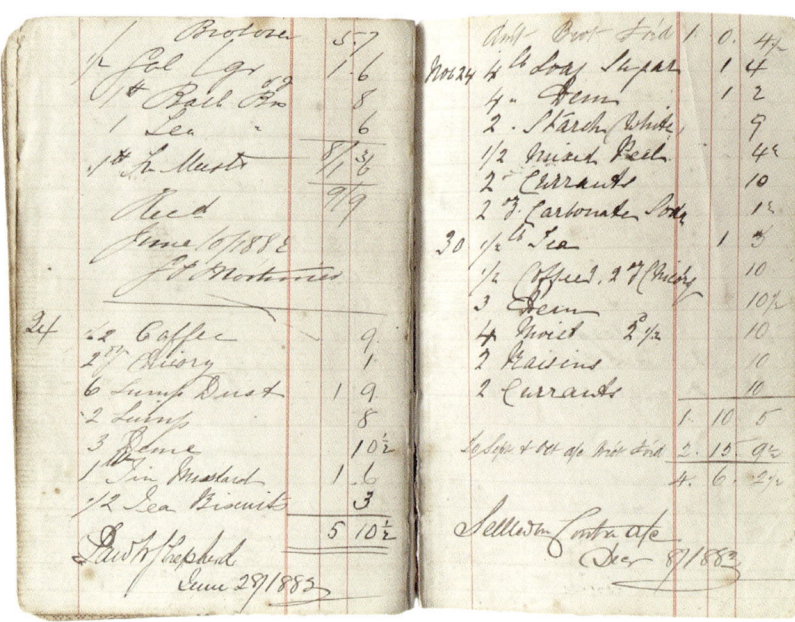

7. A grocery order book from the 1880s

companies did not extend beyond the town centre. Paraffin lamps were to arrive in the late 1850s.

Written at the foot of the bill is a barely legible message which seems to read: '9th allowed four Gallons which is more than is allowed for sperm oil per Gallon 6/6.'

Later in the century, Shepherd's had a grocery shop on the corner of Kings Road and Duke Street, opposite Jacksons Corner. Before them, an inn called the White Hart had stood on the site, which was removed around 1860 in a road-widening scheme. The grocer's shop lasted until around 1898, when Jacksons took it on as their shop selling china, earthenware, glass and leather goods – see the next chapter. This was relinquished in 1928, and from 1929 the building was occupied by the Abbey Road Permanent Building Society. The Victorian building was demolished and rebuilt for the Abbey National Building Society in 1983. The new premises, no longer occupied by the Abbey National, still bear the 'Abbey Corner' sign.

This small morocco-bound order book once belonged to Mrs Thomas Pither, of Dunt Lane Farm, Hurst. She wrote her orders in there, between 1881 and 1884, and took the book to the shop – or maybe gave it to a servant to take it the six or so miles. Then some time later the order would be delivered to her door. The bill would be settled in due course: bills bore the words, 'five per cent interest charged on overdue accounts.'

The most interesting part of the book is the aide-memoire, printed at the front, listing the various commodities that could be ordered. Among the sugars, there was raw sugar, lump sugar, moist sugar, and moist crystal sugar. As well as oatmeal, there were groats (crushed oats). There was ginger root, cayenne, and allspice. There were matches, and there were Jockey matches. And there was knife powder, important in the days before stainless steel, for scouring steel knives before they went rusty. To take the time to study the list would be a history lesson in itself.

Supermarkets began in the 1950s, and the first Reading grocer to bring in self-service was John Quality of Broad Street, in 1951. Baylis, with their flagship store on the corner of Broad Street and St Mary's Butts, whose letter-head is illustrated overleaf, were soon to follow suit.

Their shop was a familiar sight for many years. It was opened by John Henry Baylis in 1875, and by 1956, when his grandson, Derek, took over, there were branches in Caversham, Tilehurst and Erleigh Road in Reading, and others in Abingdon, Crowthorne, Mortimer, Newbury, Wallingford and Wantage.

By this time, the firm had become old-fashioned and was beginning to lose money. Derek Baylis embarked on a radical modernisation plan. He closed the less profitable branches, and converted the town-centre store into a supermarket, with self-service, bright lighting, and brightly-coloured posters advertising bargains. It had an advertising slogan: 'It pays to shop at Baylis.' Turnover doubled in the first year.

Mr Baylis had always said that he would sell the business when someone offered him a million pounds for it. This happened in 1969. The old property was demolished and rebuilt, and a branch of Caffe Nero now occupies the

Telephone Nos.
2251/2252

Directors:
R. H. BAYLIS E. W. BAYLIS
J. E. BAYLIS D. P. BAYLIS
S. E. BAYLIS

BAYLIS
THE GROCERS LTD

Broad St. & the Butts Corner, READING.
Erleigh Rd & Blenheim Rd Corner, READING.
2 & 4 Ock Street, ABINGDON.
Church St, Caversham.
90, Northbrook Street, NEWBURY.

Head Shop, Broad Street Corner - - READING

The Borough Librarian,
Central Public Library,
Reading.

April 23rd, 1952.

Dear Sir,

    Thank you for your letter dated April 17th. We do not wish to take any action for the time being.

    Yours faithfully,
    Baylis-The Grocers-Ltd.,

    Derek Baylis
    Director.

DPB/PW.

Opposite page:
8. The Borough Librarian at the time, Stanley Horrocks, was editor of the official guide-book for the Borough: Mr Baylis is here declining the invitation to put an advertisement in the next edition.

9. Green Shield trading stamps

ground floor. This was part of a national trend – the disappearance of the town-centre supermarkets in favour of edge-of-town shops with large free car parks. More recently, 'convenience' grocery stores have opened in the town centre, open for long hours.

Baylis the grocers claimed to have been the first in town to offer trading stamps, a way of securing customer loyalty in the 1960s and 1970s, rather like the plastic cards issued by shops in the electronic age. The more you spent, the more stamps you got. You licked the backs, stuck them in books, and could eventually, when you had filled enough books, send them off or hand them in to acquire products.

The Co-op had been running such a scheme, which did not involve stamp-collecting, for over a century before, offering members a dividend, usually 5% of what they had spent over a particular quarter – a shilling in the pound, returned in cash. In Reading, by 1970 they were offering 'dividend stamps' instead.

Green shield stamps were first introduced in 1958. In the 1960s you received one stamp for every sixpence spent. It took 1,280 stamps to fill a book, meaning that you had to have spent £32. At the time, an average man's full-time wage brought in around £20 a week before tax.

Tesco began to issue them in 1963, but Sainsbury's decided against. Other companies began to offer trading stamps of different colours, and there were 'stamp wars' between rival companies. Many petrol stations issued stamps, and sometimes offered double, triple and quadruple stamps in attempts to win custom from their rivals.

The green stamps were so popular in Reading that there was actually a Green Shield Stamp shop – in the Caversham shopping precinct, next to what had been the Regal cinema, before the Waitrose supermarket was built. This meant that Reading people could 'cross the water' to redeem their stamps. The shop is now a branch of Superdrug.

Eventually, people became disillusioned, believing that the shops issuing trading stamps must be adding the cost onto their prices. Tesco embarked on a policy of abandoning the stamps, and lowering prices, and eventually other traders followed suit. The Green Shield shop in Caversham opened in 1969, and closed in 1978.

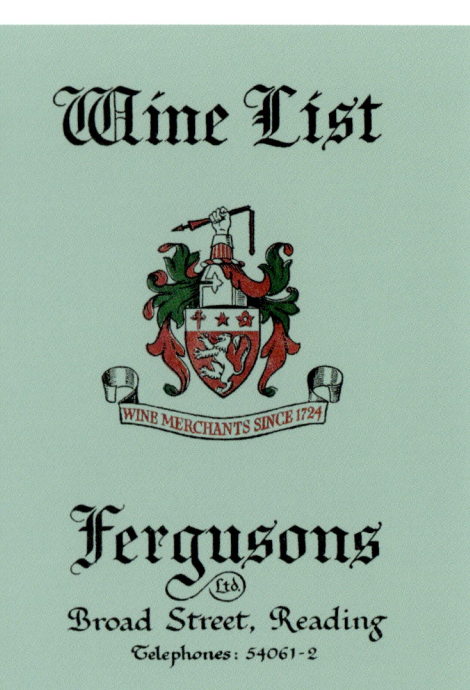

10. This list from 1958 states that the Fergusons had been in business since 1724.

Wine merchants have now largely disappeared from our high streets, and trade has been taken over by the supermarkets, with even small convenience stores and local corner shops having a selection of beers, wines and spirits.

One of the longest-lasting of the Reading wine merchants must have been Fergusons, its name disappearing from Broad Street around 1974. John Mansfield Ferguson arrived in Broad Street in 1861, when he took over the Angel Inn from William Parsons. He had previously run a 'wholesale and retail wine and spirit establishment' at the White Hart Inn, mentioned above. He died the following year, and in 1863 the licence was transferred to his brother, William Henry Ferguson. W. H. had a wine and spirit business in the Market Place. He must have had some capital behind him, for almost immediately the old Angel was demolished and rebuilt, with an Angel Brewery behind, and no longer offering overnight accommodation.

The Angel had been one of Reading's coaching inns. An Angel Inn in this part of the street is listed on Roger Amyce's survey of Reading, 1552, and the premises extended from Broad Street back to Minster Street. By the middle of the nineteenth century, the days of stage coaches were over, and The Angel must have settled down to a less hectic existence. In the twentieth century its rebuilt interior was remarkable for its glazed Doulton tiles, and the pictures of sporting scenes depicted on them. The beers included an Anglo-Saxon beer, a Nourishing Stout, and a notoriously strong Archangel 7X Stout.

The brewery side of the business was eventually taken over by Morland's of Abingdon, but the Ferguson name was retained, and their off-licence must have been thriving. When the inn closed and was demolished in 1964, a branch of British Home Stores arose on the site, with a part of the new building being a Fergusons off-licence, which lasted for around ten years.

When BHS went out of business, the building was extensively modernised, and re-opened in 2016 as a branch of Primark.

Specialist tobacconists have largely disappeared, though at the time of writing, such a shop can still be found in the Harris Arcade. In the 1960s and 1970s, like most town centres, Reading had a couple of small tobacco kiosks among the shops run by Finlay's, in Broad Street, and in West Street.

Friar Street, in the 1960s and 70s, had two rival establishments, full-sized shops you could walk into – Walter Chapman's, and William Newbery's. Chapman's

11. Learning to smoke a pipe brought the author no pleasure at all.

advertised snuff, and was on the curved corner of Blagrave Street, where O'Neill's Irish pub is now. In recent years, Newbery's shop has been home to fast food takeaways – Raavo Deli, and now Iro Sushi.

The small rectangle, not quite square, of crisp white paper, with printing to imitate copperplate handwriting, came from the latter. It was used to wrap an ounce of pipe tobacco, when the present author was required to smoke a pipe in an amateur production of *Dial M for Murder*, presented by St Laurence Players in 1974. Learning how to keep the tobacco burning took some doing.

In the shop, the tobacco was in airtight tins, and was weighed out by the ounce and the half ounce, and then wrapped in a paper twist. The most fascinating aspect of the shop was the small gas flame, constantly burning at the end of a vertical brass tube set in the counter, where customers could light their cigarettes. We tend now to forget how prevalent cigarette smoking was, before the days of government health warnings, increased taxation and the banning of smoking in public places.

Telephone - 4464-5 *(TWO LINES)*

G.G. Parslow & Son, Ltd.
DIRECTORS — G.G.PARSLOW H.T.PARSLOW B.PARSLOW W.PICKARD

BAKERS, CONFECTIONERS & CATERERS.

18, West Street.

READING.   Nov 27th 1936

ALSO AT
30, CASTLE STREET. TEL. No 4464
42, ERLEIGH ROAD. TEL No 61866
PALM LODGE, WEST STREET, TEL. No. 4465
PROSPECT STREET, CAVERSHAM. TEL. No 72572.
28, CASTLE STREET. VITAMIN D. BAKERY.

Ref 93.,
WP/VP.,

Miss Benger,
  93, Liverpool Road,
    Reading.

Dear Madame,

    We herewith have much pleasure confirmimg having booked a Wedding Reception to be held at Bartholomew's Hall, St Bartholomew's Road, Reading on Saturday Dec 19/36, time at the church 10-30 a.m.

<u>Buffet @ 2/9d.</u>

        Assorted Sandwiches
        Savoury Rolls
        Sausage   "
        Fancy Cakes and Biscuits
        Three Gateaux
        Jellies and Trifles
        Lemonade and Coffee

Flowers 3d. per head extra.

We to supply glass for the beer and wines.

    Assuring you of our best efforts to give you every satisfaction.

                          Yours faithfully,

                    For G.G.Parslow and Son Ltd.

                      G.G. Parslow

Opposite page:
12. The cost of a wedding reception in 1936

Butchers, bakers and fishmongers are also harder to find than they were in the past. This confirmation of booking for a wedding reception in 1936 comes from Parslow's the bakers, who at the time had shops in Castle Street, Erleigh Road, and Prospect Street, Caversham, as well as the headquarters in West Street. It shows that the cost of a buffet for a wedding breakfast could cost as much (or as little) as 2s. 9d. a head.

Mr Parslow had come to Reading just after the First World War to manage the Co-op bakery. He set up his own shop in West Street in 1923, taking it over from a Mr A. C. Bond. It was known as the Palm Lodge, and was presumably decorated with potted palms.

Next to the Castle Street shop was his 'Vitamin D Bakery.' Apparently, the dough for the bread was treated with ultra-violet rays – the 'vioroid' process. Since the loaves won prizes in bakery competitions, it must have tasted all right!

In later years the bakery and offices moved to Loddon Bridge Road in Woodley, and by 1970, Parslow's had 32 branches, including Ascot, Bracknell, Burnham, Henley, Maidenhead, Marlow, Newbury, Slough, Tadley, Twyford, Wallingford, Windsor and Wokingham. The bakery in Woodley closed in 2006, following a take-over by Allied Bakeries.

Our next shop is Langston and Sons, gentlemen's outfitters, with two shops in 1916, when the illustrated sheet of blotting paper overleaf was printed. Blotting paper, now a thing of the past, was in daily use in homes and offices, until ball-point pens took over from pen-and-ink in the 1950s. Ink-wells, steel pens and blotters could be found in offices, banks and post offices until around 1960.

The two shops were on the corner of Oxford Street and Cork Street, and on the corner of Friar Street and West Street, which was their headquarters.

On Cork Street corner, in their January sale, they offered winter clothes at bargain prices. Boys' overcoats could be had for between 3s. and 12s. 9d., and men's overcoats for 20s. for any style. Winter gloves are advertised, and 'fleecy front and back protectors,' were 4s. 11d., now half price, to fit anybody. They were for wearing under a coat, and suitable for soldiers (this was war time), and motorists (early cars didn't have heaters).

The history of the shop has a romantic beginning. Charles Samuel Langston wished to marry Miss Sophia Bradby of Theale, but her parents objected. The

13. Nothing cost over £1 in Langston's sale in 1916.

lovers eloped, and married in London in 1849. Then, at the age of 38, Charles was struck down by a serious illness. Realising that his days were numbered, he set up his wife in a small wool shop at 89 Oxford Street, Reading, in 1862, and died within a year.

The shop prospered, and moved to larger and more central premises on the corner of Friar Street and West Street in 1875, now the site of a slot-machine arcade called Admiral. The shop was rebuilt in 1884 as a part of one of the two lasting contributions of Alderman J. C. Fidler to the Reading townscape – the other contribution being Queen Victoria Street, a completely new street. His shopping arcade between Friar Street and Broad Street was destroyed by enemy bombing in 1943.

The Oxford Street/Cork Street shop opened around 1903, and closed in 1967 to make way for the Butts Shopping Centre (now called the Broad Street Mall). Langston's then opened up in a new shop under the multi-storey car park on Yield Hall Place, which specialised in riding gear and saddlery.

From Sophia Langston and her son Ernest, the shop passed down to Edward and Hubert, the sons of Ernest, who were both Mayors of Reading. In its later years, Langston's was not fashionable or trendy – it came to specialise in clothing and footwear for farmers, workmen, equestrians, sportsmen, and ballet dancers. The Friar Street/West Street premises remained the head office to the end. Well known and well respected, Langston's closed in 1993, after over a century. They were one of a number of family-owned gentlemen's outfitters in the town to cease trading around the end of the twentieth century, others being Silver's and Reed's on Broad Street, and Butler's in King Street.

As mentioned above, Reading's Market Arcade was wrecked by enemy bombing in 1943. It ran from Friar Street to the Corn Exchange and Covered Market, both of which also disappeared following the bombing, and on to Broad Street. It was rebuilt as the Bristol and West Arcade, which is currently (2023) awaiting yet another redevelopment.

The Arcade first appears in Reading directories in 1897, and Abel Fletcher first appears there in the 1920 directory. Other firms in The Arcade included Silver's, the gentlemen's outfitters, and Ebenezer Hill's business specialising in baby carriages. Together with Abel Fletcher, they moved out following the

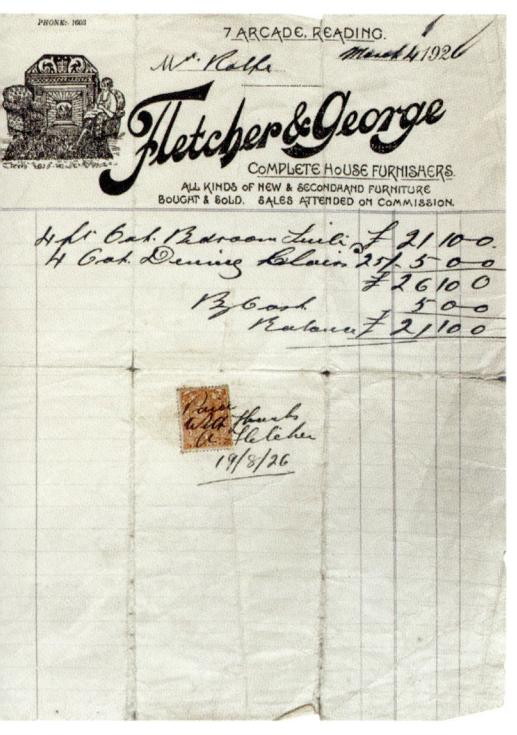

bombing, Fletcher's to 4–6 The Forbury, where they continued to trade into the 1970s. Curiously, the name 'George' which appears on this bill from 1926, doesn't appear alongside Mr Fletcher's in the old street directories.

The invoice shows that Mrs Rolfe had purchased a four-foot (or possibly four-part) oak bedroom suite for £21, and four oak dining chairs at 25s. each. She had paid £5, leaving £21 still to pay.

The document has a distinct period charm, stemming from the mixture of typefaces used, and the little vignette in the top left-hand corner. Here, a lady, wearing a necklace, sits in a comfortable fire-side armchair, knitting, her feet cosy in the deep pile of the hearth-rug.

The name of Samuel Collier will appear again in this book as a manufacturer of bricks, tiles and other earthenware products (see p. 84–5). As a shopkeeper, he sold china, pottery and glass at 15 Minster Street. The receipt illustrated here dates from 1847, the year before he took on a clay-pit and factory. He was joined in the enterprise by his son, Edward Philip Collier, who was to become the Chairman of the Reading School Board, and to have a school off Caversham Road named after him.

Samuel Collier's shop remained in the same line of business until it was demolished, around 1980, latterly as Watson and Son. It was remarkable for having, in the middle of the façade at first floor level, the carving of an eagle, perched on top of a grotto or cave, in which was a lion. Legend has it that it had once been an inn called the Cardinal's Hat, though the sculpture doesn't seem appropriate. Its site is now under the back of the Primark store – formerly British Home Stores.

This bill, signed by Mr Collier, shows that on 23 March 1847, someone purchased a sugar bowl for 8s 6d, and a 'Blue Chamber' for 1s 3d. This latter was presumably a chamber-pot.

Independent dispensing chemists are now something of a rarity. In the past, their shops tended to be passed down through a family from father to son, and J. Powell and Son lasted not quite a hundred years.

The testimonials recommending the '8 Preparations' mentioned on the front date the booklet illustrated overleaf date back to 1912, or shortly after. By then, Powell's were long-established: John Powell, dispensing chemist, first

Opposite page:
14. There was no set number of items in a 'bedroom suite' – apart from the bed: it could have included wardrobes, a dressing-table and bedside tables.

15. Camphene Vesta Lamps, advertised here, were specially designed to burn a mixture of turpentine and alcohol.

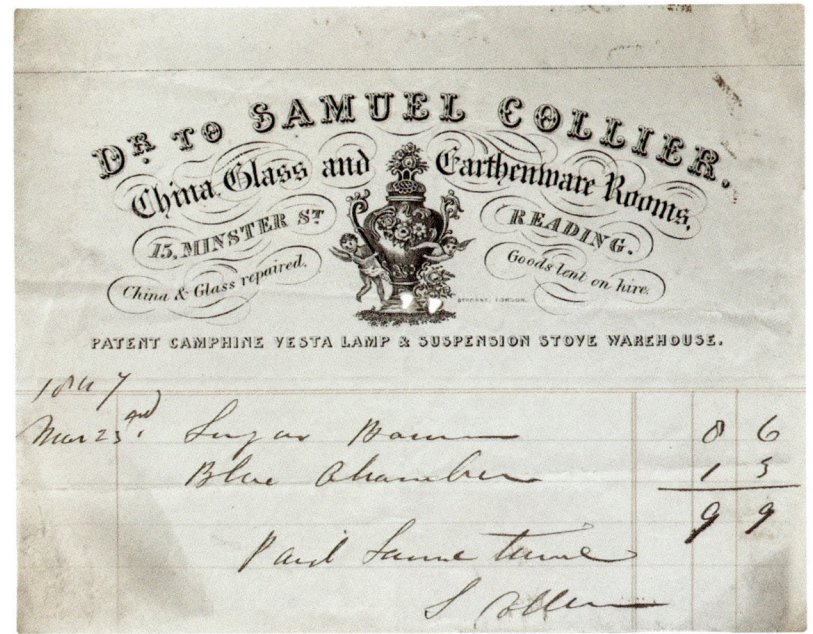

appears in directories in 1874. Besides preparations for humans, Powell's were also agricultural chemists, supplying powders, ointments, lotions and drenches for farm animals, not advertised here. The firm disappears from the directories after 1970. Their shop, in St. Mary's Butts, was demolished and replaced by a building devoid of any kind of architectural distinction. Until recently it was occupied by the 7 Bone Burger Company. The eight preparations are:

1. Indigestion Mixture – for flatulence, heartburn, dyspepsia, sick headache, etc.
2. Vegetable Hair Wash – banishes dandruff and scurf, and promotes the growth and luxuriance of hair.
3. Bronchial Linctus – for the relief of asthma, bronchitis, coughs, hoarseness and loss of voice.
4. Gripe Mixture – for babies, especially when teething.

16. Today we would wonder quite what 'chemists by exam' signified.

5. Powell's Female Pills – unrivalled as a safe and sure remedy for all female complaints.
6. Liver and Stomach Pills – they have been before the public for over half a century, which in itself is sufficient testimony.
7. Neuralgia Pills – never fail to sure neuralgia, tic, toothache and all nervous afflictions.
8. Foot Powder – for the relief of tired, tender, perspiring feet, and the prevention of chafing and blistering.

The back of the booklet advertises Powell's Medical Hall and Artificial Teeth Depot. Teeth could be stopped, scaled, or painlessly removed. Prize medal artificial teeth could be supplied, from 21s. a set.

For over a century, the most prestigious jeweller's, goldsmith's, silversmith's and watchmaker's shop in the town went by the name of Bracher. Reuben Bracher, who signed this receipt in 1867, was to become one half of the well-known Reading partnership, Bracher and Sydenham. Around 1974, they became part of the Goldsmiths chain.

Mr Bracher had come from Salisbury, where he had been apprenticed to a watchmaker. Around 1846 he came to Reading to work for James Trendell, jeweller and hairdresser, in Minster Street. The shop was on the corner of Yield Hall Lane, its site now covered by a part of The Oracle shopping centre. Bracher became the partner of Mr Trendell in 1852, and took over the business on his retirement in 1855. As may be seen from the receipt pictured below and overleaf, in 1867, Mr Bracher was a clock and watch maker, goldsmith, jeweller, optician, and still an 'artist in hair.' The partnership with Joseph Sydenham, his nephew, came about in 1874.

The shop was successful, and was noted for the silverware produced by its craftsmen. King Edward VII was a visitor, and awarded a royal warrant. From a single shop, the business expanded into the shop next door, and the shop next door to that in Minster Street. The move to a more prestigious location in Queen Victoria Street came about in 1924, and there it remained for the next 65 years. According to the old street directories, it began at Nos. 30 –30a, expanding to Nos. 26–30 in 1934, but retracting to No. 26 in 1971 and moving

17. The header of a receipt for work done, issued to the executors of the late Col. Blagrave.

17a. Invoice for putting a ring into a brooch for Col. Blagrave. He died shortly after the work was done, and the next item relates to his funeral.

to No. 24 in 1973. Though becoming a part of the Goldsmiths chain of jewellers, it nevertheless remained a high-class establishment, with a top-hatted and liveried doorman, and lit by a large chandelier, into the 1980s. Its glory days were numbered though: the business moved into The Oracle when that opened in 1999, and Bracher and Sydenham were no more.

By the early nineteenth century, Reading had several booksellers, many of whom offered other services: they were printers and stationers, and also ran circulating (i.e. lending) libraries. The best-known by far was George Lovejoy: Reading Central Library has his diaries, and his collection of ephemera.

The bill is for black-bordered notepaper and envelopes, and for the black wax with which to seal the envelopes, and was paid by the executors of the late

18. By 1867, Mr Lovejoy had been joined in his enterprise by Miss Eliza Langley, who has signed this bill.

Colonel John Blagrave of Calcot Lodge, in 1867. He had died on 21 June of that year, so the last batch of stationery was presumably bought to notify mourners of the Colonel's funeral (see p. 71–2). The bill-head carries the emblem of Mr Lovejoy's Southern Counties Library, Stamp Office and Post Office – a straw beehive, with flowers behind it and bees buzzing round it, and the motto, 'Nothing Without Labour.'

Lovejoy was indeed a busy man. The latest novels were always available from his Southern Counties Library, and the Reading establishment claimed to be the largest in the provinces. It was said to enjoy a substantial 'carriage trade' – meaning that it had customers who could afford to arrive by carriage – and several literary figures were friends of the proprietor, notably Mary Russell Mitford and Charles Dickens. The shop was also an estate agency, and an insurance agency.

Besides being a supporter of the temperance movement and the abolition of capital punishment, Lovejoy also pressed for Reading Corporation to adopt the Public Libraries Acts. The first public library in the town opened in 1882, shortly before his death the following year.

He had taken over an existing circulating library at 31 London Street in 1832, and when the property was required for the building of the Public Rooms, he moved a short way up the street, eventually occupying Nos. 33–39. Miss Eliza Langley had joined the business in 1856, and when he died in 1883, she was able to buy it, and continued to run it until her own death in 1897. It has been claimed that as well as being a bookseller, she was the country's first female estate agent, from the same premises.

The bookshop continued until 1989, at first run by William C. Long, then by William Smith and Son, and then by Blackwell's of Oxford. The subscription library continued until around 1950. The building of the Inner Distribution Road made shoppers less willing to go to London Street for their books, and the business moved to Kings Road, with the London Street premises becoming the Reading International Support Centre (RISC).

Another item relating to Mr Lovejoy is a ticket of admission to the gardens at Whiteknights, pictured opposite. The Manor of Earley Whiteknights in 1798 had been purchased by the extravagant Marquis of Blandford, who was to become Fifth Duke of Marlborough. He spent enormous sums on the gardens, as well as on his collections of pictures and books, and in 1819 was forced to sell his collections, including the rare plants. He left the area, to live at Blenheim.

Nevertheless, the gardens continued to be visited and admired. Daniel Benham, in his 1843 *Excursion to Reading...* wrote:

> I never spent two hours with greater pleasure than I did in this earthly paradise, and so it may truly be called, even now although its moveable plants had been taken away, under an auction of them which produced £10,000.

In 1849, the estate was bought by the financier, Sir Isaac Lyon Goldsmid, and passed down to his son, Sir Francis Henry Goldsmid, who was MP for Reading, 1860–1878. In 1867 Sir Francis divided Whiteknights into six leaseholds, so

19. George Lovejoy's admission ticket to the gardens in Whiteknights Park has survived in the University's ephemera collection, appropriately since it is housed in the Department of Typography & Graphic Communication at Whiteknights.

> ADMISSION TO WHITEKNIGHTS.
> BY PERMISSION OF
> SIR F. GOLDSMID, BART., M.P.
> No.   [*Not Transferable.*
> No admission without a ticket. | GEORGE LOVEJOY,
> Admission from Two o'clock; Close at Nine.
> *** It is expected that all Persons will protect the Plants, &c, from Injury.

this ticket must date from the period between 1860, and the splitting of the estate. Six very large houses were built: Whiteknights Park House (on the site of the old manor house), Whiteknights House, Blandford Lodge, The Wilderness, Erlegh Park (or Erlegh Whiteknights), and Foxhill (built for Alfred Waterhouse, the architect, to his own design). Sir Francis died in 1878 as the result of an accident when stepping from a train in Waterloo Station. By the time of the Second World War, the enormous old houses on the Whiteknights estate were becoming increasingly expensive to maintain and manage, and during the war, some of the land was occupied by the temporary buildings of the Ministry of Works. After the war, the University of Reading, with its campus on London Road surrounded by built-up areas, was seeking to expand. It was able to acquire the whole estate in 1947, and to re-use some of the old houses.

From the twentieth century comes the advertising card shown overleaf, probably intended to be used as a bookmark, from another Reading bookseller. James Golder's was one of three Reading bookshops from which the public library bought its books, when the present author started work as a librarian in 1969. The others were William Smith, formerly Lovejoy's and mentioned above,

20. Advertisement from Reading's 'Pen Doctor'

and W. H. Smith. At the time, W. H. Smith had two branches in Reading, both in Broad Street.

The bookmark states that Golder's had been in business for 100 years. The last advertisement for Golder's in the local papers appeared in 1979, when they claimed to have been in business for 150 years, giving the foundation date of 1829, which suggests that the card under consideration dates from 1929.

James Golder began his career working for Lovejoy's, and opened a shop of his own in London Road around 1862, moving to a shop in the Market Place in 1868,

NEVER MIND HOW IT HAPPENED.!

WE WILL *Repair* YOUR *Fountain Pen.*

A PEN EXPERT is in attendance.
Any make quickly repaired.

JAS. GOLDER,

Reading's Pen Doctor,

21, KING STREET
(opposite Barclay's Bank)

Phone 4169 ::: READING.

and to King Street around 1909. The King Street shop has been demolished, and the new building on the site is a Vietnamese restaurant called Pho, by the entrance to the The Village shopping arcade (formerly King's Walk).

The card invites you to browse at leisure, and assures you that you are welcome. It goes on: 'The assistants are at your service when you need them, but unless you look to them, they will leave you undisturbed.'

The side of the card illustrated here is perhaps surprising. At a time when most pens are bought with ink in them, and when they run out or dry up you throw them away and use another, the thought of taking a pen to the 'pen doctor' seems almost laughable. Younger people will never have used a fountain pen, and may never have seen one, though they'll be familiar enough with the 'qwerty' keyboard.

The fountain pen had one great advantage over the steel pen that came before it: you could write with it for an hour and more, and when the ink ran out, you could refill it with ink by Stephens, Waterman, or Parker. The disadvantage was that in time, the rubber tube inside would develop a leak, and cause a nasty stain if you'd clipped it into a top pocket.

Finally in this chapter, we look at a couple of music shops. The front of the piece of music illustrated overleaf bears the name of one of the Hickie Brothers, who came from Cheltenham and set up in business in Reading in 1864. Newspaper advertisements claimed that the business was established in 1856 – presumably in Cheltenham.

In Reading in 1864 they were piano tuners and repairers, trading from a house in Great Knollys Street. The first mention of William Hickie's County Music Warehouse in the local papers, at 38 Broad Street, comes in 1876. This makes the business the oldest in the town which is still trading under the same name – though the ownership has changed.

By 1888 the shop was Hickie and Hickie and had moved to 100–101 Broad Street. By 1904 they had moved to 153 Friar Street, where they still are. Their story is told in greater detail in the book *Airs and Places: People and Music in Berkshire*.

The business was taken over by Frank William Elphick in 1913, and has continued to be run by the Elphick family ever since, always trading as Hickie and Hickie.

In the years between the wars, pianos were their speciality. They employed eight tuners, and had 10 or 12 repairers in their workshop.

21. This piece of sheet music, perhaps not a piece of ephemera in the strict sense of the word, has the name of the seller, W. Hickie, County Music Warehouse, 38 Broad Street, printed on the foot of the front cover.

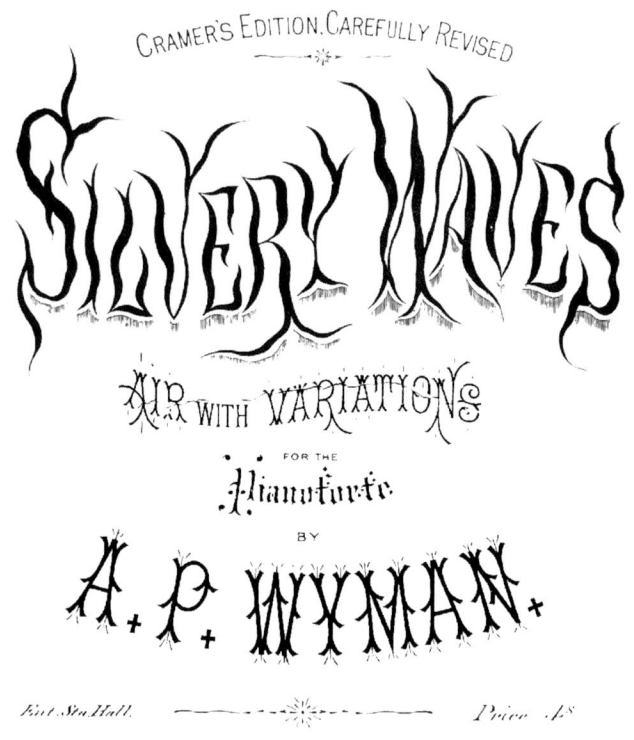

The sale of gramophones and gramophone records took off after the ending of the First World War, and it was around 1959 that vinyl records took over from the old '78s'. With the 'pop' music craze of the 1960s, Hickie's opened their mezzanine floor, with listening booths along one side, and the record racks on the others. This was extremely popular on Saturdays. Naturally, the sales of electric guitars also increased.

In the late 1930s, it was just possible to receive the television signal from Alexandra Palace, and Hickie's claimed to have been the first shop in Reading to stock television receivers. You needed a very tall mast to capture the signal – the one over the shop was said to have been delivered by water, on account of its length. In the 1950s, the demand for TV sets, rented or purchased outright, was such that they opened another shop, taking over the next-door premises on the corner of Queen Victoria Street. Early sets were notorious for going wrong, so they opened a service depot employing 10–12 people.

The emphasis now is on musical instruments and sheet music. In the 1970s and 80s, the present author remembers with fondness the classical record department on the ground floor – LPs followed by CDs. Presided over by Leonard Heeks, and later by Ken whose surname I never knew, to set foot in their department was like going into your club, where they knew you, and they knew what you liked, and were able to recommend new releases, and give you the chance to try them out. Every disc in their racks was there for a reason. It seems unlikely that any such shop exists now, anywhere in the land.

For many years the great rivals of Hickie's were Barnes and Avis. Thomas Barnes and Frank Avis took over the music shop of Thomas Waite at 5–7 Duke Street in 1911. Like Hickie's, the shop specialised in pianos, and had a special piano lift to raise and lower pianos between floors – a device which was recorded by the noted industrial archaeologist, J. Kenneth Major: there is a copy of his drawing in Reading Central Library.

Barnes and Avis were successful, and took over the next-door shop at No. 9. The premises were on the site now occupied by the office building called Dukesbridge Chambers with shops below, about where Ryman's the stationers now are.

This receipted bill from 1930, for tuning the piano of Mr A. S. Miller of Great Park Farm, Mortimer, on three occasions at 6/- a time, advertises the firm's

22. In 1939, the Barnes and Avis music shop moved into the large shop at 140–141 Friar Street, now the Revolucion de Cuba restaurant.

goods. They sold pianos, player pianos, gramophones, gramophone records and 'Marconiphone' radio sets. Programmes of piano recitals at the Town Hall and Palace Theatre around this time show that they also hired out pianos.

Just after the date of this bill, Barnes and Avis opened another branch at 35 Oxford Street, they took over a travel agency in Kings Road, and they opened another music shop in Wokingham.

The big change came about the time of the outbreak of war in 1939, when they were able to acquire a very large shop, 140–141 Friar Street. This became the head office, piano showroom, a shop selling musical instruments, sheet music, radio sets, gramophone records, and a travel agency. They were taken over by Rumbelow's around 1969, and the shop closed in 1995.

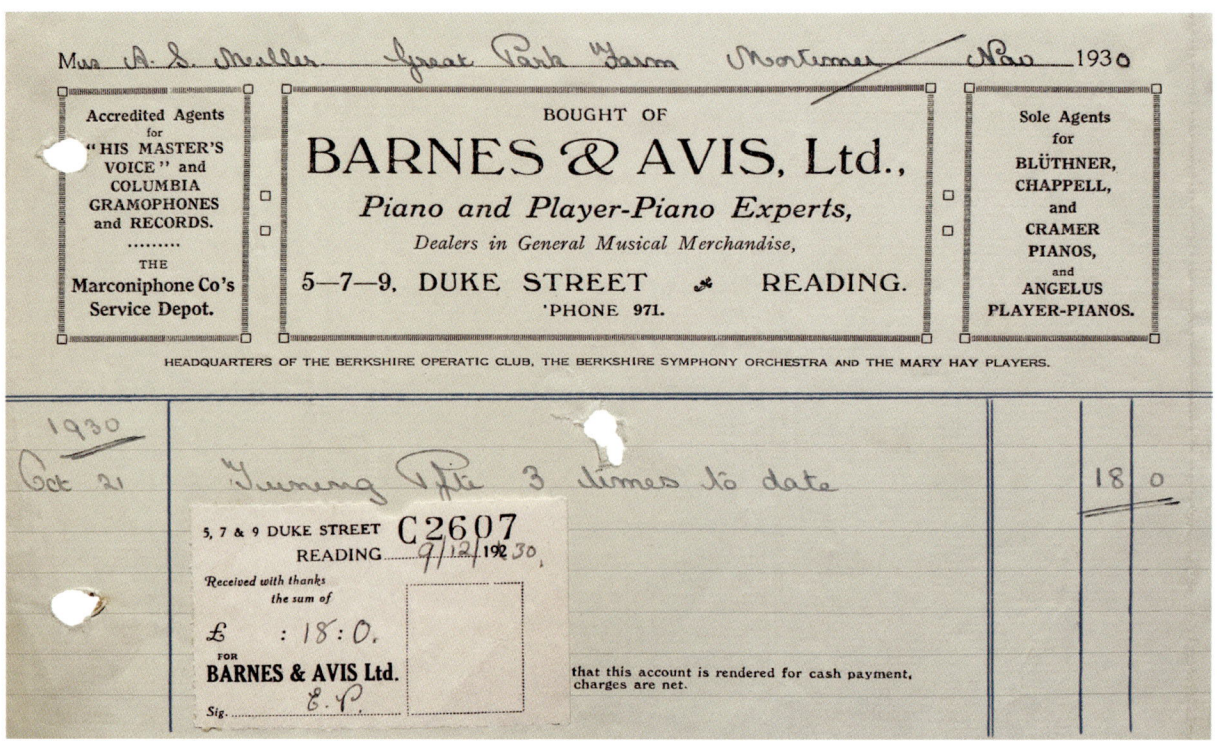

23. This receipt from 1907 from Wellsteed's, chosen for its fancy header, is for 'knickers' costing 4s. 11d., for which the customer has tendered five shillings. The firm's name was always pronounced as if it were spelled 'Wellsteads'.

III. Department stores

The golden age of the department store seems now to have passed. Fifty years ago in Reading, A. H. Bull's and McIlroy's had already gone, but we still had Heelas, Wellsteed's and Jacksons, founded by local families, and the nationally renowned Woolworths, Marks and Spencer, Littlewoods, and British Home Stores. Perhaps, among the 'home grown' department stores we should include Tutty's of London Street – 'The Store that Value Has Built', which closed in 1975. It specialised in selling goods on credit. Then the Butts Centre, opening in 1972 and later called The Broad Street Mall, gave us a branch of Wilko, and The Oracle, opening in 1999, had Debenhams (which had absorbed Wellsteed's) at one end, and House of Fraser at the other.

Wellsteed's was founded by the draper, William Hedgecock Wellsteed at 7 King Street in 1847. By 1854 he had three shops – the original one, and two more in Middle Row. This was a row of shops in the middle of Broad Street, at the eastern

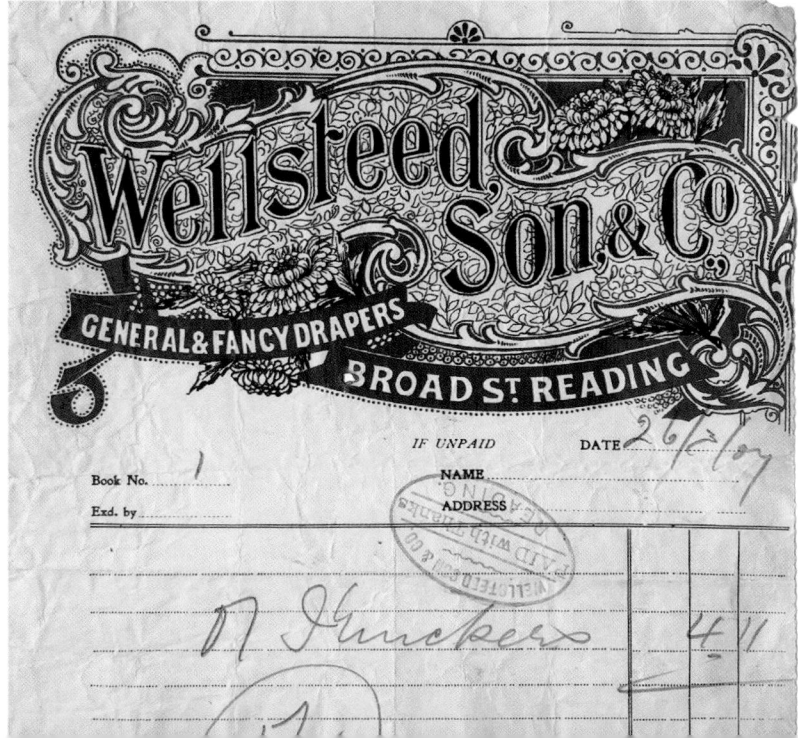

Opposite page:
24. Bill issued to Mrs Bacon of Surley House, Basingstoke, in 1899, with a bill-head dated '190-,' showing it had been printed for use in 1900 onwards.

end, which did not last long enough to be photographed, but appears on old maps. By 1870 the shop was on the south side of Broad Street, and opposite where Middle Row had been. It was in a prime location, and over time, like Heelas store farther along the street, it diversified to become a department store. After a series of takeovers, it became a part of the Debenhams empire.

The Broad Street premises were badly damaged in the air raid of 1943, and were closed until 1947. The local studies collection at Reading Central Library has a number of 'before' and 'after' pictures, which can be viewed online by searching the library catalogue.

The store changed its name to Debenhams in 1972, and moved into The Oracle shopping centre in 1999, on the side facing the river. Its Broad Street frontage, in white faience and bronze, which was new in 1905, is still there. Debenhams found themselves in financial difficulties in the twenty-first century, and the compulsory closure of 'non-essential' shops during the COVID-19 crisis seems to have been the last straw. The Reading store closed in 2020, and the last of their department stores closed in 2021.

The Heelas family of drapers from Wokingham were for many years the great rivals of Wellsteed's. They acquired their first Reading shop in Minster Street in 1854. Here, it prospered, and gradually they bought up the neighbouring properties – shops, pubs, and even the Salem Chapel. In 1875, the Black Boy pub was acquired, giving it a frontage on Broad Street for the first time.

The frontages to Broad Street and Minster Street have been altered several times over the years. On the picture on this bill-head, only the right-hand building now remains: it has had a clock inserted into the top of the central bay. The gothic styled building to the left was the firm's first shop in Broad Street.

 From being a family-owned company, Heelas came into the hands of Charles Clore, United Drapery, and from 1953 onwards, the John Lewis Partnership, with their motto, 'never knowingly undersold.' If you could find the same article on sale locally at a lower price, the Partnership would refund the difference.

The bill says on the top that the shop closed on Wednesdays at two o'clock. Wednesday was the traditional early closing day for shops in Reading, a custom which is no longer observed. It seems rather grudging from the shop assistants' point-of-view, and hardly constitutes a half-day off. In the 1970s, under the

CLOSED AT TWO O'CLOCK ON WEDNESDAYS.

110, 111, 112, BROAD STREET,
24, 25, 26, 27, 28, MINSTER ST.

BY SPECIAL WARRANT OF APPOINTMENT TO H. R. H. PRINCE OF WALES.

READING, 190

BOUGHT OF HEELAS SONS & COMPY. LTD.

DRAPERS
SILK MERCERS,
Tailors,
HOSIERS,
Gentlemen's Outfitters.

HEELAS, SONS & CO'S BROAD STREET FRONTAGE

CARPET
WAREHOUSEMEN,
Decorators,
COMPLETE HOUSE
FURNISHERS.

Bankers,
SIMONDS & Co.
Reading

Mrs Bacon
Burley House Basingstoke

3/- Folio

Mr W. Cannon

1898						
Dec	19		Repairing Machine		5	0
1899 Mch	10		Dress Length		8	9
		5	Amazon	1/4½	6	10½
		8	Flannel	1/0¾	8	6
		2½	do	1/0¾	2	8
		12	Print	4¾	4	9
		8	do	4½	3	2
	28	6 pr	Hose	1/6½	9	3
		6	do	1/9½	10	9
			[illegible]	1/4½	2	9
					8	6

25. Receipt for a remnant on winceyette – a brushed cotton material used for nightshirts, nightdresses and pyjamas – costing one shilling.

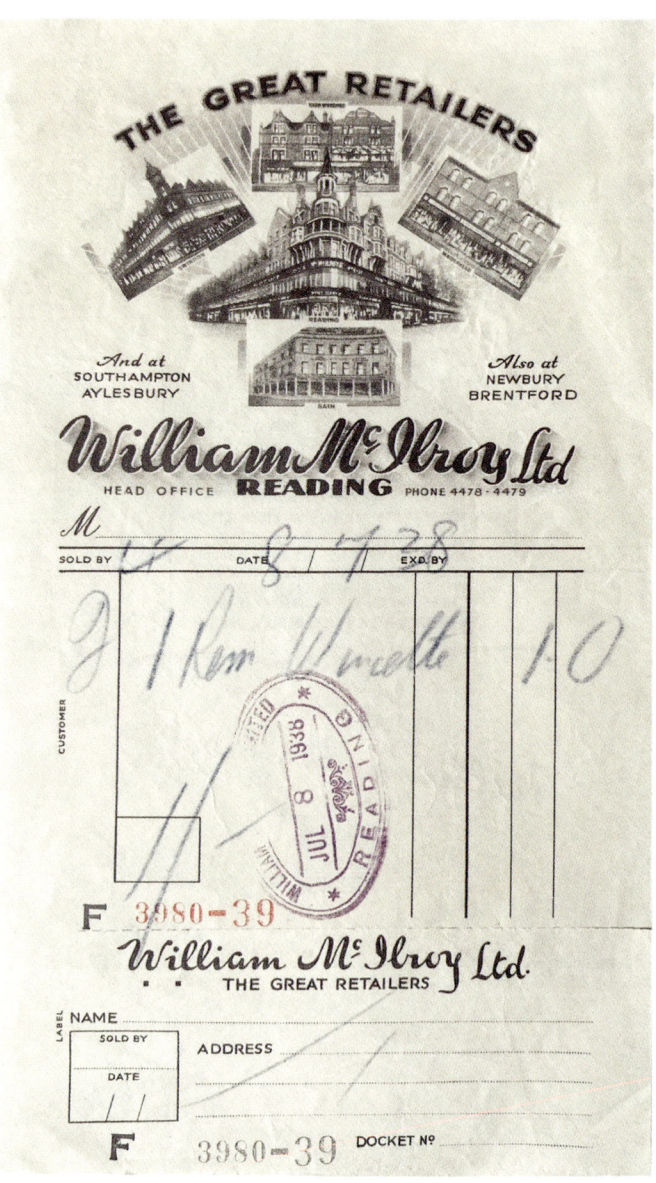

Partnership, the shop was closed all day on Mondays – but this was a time for staff training, so that the assistants knew the products they were selling, and would be able to help the customers choose between one item and another, or so it was advertised.

Besides what is mentioned here, at one time the shop included ladies' and gentlemen's hairdressers, and there was a funeral furnishing department with its own chapel of rest off Minster Street. The present author recalls the restaurant, upstairs, with a very low ceiling, so as to give it the feeling of a dining room between decks on an ocean liner of bygone days. A silver-haired gentleman showed you to a seat, and a waitress in black dress and white apron asked if you would like a drink. I always said that I would. (For the Heelas Concerts see p. 155–7.)

When William McIlroy's new store opened in 1901, it claimed to be the largest department store in the south of England – presumably outside London. Its architecture was eclectic and exuberant, with red and yellow glazed bricks, corbelled balconies, crow-stepped gables, and a large clock on a bracket over the pavement. It had more window than wall, and was nicknamed 'the Crystal Palace,' or more simply, 'Mac's.'

The McIlroy family had come from Derry/Londonderry to open a shop in Friar Street in 1875. They were successful, and were buying other shops in Oxford Street – the stretch of road that was later called Oxford Road, and then Broad Street West when The Butts Centre changed its name to the Broad Street Mall.

By the time this bill-head was produced, they had branches in Aylesbury, Bath, Brentford, High Wycombe, Maidenhead, Newbury, Southampton and Swindon.

But it was not to last. Post-war depression took its toll, and the shop was becoming old-fashioned. It had overhead wires along which canisters whizzed from the counters to a central cash desk. Once the latest thing, by the 1950s they were outmoded. Even so, the closure of the Reading store came unexpectedly in 1954. The stores in other towns lasted for some years longer.

The Reading building still stands on the western part of Broad Street and Cheapside, shorn of its clock and architectural embellishments, the ground floor now home to a variety of shops.

26. Detail from of an advertising poster from the 1920s, when Jacksons had two shops across the road from one another

Also founded in 1875 was Jacksons department store, initially on High Street. There was a feeling of sadness and loss when it closed, by now round the corner on Kings Road, in 2013. Edward Jackson had started as a tailor and gentlemen's outfitter. He went on to become Mayor of Reading. At the time, there were great changes afoot in this part of town, where the crossroads formed by King Street, Kings Road, High Street and Duke Street was being widened, involving the demolition of the Saracen's Head pub on the High Street/Kings Road corner. Mr Jackson had a much larger shop built, partly over the site of the pub, but set back to give a wider carriageway to Kings Road. The new Saracen's Head was built next to it, a little farther along Kings Road, and then Jacksons built another large store beyond that. Their publicity never gave any intimation that the main building was divided in the middle by a pub, which is the case with the picture on this poster. The Saracen's Head closed in 1960, and Jacksons was then able to use its ground floor as their main entrance.

On the poster, the building to the left is the present one, with its extent along High Street exaggerated and no suggestion of a pub on Kings Road. This was Jacksons main shop, for clothing and footwear. The building to the right was on the corner of Kings Road and Duke Street. Before ever Jacksons took it on, it was Shepherd's, the grocers (see p. 14–15). It became Jacksons household department, selling china, glass, cutlery, leather goods, stationery, and toys, until 1928.

At the height of their prosperity, Jacksons had shops in Oxford Street and London Road in Reading, in Prospect Street in Caversham (closed 1994), and branches in Bracknell, Camberley, Goring, Henley and Oxford.

The Kings Road store was fitted with a Lamson pneumatic system whereby cash was moved in tubes between the counters and a cashier in another part of the building. It was in use until the day the store closed – the last one in the land. There were other quirky things about this shop, such as the device for stretching felt hats that were just a fraction too small, and the potted aspidistra in the gentlemen's changing room, remembered by the present author from the 1980s.

With the opening of The Oracle shopping centre, and the old buildings in need of repair and refurbishment, the family-owned business came to an end. It had become something of an anachronism, sometimes being compared with the Grace Brothers department store, the setting for television's situation comedy, *Are You Being Served?* At the time of writing, there are apartments on the upper storeys, with shop units, awaiting tenants, on the ground floor.

Alfred Holland Bull first appeared in the Reading street directories at 6 Broad Street in 1886. By the time of the bill illustrated overleaf, the main shop was at 52–59 Broad Street, and had been extended through to Friar Street in 1898, in a building designed by two local architectural practices, F. W. Albury, and Millar and Naysmith. But the building shown on the bill-head to the right was in fact several doors away, at Nos. 47–48. By 1914 it hadn't been part of Bull's for some years – it was the Vaudeville cinema (see p. 151), but had previously been Bull's boys' and gentlemen's outfitting department.

Mr Bull himself was Mayor of Reading 1901–1903; there is a small portrait of him on the front of the programme of the coronation celebrations of 1902 (see p. 178).

27. Bill from 1914, which was printed by Lamson Paragon, the firm which built the pneumatic system for moving cash through the store.

The back of the bill mentions household goods, ladies' fashions, and the availability of black dress material for mourning clothes. The payment terms are 'ready money only – no discount,' but 'lowest prices.'

Like Jacksons department store, Bull's had a system of vacuum tubes running through the store between the counters and a central cash desk. The bill and the cash would be placed in a canister, which would have been placed in the tube, the tube closed, and the canister sucked across to the cashier. The cashier would have checked the bill, found any necessary change, stamped the bill, and sent it back to the shop assistant.

In 1940, Bull's was taken over by the John Lewis Partnership, and in 1953, the Partnership decided to take over Heelas, and to sell Bull's former premises to Littlewoods. Eventually, a new store for Littlewoods was built over part of the site, and part of the old building remained as a furniture shop, Wolfe and Hollander, which became Waring & Gillow. Waring's had a disastrous fire in 1979, after which the rest of the 1898 building was demolished. Littlewoods decided to close all their stores in 2005. Shops in Broad Street which are now on the site include Superdrug, and Schuh.

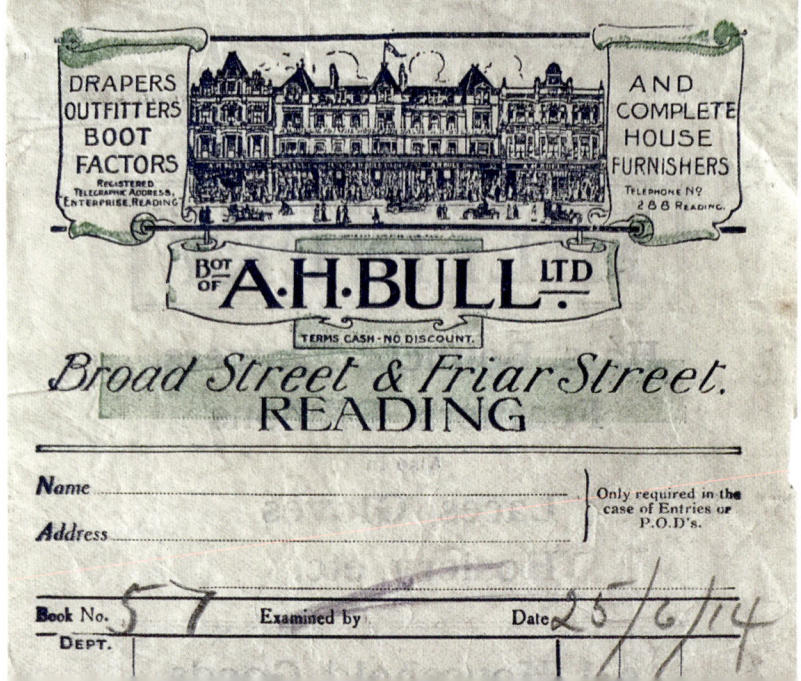

28. Banknote from Reading's earliest bank, founded in 1788

IV. Trades and services

This chapter is reserved for establishments which provided services of different kinds – maybe financial, or firms which actually produced or manufactured what they sold direct to the public. Large-scale manufacturers appear in the next chapter.

Whether or not a banknote counts as a piece of ephemera or not is arguable – some would argue that it is particularly ephemeral! It now seems odd and decidedly risky to have a bank in a provincial town issuing its own banknotes. The Bank Charter Act of 1844 prevented new banks from issuing them, and bank closures and takeovers meant that the practice gradually died out.

Here are the crumpled remains of a one pound note from Reading's earliest bank, signed by Richard Westbrook just two years before the bank failed in 1815. It occupied a building with a balcony in the Market Place, which was later occupied by an upholsterer named Ford. Around 1840, it was damaged by a storm, and demolished.

Opposite page:
29. A Post Office telegram, sent from Castle Cary in Somerset at 9.10 am, and delivered to Mr Ross, the auctioneer, in Reading at 9.40 am.

The Reading Bank had been founded in 1788, and the partners were Sir Charles Marsh, a retired army officer; Henry Deane, son of a partner in the Castle Brewery; and Eyre Evans Crowe, a chapman, of Sindlesham. They each put £1,000 into the business. Crowe was declared bankrupt in 1798, owing to a private loan he had made, so he was unable to continue as a director. Marsh died in 1805, and Richard Westbrook took his place. Westbrook has signed this surviving note, bottom right.

The bank seems to have been poorly managed by people without the necessary experience. The winter of 1813–14 had been severe, and the harvest of 1814 was poor. Creditors were calling in their loans, and the bank was forced to close its doors, literally, in 1815. The directors had their property and assets seized by the Commissioners in Bankruptcy, and the debtors were ordered to make repayment. Interestingly, a number of the debtors were silk manufacturers in Reading.

Other early bankers were more prudent. The partners in both Stephens, Blandy & Company and J. & C. Simonds were brewers, but employed professional bankers. Stephens, Blandy eventually merged with Lloyd's Bank, and Simonds with Barclay's.

The next piece of ephemera illustrates two services – that of W. R. Ross, the auctioneer, and the telegram service run by the Post Office.

When very few people had access to a telephone, the telegram service was important, though expensive, for conveying urgent messages that couldn't wait for the post. You could dictate your message at a main post office, and pay for it there and then, knowing it would be on its way within minutes, carried by a uniformed messenger-boy on a motorbike. Early telegrams were hand-written: this example from 1933 has the message produced by a teleprinter on a strip of sticky paper that was cut into sections and stuck onto the telegram itself. The Post Office compulsorily took over all pre-existing telegraph offices in the country in 1870, and British Telecom ended the service, which was by then not much used, in 1982.

The recipient in this case was William R. Ross, an auctioneer specialising in farm auctions, who was at 18 Blagrave Street from around 1929. Although Mr Ross left the firm around 1936, it continued in his name until around 1969, when it became a part of Cooksey, Walker, Ross & Co., in the Market Place. If

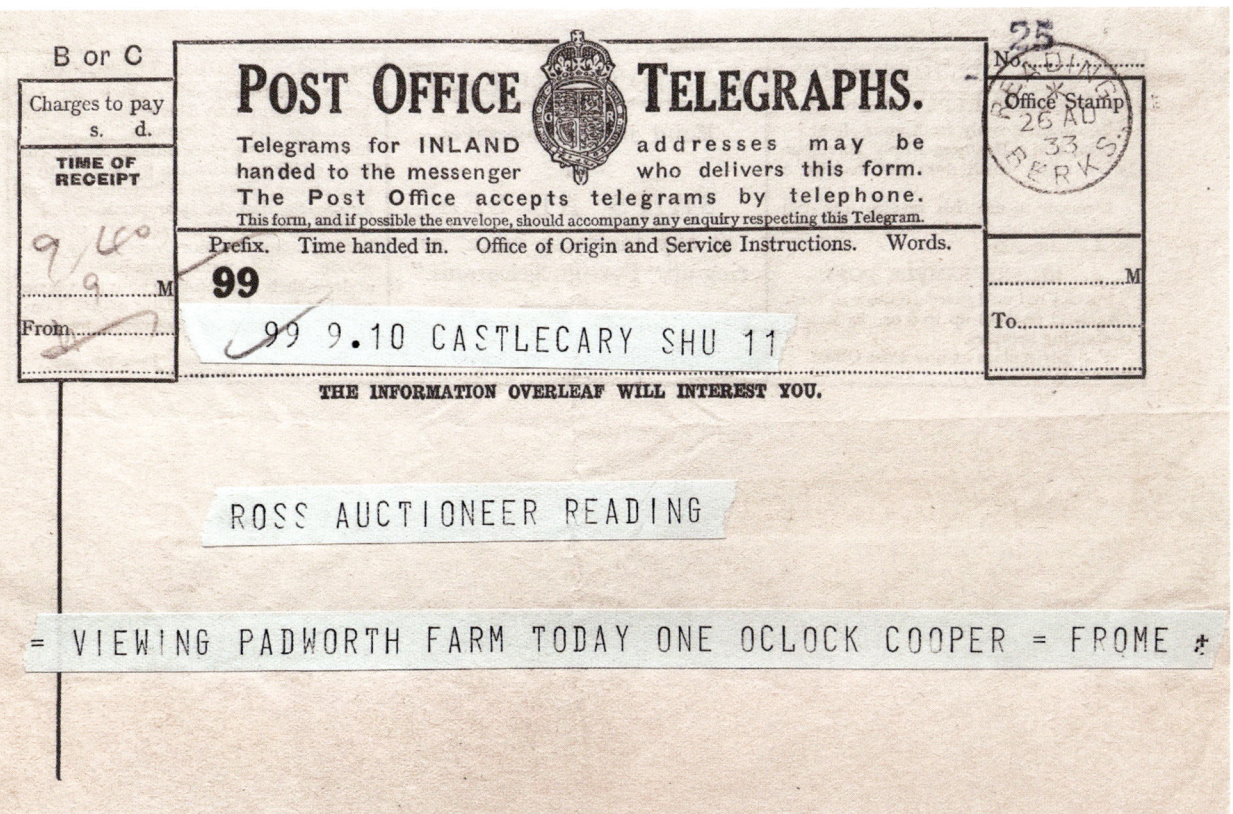

their name sounds slightly amusing, one of their rivals at the time went by the even more fulsome name of Vanderpump & Wellbelove (incorporating Wellesley-Smith & Co.)!

Before the internal combustion engine became widespread, one of the most important trades must have been that of the blacksmith. At the time of the bill illustrated overleaf, in 1930, motor transport was becoming more common on the roads, but horses continued to be important, especially on farms. Hugh Miller, the farmer at Great Park Farm, Mortimer, must have been a relative of

Private Address: Willesborough, Conisboro' Avenue.

Repairs Promptly Executed.

Works—NORTH STREET, CAVERSHAM, 31st Jan. 1921.

Mr H. Miller

DR. TO **W. A. PAGE & SON,**
(MRS. W. A. PAGE, W. A. PAGE.)
SHOEING & GENERAL SMITHS.
- PRACTICAL BOAT SMITHS. -
Lawn Mowers Ground & Overhauled.
Kitchen Ranges and Grates of all kinds Repaired.
ACCOUNTS MONTHLY. Ornamental & Plain Fencing.
PHONE No. 3142.

229-20

			£	s.	d.
Dec 1920	To a/c rendered.		5	15	
Jan. 2nd	2 shoes 1 steeled & screwing 4 holes Daisy			5	6
"	2 dz 3/8" frost studs to Reg.			3	
" 3rd	2 hind shoes & screwing 4 holes brown pony			4	6
" 7th	2 F shoes & screwing 4 holes Daisy			4	0
" 9th	2 hind shoes 1 steeled & screwing & holes			5	6
" 14th	2 front shoes & screwing & holes brown pony			4	6
" 15th	2 hind shoes 1 steeled & screwing & holes Daisy			5	6
" 17th	2 hind shoes & screwing & holes brown pony			4	6
" 21st	2 hind shoes 1 steeled & screwing & holes Daisy			5	6
" 24th	2 front shoes & screwing & holes brown pony			4	6
" 28th	4 shoes 1 steeled & screwing 8 holes cob Daisy			10	6
" 30th	2 hind shoes & screwing & holes Brown Pony			4	6
" 31st	Shutting up 1 billhook & fixing on bills shutting & mending handle & sharpening fold bar			5	6
		£	9	2	6

Mrs A. S. Miller of Great Park Farm, who in the same year was having her piano tuned by Barnes and Avis of Reading (see p. 35–6). It seems rather a long way to come, from Mortimer to Caversham to have your horses shod.

North Street is one of the two cul-de-sac streets off the eastern side of Prospect Street in Caversham: North Street is the one nearer Peppard, and South Street the one nearer Reading. In 1930, the Page family were living in Conisboro' Avenue, on Caversham Heights. Edmund Page had been a smith in Westfield Road, Caversham, in 1899, and he took over the forge of George Francis in North Street in 1901. E. Page and Son changes to W. A. Page and Son between 1918 and 1937.

During the month of January 1930, Mr Miller was at the forge on 12 occasions, usually to have one of two horses shod – one called 'Daisy,' and the other a brown pony. A pair of front shoes, secured by four screws, cost 4s. 6d. and a pair of hind shoes, 5s. 6d. When fitting hind shoes, one of them is sometimes described as 'steeled.' Not everything on the bill is legible and understandable to an outsider. On 2 January 2 dozen 'front studs to Reg.' were supplied, and on 31 January, 5s. 6d. was charged for 'shuttering up 1 bridle ring and fixing on bridle shuttering and mending handle and chamfering fold bar.'

Mr Miller owed £5 15s. for December, and £3 7s. 6d. for January, bringing the total to £9 2s. 6d.

The bill is enlivened by images of a farrier shoeing a horse at the forge, while another horse awaits his attention, and two rowing-boats, each containing eight oarsmen and a cox, of the kind seen at regattas, indicating that the Pages were also boat smiths. In addition, they advertise the servicing and sharpening of lawnmowers, repairs to kitchen ranges and fire grates, and 'plain and ornamental fencing', presumably of cast and wrought iron.

One of the last smiths in Reading itself must have been Tibbetts, Son and White, who had their forge in Merchants Place, off Friar Street, until 1996.

30. A bill for shoeing horses and work done on their bridles from 1930

The arrival of motor transport saw garages beginning to take over the work of blacksmiths and stables, and coachbuilders were becoming vehicle body builders. One of the Reading firms which successfully managed the transition from horses to motors was Vincent's. When the receipted bill illustrated overleaf was issued, in 1914, they were in Castle Hill, just below Coley Place – a site now occupied by

31. The wording in the small box to the left of the header says that W. Vincent will take every precaution, but accepts no liability if vehicles are damaged by fire or any other cause, including accidents which might occur while they are being driven by his engineers.

the roundabout with the Inner Distribution Road below. They were agents for some of the more luxurious makes of car, they built car bodies to customers' requirements, they repaired cars, and hired out cars. By 1908, they had started the first motor taxi service in the town. One aspect of their work, not advertised here, was the building of horse-boxes, for which they were to become particularly famous: they built the first motorised horse-box in the land, and built them for the aristocracy and royalty.

The main job outlined on the bill involved modifying a new bracket for a searchlight, and bending and fitting a pipe from the gas generator to the acetylene lamp. At the time, acetylene lamps were still considered better than the electric lamps which would soon overtake them. The customer was a Lieutenant Johnson, and below the receipt is written in red ink: 'please send receipt to Carter, Clay and Lintott, The Broadway, Woking' – showing that Vincent's were attracting customers from miles around. The Woking firm were accountants.

32. One can't help wondering how useful the 50 pins on this card would have been.

William Vincent started to work for a wheelwright in Arborfield in 1806. He was able to take over the business, and was joined in it by his two sons. The firm moved over from building horse-drawn vehicles to motorised ones, and their showroom and works in Reading opened in 1899. When the Grand Cinema closed in Broad Street in 1922, William James Vincent took over the building as a car showroom. This building was later the Cadena Café, and is presently a branch of Santander. Then in 1928 they moved to a new showroom and works on Station Square – the Thames Tower office building stands on the site of the showroom. It had large windows of curved glass, which gave window-gazers the impression that there was no glass there. The works were described as 'the largest, most complete and most modern works the motor trade has yet seen in this country.' Vincent's were kept busy during the Second World War, building vehicles of different kinds, including ambulances, and manufacturing aircraft parts. They moved to Oxford Road around 1972, and in 1987 became a part of the Penta Group. The showrooms moved back to Castle Hill, but the name of the firm disappeared from the Reading phone book between 1989 and 1990.

Before we had laundries, laundrettes and automatic washing machines, there were washerwomen, or laundresses, to do your washing for you, and the old Reading directories list them. The Reading and Caversham Laundry claimed to be 'the oldest and most reliable laundry in the district' – it first appears in directories in the 1884 edition, in George Street, Caversham, then as now.

By the time this advertising card appeared, around 1914, its vans were going round, collecting and delivering laundry in Ascot, Blackwater, Bracknell, Goring, Henley, Pangbourne, Shinfield, Shiplake, Twyford, Wargrave, Wokingham – and even London. As well as washing and ironing, it undertook dyeing, dry cleaning and carpet beating. This was before the time when households had fitted carpets and vacuum cleaners.

Many still remember the disastrous fire of 1988, when the laundry buildings were severely damaged. It was said to have been caused by the spontaneous combustion of a pile of particularly greasy laundry. At the time the business was owned by a firm called Whiteknights, who quickly had their laundry rebuilt. Subsequently it was owned by Berendsen, and now (2023), the sign says 'Elis.'

33. Leaflet from around 1960, advertising the fact that the milkman was now delivering groceries as well as milk.

Besides the laundry near the Caversham end of Reading Bridge, there was a 'receiving office' in a different part of town, at 421 Oxford Road. It was still listed in the 1971 directory. The advertising card, crimped so that it could hold 50 pins, was presumably offered as a free gift to customers. The Oxford Road receiving office is now the Hot Stuff tandoori take-away.

Another trader who came to your door was the milkman, who until the early twentieth century was often the farmer who had looked after the cows, and brought the milk in churns on a horse-drawn float, to be ladled into customers' own jugs. Milk in pint bottles was the order of the day by the 1950s.

This leaflet, from around 1960, was a reminder that the milkman, besides delivering milk and cream, could also bring butter and cheese, yogurt, and a host of groceries, in boxes, cans and bottles.

Job's started in Middlesex, with a dairy run by Mrs Roberts. In 1819, Mrs Roberts married a Mr Job, and the business was passed on down the family. In 1930, they opened a modern milk pasteurising plant at Hanworth. This was at a time when tuberculosis, or consumption, was still striking people down, and there was concern that tuberculosis in cattle could be passed on to humans who drank their milk, so stress was laid on the routine testing and pasteurisation of milk. The pasteurisation process in the 1930s was known as HTST – High Temperature, Short Time. The milk was heated to 161 degrees F., the temperature was held for 15 seconds, and then the milk was cooled rapidly to 40 degrees.

The firm opened their second milk pasteurising plant at Didcot in 1935, and were able to expand their business.

They arrived in Reading in 1943, during the Second World War, and by 1960 they had offices on Shinfield Road Reading, School Road Tilehurst, and Headley Road Woodley.

They were bought out by Unigate, who in turn merged with Dairy Crest, who still provide a doorstep delivery service in the town.

Since the 1950s, the economy of Reading has sometimes been described as 'beer, bulbs and biscuits' – a search of the online British Newspaper Archive finds it first used in 1957. One might quibble, and say that biscuits should come first, and that Sutton and Sons were famous for seeds, rather than bulbs. They produced seeds for amateur gardeners, but for farmers as well, and grass seed for sports grounds was a speciality. Their seeds were shipped around the empire. Suttons were in the Market Place, but for a while they had a formidable rival in Friar Street, in Fidler and Sons. The name of Mr J. C. Fidler, entrepreneur and benefactor, appears several times in this book.

The 1851 bill for Suttons illustrated overleaf shows the original shop, and the sign just below the guttering reads: 'Established 1806.' These premises in the Market Place were later rebuilt in Victorian Gothic style in 1872, but the site is now occupied by the bland Soane Point office building.

The business expanded greatly under Martin Hope Sutton, the son of John Sutton, the founder. He was able to take advantage of the railway and the penny post, which both arrived in 1840. The site in the Market Place, where farmers gathered regularly to sell their produce must also have been advantageous.

The bill is made out to 'Higgot, Esq.,' who must have been a farmer, though despite his unusual name, has proved elusive in directories and old newspapers. He was buying vegetable seeds, such as 'Coss Lettice,' 'Suttons Imperial Cabbage,'

Reading, Berks Mids 1851

— Wiggot Esq

BOT. OF JOHN SUTTON & SONS
Nurserymen, Seed Growers
& Contract Planters

ESTABLISHED 1806
READING SEED WAREHOUSE
SUTTON & SONS

Great attention Paid to the growth of the most approved kinds of Turnip and other Agricultural Seeds

Natural Grass Seeds in great variety for permanent Pasture, Grounds laid out & planted with taste and economy

Nos 7 & 8, Market Place.

1851			
April 12	2 qts Purple top Swede	3	0
	1 ℔ Large White Belgian Carrot	1	0
	½ ℔ Yellow Globe Mangold Wurzel	–	4
	4 oz Electrine long red do	–	6
	½ ℔ Guernsey Parsnip	–	6
	4.3 ℔ Broad Clover	1. 5	1
	1 pint Marrowfat Pea	–	6
	1 oz Dark red Beet	–	6
	1 — Short Horn Carrot	–	4
	½ — Suttons Imperial Cabbage	–	6
	½ — a Superb green		

Opposite page:
34. Some of the seeds seem to have been sold by weight (1 lb. Large White Belgian Carrot) and sometimes by volume (2 qts. Purple top'd Swede).

and 'Short Horn Carrot,' but he was also buying seeds for animal feed – 'Yellow Globe Mangold Wurzles,' 'Elvetham Long Red Mangold Wurzles,' and 43 lb. of 'Broad Clover' seeds. The last of these was by far the dearest item on the bill, at £1 5s. 1d. The date, top right, reads 'Midr. 1851' – signifying midsummer – though lower down, it appears that the seeds were actually supplied on 12 April. This indicates the long periods of credit allowed to regular customers.

The firm built up an enviable reputation, breeding their own varieties and testing them in trial grounds. Family members were driven by Christian ideals, and they expected their employees to follow their lead. Among their extensive buildings in the Market Place, The Forbury and Kings Road was the Abbey Hall, in Abbey Square, near the present-day Central Library. Here, a short act of worship (not compulsory) took place for the employees, before the start of each working day.

Suttons left Reading in 1976, and moved to Torquay, where there would be no shortage of part-time labour outside the tourist season, when the firm was at its busiest. Their trial grounds between London Road and the railway at Earley became the Suttons Business Park.

At the time of the great Victorian expansion of Reading, house building was in the hands of many small building firms, each of them building a terrace here and a terrace there. Contrary to popular belief, the big Reading employers, Huntley & Palmers and Suttons, did not themselves build houses for their workers on a large scale. Following the First World War, Reading Corporation was a major housebuilder, building 'homes for heroes.' By the 1940s, housebuilding firms were bigger, and might build whole streets, and now, building firms are national in scope.

The leaflet illustrated overleaf is undated, but was probably issued by J. T. Cook and Son around 1946 to advertise houses for sale on their Berkeley Estate, though some of the houses were built just before and during the Second World War.

Berkeley Avenue was constructed around 1908, coming off the Bath Road and crossing the Holy Brook and the River Kennet to join Pell Street. The Coley goods branch railway line also passed beneath it, and was being constructed at the same time. The new avenue gave traffic on the Great West Road a way through Reading which avoided the town centre – Pell Street led to Crown Street, and Crown Street to the London Road.

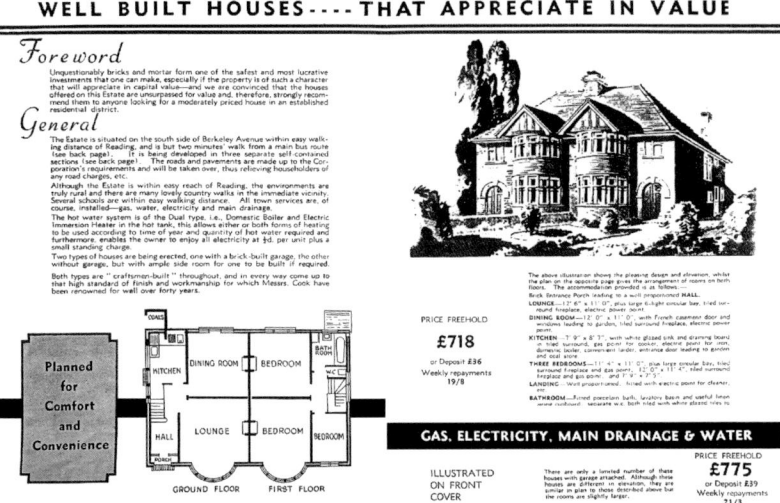

35. Advertisement for 3-bedroomed semi-detached houses, available with or without garages

Cook's Berkeley Estate comprised what are now Baydon Drive (some houses occupied by 1939) and Hungerford Drive (1941) off Berkeley Avenue, and Froxfield Avenue off Coley Avenue (houses occupied by 1949). All were dead ends: the leaflet states that 'at the end of each road there is a convenient 'round about' for cars to turn.' The use of inverted commas suggests that traffic roundabouts, at the time, were something novel. The roads also boasted pavements and grass verges with ornamental trees, which would be tended by the council at public expense.

All the houses were semi-detached, and had the same basic layout, but were of two types. The more expensive type had slightly larger rooms, and a garage at the side. Those without a garage had ample space at the side to build one, should it be needed. All had a front porch, a lounge, a dining room and a kitchen downstairs, with a lean-to coal store at the back. The two reception rooms had fireplaces, as had the two larger bedrooms above them. Also on the first floor was a smaller bedroom without a fireplace, and a bathroom and separate wc. Houses with garages cost £775, or a deposit of £39 and weekly payments of 21s. 3d., presumably for 25 years, although the leaflet doesn't state this.

36. Milsom's, the builders' merchants, gave the address of their premises on Caversham Road as the Britannia Wharf, though they were nowhere near waterways.

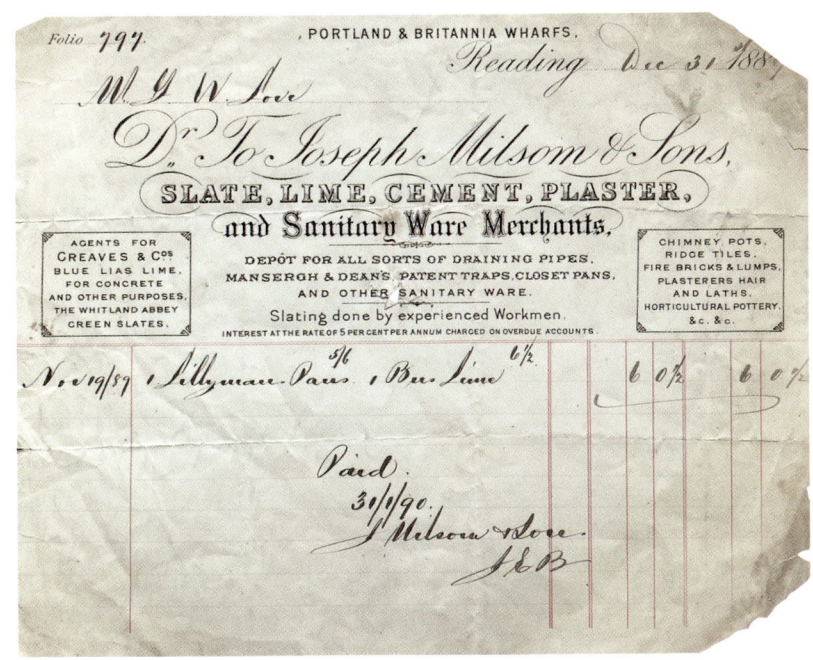

Naturally, builders would have needed bricks, which could be sourced locally, but timber and slate were brought in, often by water until well into the twentieth century. Joseph Milsom, whose bill is illustrated here, started in business as a coal merchant, at Dyson's Court, Friar Street, in the 1840s. By 1855 he had his own wharf – the Portland Wharf, on the corner of Kings Road and Watlington Street, by the Silly Bridge (now called Watlington Bridge) – and by 1888, Milsom and Sons were also at Britannia Wharf, Caversham Road, on the corner of Great Knollys Street.

To find a 'wharf' so far from a waterway seems strange. The name was probably because in Reading, coal, timber and builders' merchants often brought in their materials on barges, and the Britannia and Britannia Tap public houses were on the opposite side of Caversham Road. The Portland Wharf was one of a number of wharves on Kings Road, backing on to the New Cut of the Kennet Navigation. Another of them was called the Bangor Wharf, presumably where roofing slates

Opposite page:
37. The lower part of the calendar for 1898 has unfortunately been torn off, but even so, it is an interesting relic.

from North Wales were unloaded, and it seems likely that at the Portland Wharf, Portland cement, if not Portland stone, would have been unloaded.

By the twentieth century, the Milsoms were builders' merchants as well as coal merchants, but they sold their Portland Wharf to Huntley & Palmers shortly before the outbreak of war in 1914. The biscuit bakers were buying up the land along Kings Road opposite their factories, where they had plans for a 'Great Social Scheme.' One large building was to contain kitchens, dining-rooms and rest and recreation rooms, while another building was to be a 'Great Hall' seating 2,500 people. The idea was that the facilities were to be made available to everyone living in the area, but war intervened and the vision did not materialise. The land became a garden, for the enjoyment of H & P employees, but with the closure of the factories and offices, it was given to the Borough, and the garden is now open to all.

The Milsoms remained in business for a further 50 years or so, with their last advertisements appearing in the local papers in the 1980s. For many years the yard was disused and the buildings boarded up, but the site is now (2023) being redeveloped.

The Lillyman Pan on the invoice was a type of toilet pan made by Twyfords of Stoke-on-Trent: the exact significance of the other item, which looks like '1 Bus Lime,' is not obvious, but may have been a kind of cement to fix the pan to the floor.

Since this book is a compilation of the work of printers, mainly from Reading, it seemed appropriate to have a section of the book dedicated to them (see Reading printers, p. 243–7). However, four examples have been chosen for this chapter, where the printers have advertised themselves, or sent out correspondence, rather than printing things for others.

The earliest printers in the town would seem to have been Parks and Kinnier, printers and publishers of the *Reading Mercury* newspaper, which began publication in 1723. Since then, many printers have operated in Reading, some of them small jobbing printers, but also some firms with a national reputation. Until recently, Cox and Wyman were printing paperbacks by the tens of thousands from Cardiff Road, and we had the Eastern Press in Katesgrove Lane; the Berkshire Printing Company in Oxford Road (a subsidiary of Brooke Bond Liebig, who did the printing for Brooke Bond tea, including the tea-cards, and for Oxo); and the Co-op Printing Works on Elgar Road.

Whether or not a calendar could be called a piece of ephemera is perhaps debatable – though its usefulness is certainly time-limited. This calendar for 1898 – or what remains of a calendar – is interesting on several counts. Diana Mackarill has written about it at greater length (see Sources, p. 248).

Joseph John Beecroft, a printer, came from Lowestoft to Reading in 1859, and with his partner, began the firm of Barcham and Beecroft, in Broad Street,

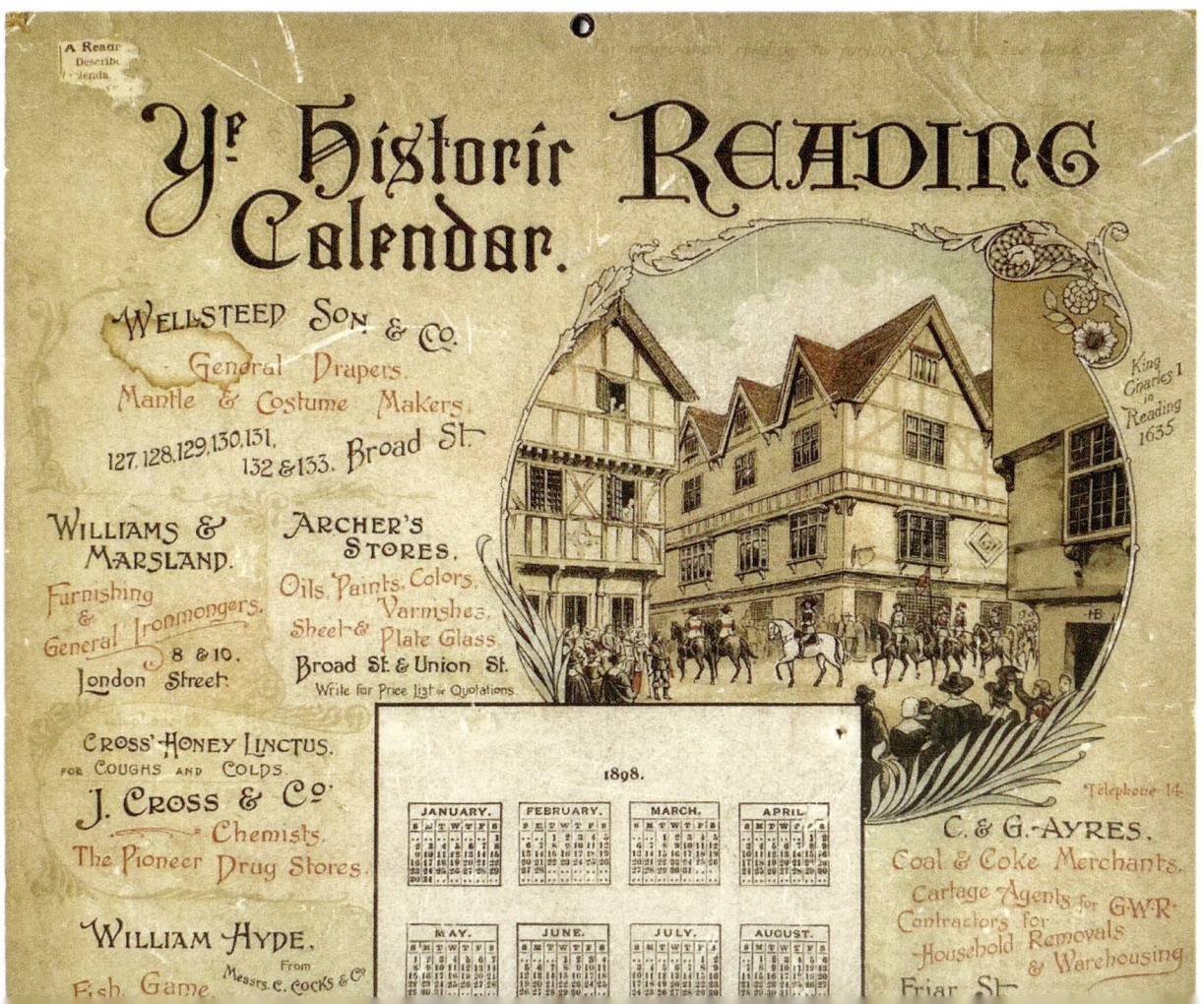

Opposite page:
38. It has not been possible to date the letter exactly, but it is addressed to another character with an extraordinary name – W. S. Clutterbuck. He was the Deputy Town Clerk of Reading from 1900, and Town Clerk 1904–1919.

where Waterstone's bookshop now is. He was a Methodist local preacher who worshipped at Wesley Church when it opened in 1873.

His more famous son, Herbert Beecroft, was born in 1864 and became an artist and lithographer, studying at the Reading University Extension College, and then in London and Paris. Herbert also became an entertainer, with his 'Sketching Lectures' in which he produced lightning sketches of members of the audience, interspersed with humorous patter. Both Reading Central Library and Reading Museum have examples of his art work, and that of his father. And, of course, the design of this calendar, and the printing of it, are the work of the Beecroft family.

In 1904, Herbert emigrated to Sydney, Australia, where much of his best work was done. His most famous painting was a portrait of Christ, said to have been painted in 1927 as a result of experiencing a vision of that face. In it, Christ has piercing blue eyes and reddish long hair and beard, and is remarkably European in appearance. The painting was much copied, and reproductions of it hung in many a parlour and Sunday school classroom in England.

Part of the appeal of the calendar, or what remains of it, is the advertising for various Reading firms, many of them still well remembered – and another is the picture itself, representing Charles I, entering Reading on horseback during the Civil War. The building to the left must be the George Inn, and its appearance must be conjectural. But on the other side of Minster Street is Walsingham House (later known as Hounslow's Corner), which was much photographed before being unceremoniously demolished in 1905. It had fine plasterwork inside, and was said to have belonged to Sir Francis Walsingham, Queen Elizabeth's spymaster. The Queen herself was said to have slept there – though this is probably legendary. The sacrifice of a fine old house for a cake shop seems a poor exchange.

When new shops were built in front of the Broad Street Chapel in 1892, Barcham and Beecroft's printing works moved to Station Road, where it remained in business for a few more years, until around 1898 – the date of the calendar.

Members of the Poynder family of printers were also artists. This enterprise began with the take-over of Macaulay's around 1880. It was Mrs Elizabeth Poynder who ran it: her husband, John Andrew Poynder, worked in banking.

There were three sons, each artistically gifted, who worked for the firm – Robert Blake Poynder, George Andrew Poynder, and Thomas Henry Poynder. All three

W. S. Clutterbuck, Esq.

Dear Sir,

    Herewith we send you ROUGH PROOF of your kind order, we hope it meets with your approval. To prevent errors occurring will you please mark plainly any corrections or alterations you desire. The Paper or Colour of Ink can be altered if necessary.

    We await your reply and are,

        Yours faithfully,

          Poynder & Son.

trained at the Reading School of Art and Science in Valpy Street, which became the University Extension College, and eventually the University of Reading. It was the youngest, Thomas Henry, who designed the Poynder Series of Type and Ornaments, and the Reading Old-Face typeface, and it seems likely that he designed the letterhead illustrated here.

The original shop was in Broad Street, on the corner of Chain Street – which afterwards was occupied by Silver's menswear for many years. The Poynders were printers, stationers and booksellers, but in the early years also seem to have run an employment agency and to have sold tickets for various events, calling the shop a 'Library and Timetable Office.'

For a brief period from 1896, George Poynder sold second-hand books from a shop at 23 Cross Street, but by 1902 was back in Broad Street. The big change came about in 1906, with the move from Broad Street. The printing works moved to 3–4 Gun Street, and was called the Holybrook Press, because the brook ran directly behind the building. A new stationery and fancy goods shop opened at 4 Queen Victoria Street.

As printers, the firm was in great demand for the production of books, brochures, posters and handbills. They advertised 'Printing of Taste,' with the text, of course, set in Poynder type. The printing operations were taken over by Lamport Gilbert in 1944, but continued in the same building. It is now occupied as the Zerodegrees restaurant and microbrewery. The stationery and gift shop continued, with its last advertisements in the local press appearing in late 1968. For its last years, it was run by the extraordinarily-named P. M. Tiffin.

The letterhead seems to show a saint, with a halo round his head, seated under an apple-tree, reading an ancient book.

Tom Morley (1862–1951) was educated at the British School in Southampton Street, and then at the School of Art in Castle Street, under Charles Havell. Despite this, he started work as a pawnbroker's assistant, and then worked for 14 years for a timber merchant. At the end of his time there, he was in charge of more than 100 employees. He left to start his own business, as a printer, designer and artist. In 1924, his address was Electric Press, 40 Kings Road. He was also an entertainer, calling himself 'Henri' – his full name was Henry Thomas Morley. In December 1897, he advertised in the *Reading Mercury*

39. Tom Morley, over his long life, was a man of many parts.

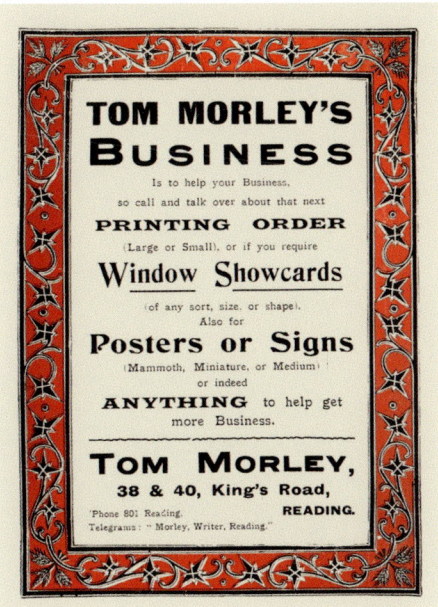
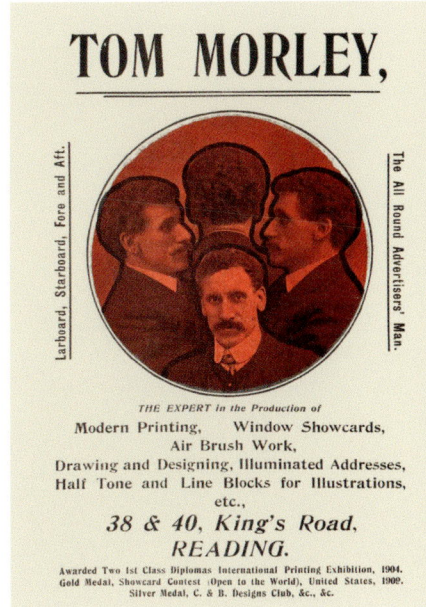

that he was available for 'Christmas parties and entertainments, with cinematograph and Punch and Judy, and as conjurer, ventriloquist, etc.' He also had a reputation as a 'lightning' cartoonist. The newspaper advertisement seems to be the first mention of a cinematograph in Reading – the first moving picture demonstrations in London were in the previous year.

On top of this, over the years he was a magistrate, a Freemason, a member of the Borough Council, on the Board of Management of the Royal Berkshire Hospital, Secretary and Treasurer of the Queen Victoria Institute for District Nursing, Treasurer of the Reading Tuberculosis Dispensary Care Association, Secretary and Treasurer of the Berkshire Archaeological Society, Fellow of the Royal Historical Society, Fellow of the Royal Society of Antiquaries of Scotland, and Honorary Curator (Medieval Antiquities) of Reading Museum.

40. An apartment block now stands on the site of Greenslade's factory, by King's Bridge, otherwise known as Factory Bridge.

He lectured on archaeology and kindred subjects, and his publications include *Rides and Rambles around Reading* (in four volumes), *Monumental Brasses of Berkshire*, and *Old and Curious Playing Cards*. The online catalogue of Reading Borough Libraries has a fuller list, and from it, a number of drawings of old buildings in the area by him can be seen.

Greenslade's were founded by Henry E. Greenslade in 1871, and closed in 1970, just short of their centenary. The works was in Kings Road, next to King's Bridge, or Factory Bridge, diagonally opposite Huntley & Palmers, and handy for the Borough Arms pub. They specialised in the printing of colour labels for grocery products. The works bordered Kennet Side, so that the employees on the upper floors were able to fish in the Kennet by holding their rods out of the windows.

It was rumoured, when they closed and the works had been demolished, that tons of contaminated earth had to be removed. They had printed banknotes for a foreign country, the green ink they used contained some compound of cyanide, and it had found its way into the ground – but this may be a myth. There was a neighbouring firm called Reading, Green and Marvell, who made colour from metals for paint, who may also have been responsible. This letter is, appropriately, on green paper.

The making of brushes and brooms may seem a humble occupation, though if one considers just how many brushes one has in the kitchen, under the stairs or in the garden shed, it becomes apparent how important it still is. Over the centuries, every town must have had at least one brush-maker, and Mr Knott's establishment at 35 Southampton Street existed between 1885 and 1964, according to the old street directories. It was adjacent to the graveyard wall of St Giles' Church.

The bill shown overleaf, dating from 1886, is interesting on account of the different kinds of brush mentioned, and because of the curious way in which the money is calculated. The customer, George Love, was an ironmonger, plumber, gas and water fitter and locksmith in London Road. He was probably re-selling the brushes he was buying wholesale from John Knott.

The brush-making industry obviously had its own vocabulary. The kinds of brush listed here are the flat dust, the bass broom, the hair broom, the union scrub, the imp. solid back union scrub, the round oils, the hair banister and the fibre carpet banister. The *Oxford English Dictionary* says that 'bass' was originally the inner bark of a lime tree, but came to mean 'any other similar fibre.' It doesn't have 'banister' as a kind of brush.

The prices are given as so much per dozen, and the quantities are sometimes expressed as a figure, and sometimes as a quarter dozen – i.e. three brushes.

One of the more unusual trades in the high street must be that of umbrella makers. Today, umbrellas can be bought in outfitters' shops, department stores and even supermarkets, but are likely to have been manufactured far away in countries with low labour costs.

Many will remember the large metal umbrella, red with a yellow border, that projected over the pavement on a bracket over the shop at 33 Friar Street, until the 1970s at least.

The umbrella and walking-stick business had been founded in 1847, as it says on the bill overleaf, but it was founded by Joseph Beard, and in a much older building in the street. Ten years later, and the firm was Ford and Beard, with John Cox appearing in directories in 1877. He was at No. 33 from 1897, or just before.

The bill, written out in January but not paid until July, was for 10s. 8d. One umbrella had been repaired, and another re-covered. Silk was used for umbrella

Feb 10 1886

Mr Love London Road

Bo.t of J Knott Brush Maker
35 Southampton St Reading

No			at per 3		£	s	d
1/4 3	1	flat dust	3/6	x			10½
1/4 "	2	do do	4/6	x		1	1½
2	0	Bass Broom	6/	x		1	2
2	1	do do	7/	x		1	2
2	2	do do	8/	x		1	4
1	3	do do	10/	x		1	10
1/4 "	2	union scrub	4/	x		1	9
1/4 "	4	imp solid back union scrub	7/				
1/4 "	1	Round oils	8	x			2
1/4 "	3	do do	1/6	x			4½
2	2	Hair Banister	8/	x		1	4
2	3	do do	10/	x		1	8
1	4	Hair Broom	8/	x			8
1	5	do do	10/	x			10
			12/			1	

Opposite page:

41. Frederick Knott followed his father John in the brush-making trade.

42. A bill for re-covering and repairing umbrellas

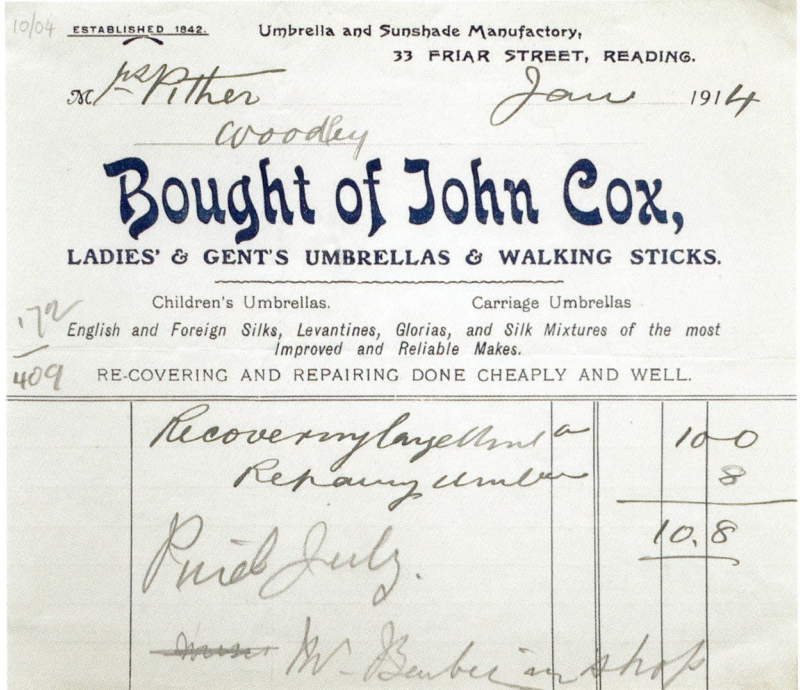

coverings, and a variety of English and foreign silks was on offer, including levantines, a stout, close-woven and twilled black silk, and glorias, a mixture of silk and wool.

As time went by, making and repairing umbrellas by hand presumably became less profitable, and John Cox's firm began selling toys in the 1950s. The last entry for the shop in the Reading street directories was in 1967.

The building is still there in Friar Street, until recently a pawn shop called Cash Converters but empty in 2024.

Then as now, firearms are held by farmers, for controlling pests, and by sportsmen for their amusement. Following the Boer War, rifle clubs, sometimes attached to pubs, were encouraged, to teach men how to shoot, and some pubs

43. Thomas Turner's firm was in business for over 170 years, at four different locations over the years.

had their own shooting galleries: the Boers had proved the more experienced shots. Gunsmiths like Thomas Turner were there to supply the town's needs for over 170 years.

This bill is made out to Captain Pigott-Carleton, who lived at Greywell Hill House in north Hampshire. In full, he was the Rt. Hon. Guy Pigott-Carleton, Third Baron Dorchester, who had died on 3 December 1875. As may be seen here, an account from 1873 is still outstanding, and on 22 December, presumably in 1875, 200 Green 12 cartridges were bought. A note at the foot of the bill states that the 1873 amount has not been paid, and on the back is a pencilled note to say that 'The Executor has nothing to do with the item of 22nd December', probably because the cartridges were purchased after Baron Dorchester's death. All rather curious.

Mr Turner claims that he makes 'improved breech loaders. Rifle & air-guns, air-canes & revolving pistols' and can supply 'Powder. Shot. Flasks. Pouches and every Sporting requisite. Equal to any house in London'. (An air-cane was a kind of air-gun with a long straight barrel, which looked like a walking-stick.)

The illustration shows a man loading his gun, with a dog on either side of him. The impedimenta of shooting lie on the ground, and hanging from the tree are a brace of dead birds, a hare, and a pheasant. In the distance to the right, two men are firing at a flock of birds.

Turner started in business in Middle Row, Broad Street, in 1838. He was later at 8 Butter Market, and between 1969 and 1971 had a second shop at 21 Whitley Street. After that he was at Whitley Street only. Finally, in 1984, his firm moved to Gosbrook Road in Caversham. Here, it had the advantage of car parking round the back, but the decline in its fortunes seems to have been inexorable. The last edition of The Phone Book in which it is listed is that for 2012, and the shop is now that of A. B. Walker and Son, funeral directors.

Perhaps even more unusual than the making of umbrellas is the art of the taxidermist, which has now almost disappeared. At the time of the bill overleaf, from 1859, taxidermists were called 'naturalists,' and in Reading there were three of them. As well as Thomas Harbor there was W. J. A. Hambling at 113 Friar Street, and William Ravenscroft at 11 Minster Street.

44. Mr Harbor's premises are in an attractive row of old buildings with tiled roofs and dormer windows, still standing.

Mr Harbor appears first in directories in 1837, at 115 London Street, which with the change from consecutive to odds-and-evens numbering became No. 41. By 1859 he is at No. 23, which is now No. 48.

The two cherubic figures, which appear on either side of the cartouche, appear to have sheaves of arrows on their backs, suggesting hunting, whilst the two exotic birds put one in mind of those stuffed birds under glass domes which decorated many a Victorian drawing-room.

Mr Harbor's customer would seem to have been William Clark Merriman (1805–1877), of Lockeridge House, near Marlborough. Newspaper obituaries mention his interest in fox-hunting, but perhaps his hunting expeditions went farther afield. The wapiti deer mentioned on the bill is like the European red deer, but rather larger, and is native to North America. As well as mounting the stag's head, Mr H. charged ten shillings for 'brushing up and cleaning 2 antelopes.' Mr Merriman was Town Clerk of Marlborough and several times Mayor, with interests in law, banking and railways.

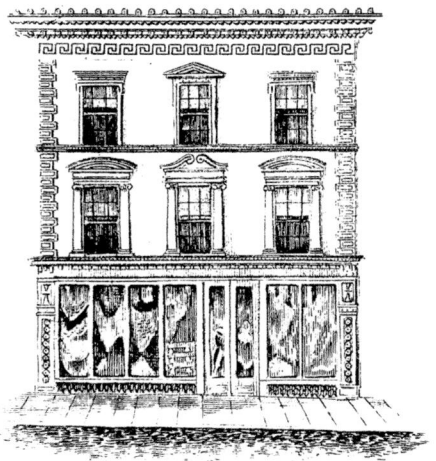

45. Mr Lediard's shop was where the building called Soane Point now stands.

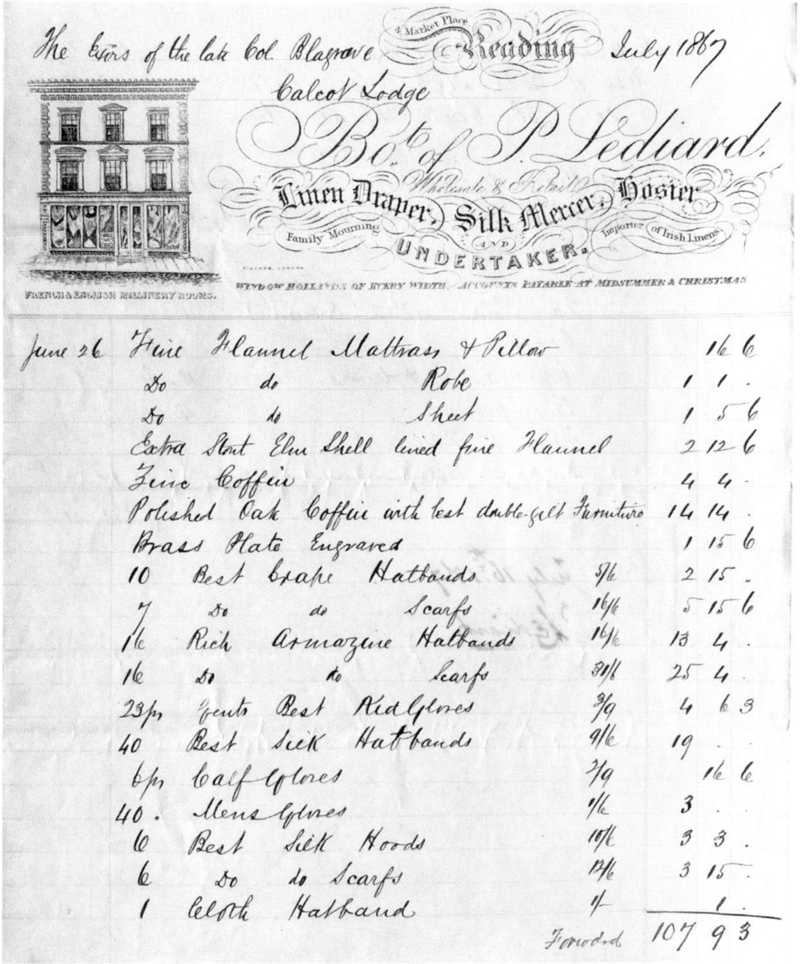

The Exors of the late Col. Blagrave — 4 Market Place Reading July 1867
Calcot Lodge

Bot of P. Lediard.

Wholesale & Retail Linen Draper, Silk Mercer, Hosier
Family Mourning — and — Importer of Irish Linens
UNDERTAKER.

FRENCH & ENGLISH MILLINERY ROOMS.
WINDOW HOLLANDS OF EVERY WIDTH. ACCOUNTS PAYABLE AT MIDSUMMER & CHRISTMAS

June 26	Fine Flannel Mattrass & Pillow			16	6
	Do do Robe		1	1	.
	Do do Sheet		1	5	6
	Extra Stout Elm Shell lined fine Flannel		2	12	6
	Zinc Coffin		4	4	.
	Polished Oak Coffin with best double-gilt Furniture		14	14	.
	Brass Plate Engraved		1	15	6
	10 Best Crape Hatbands	5/6	2	15	.
	7 Do do Scarfs	16/6	5	15	6
	16 Rich Armazine Hatbands	16/6	13	4	.
	16 Do do Scarfs	31/6	25	4	.
	23pr Gents Best Kid Gloves	3/9	4	6	3
	40 Best Silk Hatbands	9/6	19	.	
	6pr Calf Gloves	2/9		16	6
	40. Mens Gloves	1/6	3	.	.
	6 Best Silk Hoods	10/6	3	3	.
	6 Do do Scarfs	12/6	3	15	.
	1 Cloth Hatband	1/-		1	.
	Forward		107	9	3

Finally in this chapter, we have an undertaker's bill for the funeral of a wealthy Victorian. Mr Lediard, as well as being a linen draper, silk mercer and hosier, was an undertaker. Col. John Blagrave of Calcot Lodge, was described in the notice of his 1867 death in the local paper as 'late Colonel of the Berkshire Militia' (see

p. 28), which also has connections with his funeral. The Lodge was the lodge to Calcot Place, and next to Ford's Farm. At the time, it was usual for fashionable funerals to be arranged by drapers; for the less wealthy, carpenters usually provided this service.

Funerals for the wealthy were very much a matter of following fashion and putting on a good show, with the number of carriages and black horses with ostrich plumes on their heads, and the number of attendants and mourners a measure of the earthly success and popularity of the deceased. Col. Blagrave's funeral warranted a hearse drawn by four horses, and three carriages, each drawn by two horses.

Some of the items of clothing for the attendants were hired, and others were purchased, and this, presumably, is where much of the profit for the draper arose. No fewer than 38 black coats and cloaks were hired, but hat-bands, scarfs and gloves had to be bought, it would appear. And these items came in different qualities and varied in price. Cloth hat-bands cost 1s. 6d., but hat-bands of rich armazine as much as 16s. 6d. Scarfs could be of crape, best silk, or rich armazine, and gloves calf or kid. 49 pairs of gloves were required. (Armazine, or armozine, was the rich black silk material used in mourning dress and clerical gowns.) The six best silk hoods were presumably for the pall-bearers.

The polished oak coffin with double gilt furniture cost 14 guineas, but within that were a zinc coffin (4 guineas) and an extra stout elm shell lined with flannel (£2 12s. 6d. – total cost £21 10s. 6d.). Soldering up the coffin cost 10s.

The fees payable to St Michael's Church in Tilehurst were £3 1s. 6d., but in order to get there they must have had to pass a toll gate, presumably on Bath Road, which cost 4s., or 1s. per vehicle.

The total amount owing to Mr Lediard was £131 4s. 9d. An unskilled workman at Huntley & Palmers, the town's biggest employers, could expect to earn around 30s. a week. There is a great deal of social history exemplified in this document.

Mr Lediard had taken over the business from a Mr W. Harris around 1850, and by 1876 it was being run by Morris and Sons.

V. Manufacturing

With Huntley & Palmers being the largest employers in the town for a century and more, it seems appropriate to begin this chapter with biscuit-making. The firm must have been one of the first to apply mass production methods to the baking of biscuits, and in this they worked hand in hand with the engineers, the Reading Ironworks Company (see p. 77–81). They moved from their premises in London Street to a larger site on Kings Road in 1841 – a silk mill which had failed – and bought up the nearby land for future expansion.

For all their Quaker background, the Palmer family do not seem always to have treated their workers well. The first document under consideration shows an unhappy time in labour relations at the factory during the winter of 1911–1912. The episode is recorded in Tony Corley's history of the firm, where he mentions the survival of five documents in the local studies collection at Reading Central Library, of which this is the first.

It was issued by the Reading Trades and Labour Council in December of 1911. It complains of low wages and poor working conditions. Members of trade unions, those suspected of being members of trade unions, and anyone who dared to complain, were summarily dismissed, regardless of their length of service. Anyone who was 'sick or broken down' was told to 'clear off, they are of no use.' This 'heartlessly unscrupulous' company had, 'like an octopus, strangled and crushed out the manhood and the womanhood of its employees.' Strong words indeed, and not how Quaker employers were expected to behave!

Other papers report on a mass meeting of employees, and include a 'supplementary manifesto' in support of the employers, contradicting the 'slanderous and lying statements.' The management responded by issuing a paper on 12 January 1912, expressing gratification at the sentiments expressed at the mass meeting. Wages were raised, for the first time since 1900, in October 1912.

On a happier note, the firm's success in running the biggest biscuit factory in the world was due in no small part to clever advertising. Older people will still remember 'Johnny Ginger' who advertised ginger nut biscuits, and rows of large, airtight tins, with labels displaying the firm's garter motif, which lined the shelves of confectioners' shops before days of pre-packed biscuits. Later came their tag-line, 'The first name in biscuits.'

THE VICTIMISATION AT HUNTLEY & PALMERS'.

A Fight for Life and Liberty.

FELLOW CITIZENS,

This is Christmastide, the time of peace and goodwill to all men !! Yet this very season is the time chosen by this rapacious firm to strike **a ruthless blow** at scores of their workers, a blow causing tears, anxieties and sorrows to many families and fear of desolation in their homes.

The low wages and conditions of employment of their workers **have long been** a bye word, **a scandal to this town and a disgrace to this country.** Like an octopus this heartlessly unscrupulous company has for too long strangled and **crushed out the manhood and womanhood of their victims,** robbed them, and their children too, of joy and happiness, robbed them even of decent food and clothing, robbed them of real life and liberty itself.

Tradesmen have suffered terribly and can scarcely keep their heads above water, whilst many go under, simply because of these workers low purchasing power.

Girls are speeded up, put on new machines and **made to do the work previously done by 3 or 4,** subjecting them to fearful nervous and physical strain and **permanently injuring their eyesight and health.**

Deputations on this and other grievances are peremptorily dismissed, **told to** do this work, accept less wages or **get out** and then **when** sick or **broken down** told they **must clear off,** they are of no use !

Other **girls** are put **on men's work** at half the money, while ventilation is disregarded and factory inspectors hoodwinked.

The same vile treatment and even worse speeding up is **the lot of the men.**

The **only way to alter this** wicked state of affairs **was to organise** as trade unionists, **not for** the purpose of **wanton strikes but** to enable themselves **to make a fair bargain** as sellers of their labour power with the buyers of it.

The low wages and evidence we have also, proves this to be **the only way,** anyone acting as **spokesman** for others or ventilating any grievance is at once **marked down and penalised.**

Two trade unions were formed, many of both sexes joining, and now this dastardly blow is struck. Some 40 or more **men with length of service 40, 30, 27, 22, 21, 15, 14, 13½, 12½ years, and many girls,** tried and faithful servants for 14, 13, 12½, 12, 11, 10½, 10 and 9 years are summarily dismissed because forsooth their loyalty is suspect ! !

Members of the union and even **suspected members too** are **turned away** after all these long years of faithful and profit-yielding service **at a moment's notice.**

Men and Women of Reading of all classes, creed or political faith, **we** earnestly **appeal to you,** for the sake of the mothers and fathers, **for the sake of the helpless little children** whose hungry sobs will strike deeper than a strong man's curse, for the sake of **Reading's reputation** and for our country's fair name and traditions of liberty and fair dealing, **stand by, help** and work for these your brothers and sisters in their time of trouble, in **their great fight** for freedom and **a living wage !**

Money is urgently **needed** for these victims. No man or woman with human instincts should be content to enjoy this festive season's delights unheeding and not helping **to** alleviate this misery and **right these wrongs.**

Workers, join the unions, be real men and women, it is now or never, **freedom or slavery,** choose now, **demand freedom,** a living wage and some joy in life.

Cheques and money may be forwarded to the Hon. Treasurer, Mr. B. Russell, 171 Caversham Road, Reading.

THE READING TRADES AND LABOUR COUNCIL.

Opposite page:
46. A rare survival from 1911, showing the poor state of labour relations at the biscuit factory

47. The sleeve of a small gramophone record – though unfortunately the record itself is missing.

Now torn and battered, this small buff envelope once contained a gramophone record which presumably contained an advertising jingle when you played it. Unfortunately, the record is now missing. At only four inches in diameter, it cannot have played for very long!

Portable wind-up gramophones like the one in the picture were fairly widespread until the 1950s. Normal records then revolved at 78 revolutions a minute, and were ten or twelve inches in diameter. Even twelve-inch records played for only around two-and-a-half minutes.

MEABY'S READING BISCUIT FACTORY

READING, MAY 17 1897 18

Mr W N Coates Old Market Place Grimsby

Dr. to Meaby & Co Ld MILLERS AND SOLE PROPRIETORS OF THE CELEBRATED "TRITICUMINA" (PATENT) ENTIRE WHEAT MEAL BISCUIT MANUFACTURERS

TELEGRAPHIC ADDRESS, "TRITICUM READING" TELEPHONE No. 142.

BANKERS:- J. & C. SIMONDS & Co. READING.

TRADE MARK

	£	s	d
To License due.	1	0	0
June 17th 8½ sacks Meal.	6	12	.
	7	12	0

No. A 2804 Received £ 7 s. 10 d. -
With thanks
MEABY & Co., Limited.
H Marsland

Opposite page:
48. The 'License' referred to on this bill presumably gave Mr Coates permission to use the trade name 'Triticumina'.

But H & P were not the only large-scale biscuit bakers in Reading, as this receipted bill attests. It is for 8½ sacks of meal, and for a licence, sent to a Mr W. N. Coates of Grimsby, in 1897.

Meaby & Company were producing 'Triticumina', a patent wheat meal in which the grain was malted before it was milled. Their mill can be seen in the inset picture: it was in Queens Road, and the spire of Wesley Methodist Church can be seen behind it. 'Triticumina' took its name from the Latin name for wheat – *triticum* – and was marketed nationally, in much the same way as 'Hovis' was being marketed. (The name 'Hovis' was a combination of two Latin words – *hominis vis* – meaning the strength of man, coined in 1890.) Triticumina was easily digestible, and suitable for invalids, according to testimonials from *The Lancet*.

The much larger building in the picture was a biscuit factory, built by Meaby's in South Street in 1892. It isn't known for how long they produced biscuits, but in 1893 they were taken to court by Huntley & Palmers for calling them 'Reading Biscuits.' Although H & P had never registered 'Reading Biscuits' as a trade name, they won their case, so by the time this bill was issued, Meaby's biscuits may have been a thing of the past.

In 1899, the large factory was bought by another biscuit manufacturer, H & O Serpell of Plymouth, who were seeking to expand production. Their activities were temporarily curtailed when the factory was badly damaged by fire in 1904, but they survived, and were a major supplier for Marks and Spencer. The factory was rebuilt, but not to its full height. Serpell's came to grief in 1959, when they were forced into liquidation, after which their building was used by a number of smaller manufacturers, including a metal plating firm. It was finally demolished around 1995, to be replaced by a number of small office units.

Thomas and Joseph Perry came to Reading in 1818 to set up an ironworks, producing agricultural machinery and implements in Katesgrove Lane. As time went by, other partners joined the firm, and it became Barrett, Exall and Andrewes, the Kates's Grove Iron Works, and the Reading Ironworks Company, making a larger range of products. In 1836 they moved to a site across the river, immediately south of where the Inner Distribution Road now crosses the Kennet, where Lower Brook Street, Temple Place and Capital Point now are. Eventually

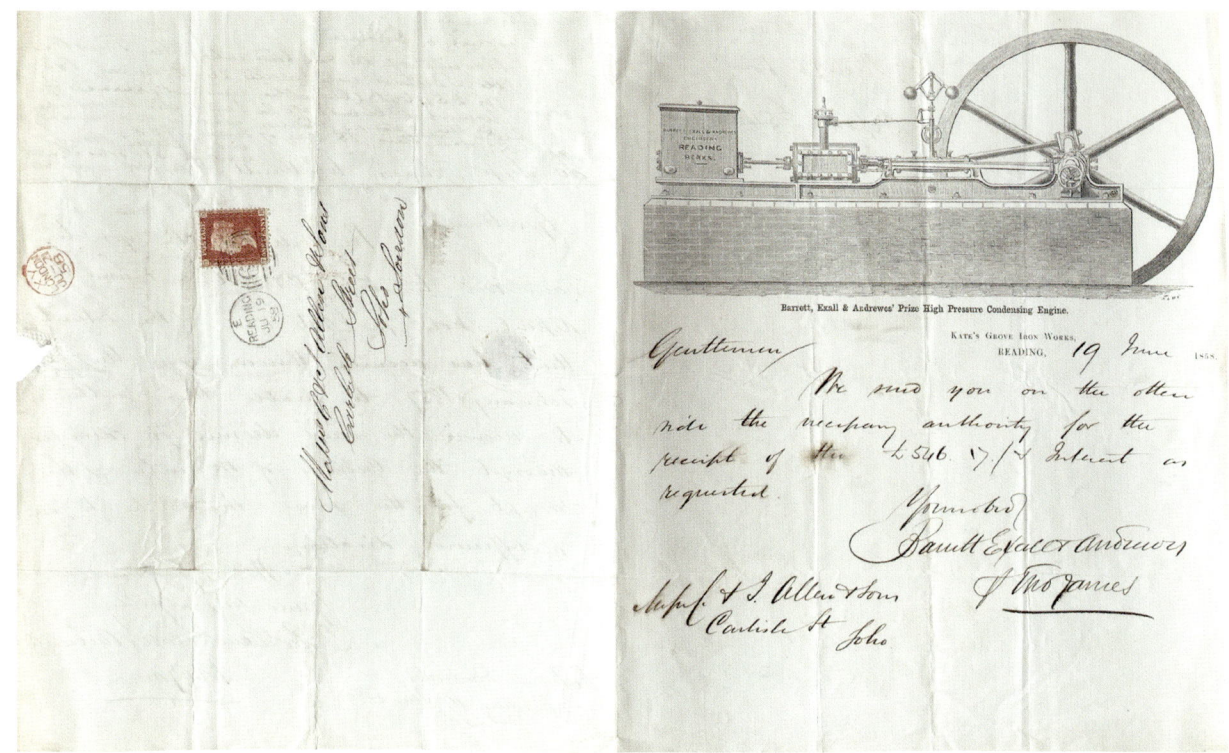

49. Letters from 1858 from what was to become the Reading Ironworks Company

they had buildings on both sides of the river, and built a bridge across. The site enabled them to bring in coal, pig iron, sand, timber, and other necessities by water.

The firm acquired a good reputation over a wide area, winning prizes at exhibitions of engineering, and exhibiting at the Great Exhibition in 1851. Besides general foundry work, they built agricultural machinery, bridges, stationary and locomotive steam engines, and biscuit-making machinery for Huntley & Palmers. For a time, they employed more workers than H & P.

Unfortunately, they failed to move with the times. They faced stiff competition, their designs became seen as outdated, and there were management problems. The firm failed suddenly in 1887. There was no-one to pick up the pieces and everything was sold off. To remind us of their existence in the area there are a couple of milestones on the Bath Road, a village pump at Sonning, some lamp standards, and the monuments, appropriately in cast iron, to Sarah Barrett and Joseph Andrewes in the old Reading Cemetery at Cemetery Junction.

There is a published history of the firm, by Roy Green, Jonathan Brown and Tony Corley.

This surviving letter had been folded four times and sealed along one edge, so that it could be sent by post without an envelope. It has on it a red penny stamp, and there are three postmarks – one from Reading, one from London, and one over the stamp, a roundel with the number 635 in the centre. It was addressed to Messrs. C. and J. Allen and Sons of Soho, London, and on the

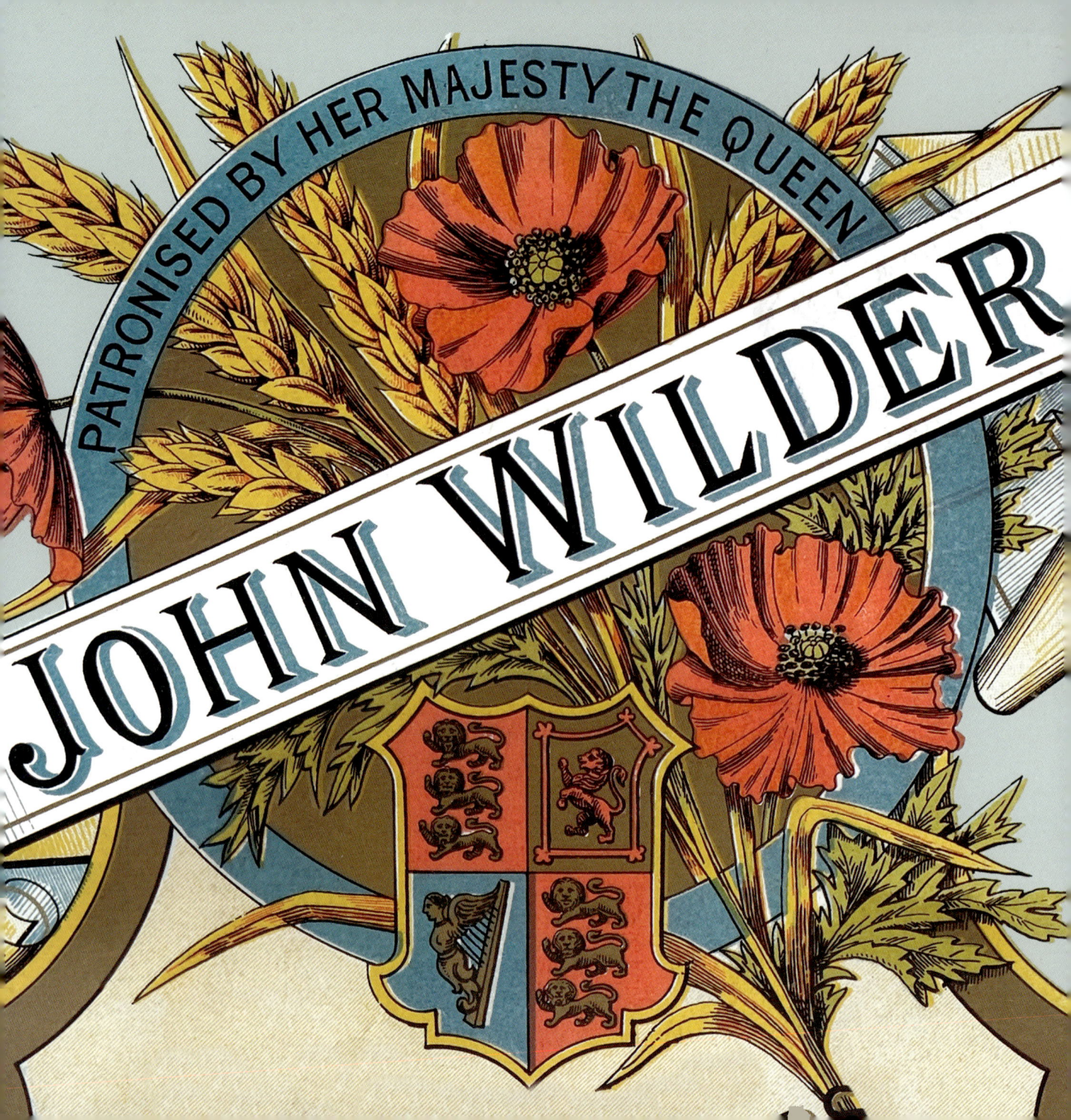

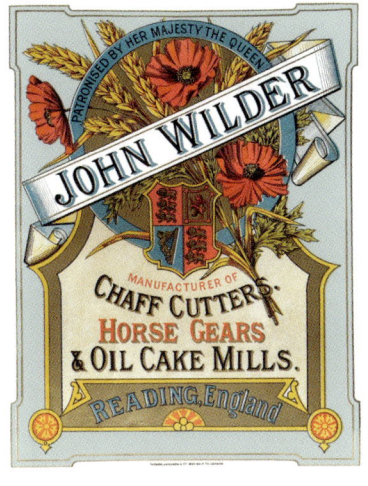  

50. The Wilder family started as iron-founders in the eighteenth century, and have run foundries in several towns and villages over the years.

back of the first letter is another one to a firm of solicitors authorising them to pay £546 17s. to C. and J. Allen, and a receipt, signed over a large violet stamp bearing Queen Victoria's head. 'C. & J. A. & Sons'.

The Wilder family ran foundries around the area from the eighteenth century onwards – at Ipsden, Crowmarsh, Aldworth, Wallingford, Henley, and even for a time in Guildford. The connections between the different branches of the family are outlined in a small book by William C. Wilder. It was a James Wilder who took on the Yield Hall Foundry in Reading in 1810.

By the time of the 1887 catalogue, the front cover of which is illustrated here, John Wilder was employing 56 men and 10 boys at the Reading establishment. His speciality seems to have been the chaff cutters, horse gears, and oil cake mills which are illustrated on its pages. They were all used in producing animal feed by cutting and crushing chaff, corn and roots.

The smaller machines were turned by hand, and the larger ones, suitable for 'large employers of horses, omnibus and tramway companies, cattle breeders, forage contractors, &c., &c.', were turned by horses. They had to walk round

51. The words 'Nine Elms Iron Works, Reading', printed very small at the bottom of the page, refer to the part of south-west London where the company was first set up.

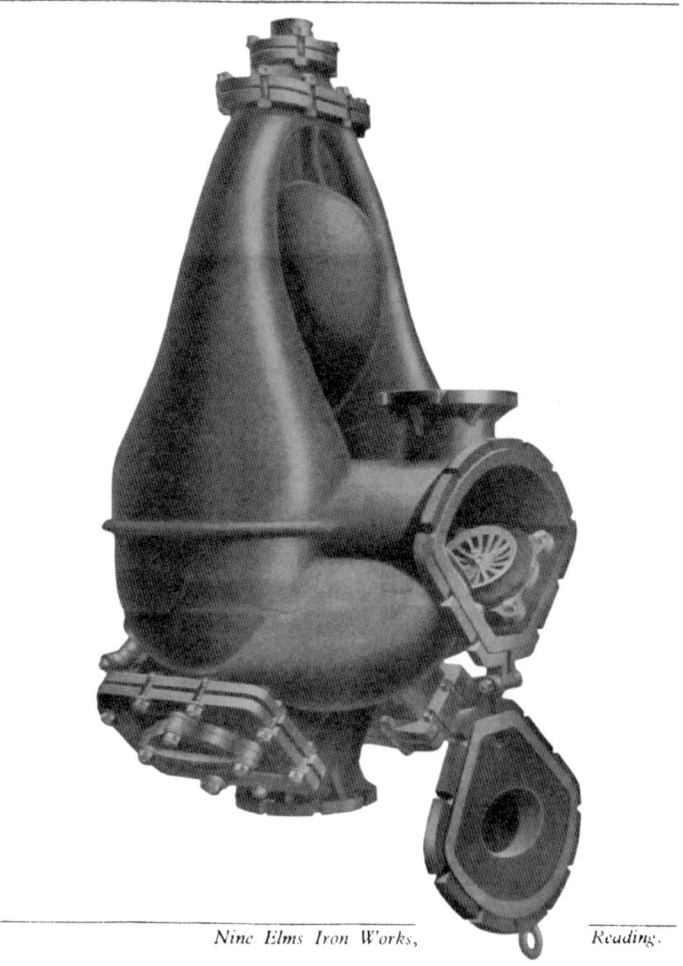

in circles, turning 'gear'. Each animal was connected to a 'draught pole' with a 'case' of cast iron in the middle of the circle. Within the 'case', a circular domed object, were the gears, which turned a revolving shaft, which was connected to the machine. The gearing could be altered to change the speed of the shaft, and besides chaff-cutters and oil cake mills, the device could drive elevators and stacking machines, and could be used to churn butter. There were smaller models turned by ponies, and larger ones for turning by two horses.

Besides what is in this catalogue, the firm also made other agricultural implements, and were general ironfounders, making everyday objects such as ovens, grids and manhole covers. They successfully made the transition to the motor age, but in the 1930s agreed to merge with the Wallingford foundry, run by another branch of the family, R. J. and H. Wilder. The Yield Hall Foundry closed around 1938, and in Reading, the firm moved its operation to Great Knollys Street, near the Cattle Market and the pubs frequented by farmers, still supplying agricultural machinery. Around 1996, they left the town centre, and in the phone books, Walter Wilder and and a firm called Lister Wilder appear, based at White House Farm, Spencers Wood.

The site of the foundry, in Yield Hall Place, is now a part of The Oracle shopping centre, reached from Minster Street by the side of the George Hotel, or from the river side near the High Bridge.

Arriving in Reading from London in 1901, the Pulsometer Engineering Company manufactured pumps in Reading until 1986. The Pulsometer Pump was a steam pump with almost no moving parts except for the valves, which made it reliable, easy to maintain, and capable of dealing with muddy water and sewage. It was invented in the United States, and the patent for this country was bought by John Hodgkin, who set up a factory at Nine Elms, in 1878. The company decided to move to Reading in 1901, to a site on Oxford Road which is now occupied by Reading Retail Park, near the corner of Norcot Road.

The illustration is of a page from their 1927 catalogue, showing a Pulsometer pump, looking something like an elongated human heart. With the coming of electricity, they developed centrifugal pumps and vacuum pumps, and their equipment was installed in water works, sewage works and on oil rigs around the world.

Opposite page:
52. Page from a catalogue of around 1911. It lists hundreds of items – bricks, tiles, chimney-pots, ornamental terracotta panels, balustrades, urns on pedestals, drainpipes and more.

In 1961 the company merged with Sigmund Pumps of Gateshead, to become Sigmund Pulsometer Pumps, or SPP, though in Reading, the works was still often referred to as 'The Pulso.'

Soon after this came a management buyout, and the firm was floated on the Stock Exchange in 1985. It was acquired by Sykes Pumps of Coleford in Gloucestershire, and in 1986 the decision was taken to move all manufacturing to Coleford, with the Reading factory closing a year later. But the name SPP has not quite disappeared from the area: their headquarters are at Arlington Business Park, Theale.

Mention has already been made of Samuel Collier (see p. 24–5) and his earthenware, china and glass shop in Minster Street. He moved over to the manufacture of earthenware in 1848, when he leased one of the kilns in the Coley area. He was joined in the business by his son, Edward P. Collier, in 1863. When the clay at Coley became worked out, he bought land off Water Road, in the Grovelands area, in 1872 and built a large works to produce the hand-made bricks, tiles, finials and terracotta panels for which the firm became famous. With the acquisition of the Waterloo Kiln they were employing 300. When the clay at Grovelands became worked out, land was bought in the Norcot area, and the clay was transported to the Grovelands works via an aerial cableway, well remembered by local residents since it spanned Norcot Road. The names of the streets on the Potteries Estate recall this era.

Around 1930, Collier's hand-made bricks found their way to Stratford-on-Avon, for the new Shakespeare Memorial Theatre (now the Royal Shakespeare Theatre).

Of all the Reading potteries, Collier's became the largest, and was the last one to close. Others included the Emmer Green Brickworks between Peppard Road and Kiln Lane, Wheeler's Tilehurst Potteries in Kentwood Hill which specialised in roofing tiles, and the Prospect Park Brickworks in Tilehurst Road. By the time of this catalogue, Collier's had taken over Poulter's Waterloo Kiln in Elgar Road. Earlier brickmaking enterprises in the Coley area gave rise to subsidence in Field Road, especially in the late twentieth century. The chalk needed to make the bricks had been mined, and the abandoned underground workings had been long forgotten and then built over.

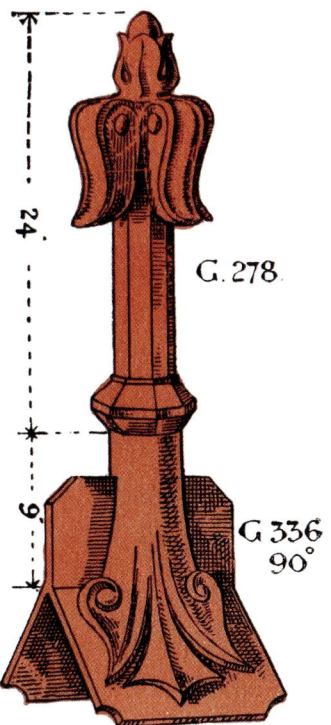

S. & E. COLLIER, LTD.,
MANUFACTURERS OF ALL KINDS OF
RED BRICKS, TILES, CHIMNEY POTS, RIDGE, & POTTERY.
GROVELANDS, READING.

SHEET No 15
SECTION No 3.

RIDGE TILE FINIALS (continued)

In ordering finials please quote the No both of Ornament & Base & also state pitch required. Ornaments will fit any base of the same letter.

Scale

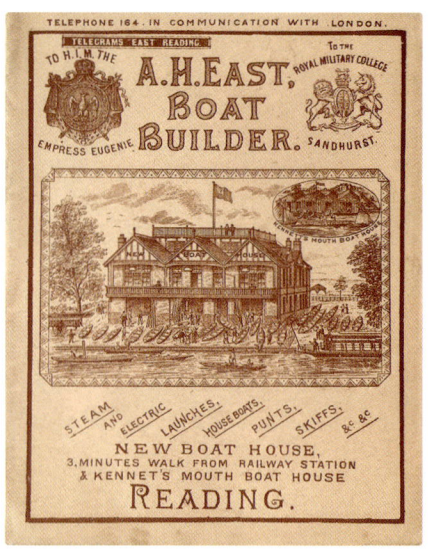
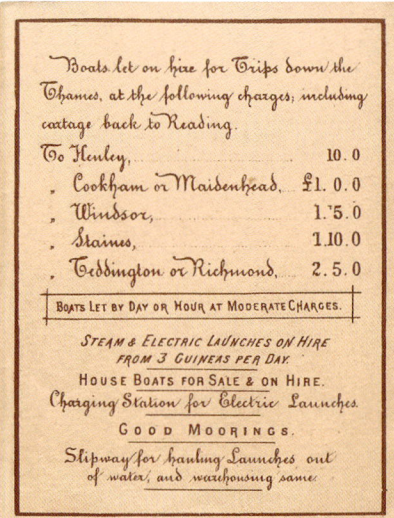

53. East's new boat house opened in 1890.

There was no longer the demand for hand-made bricks after the Second World War, and decline set in, with the works finally closing in 1967. The kilns and their towering chimneys were removed from the landscape, though the firm's small war memorial still stands on Water Road. A set of photographs, taken by the late J. Kenneth Major about the time the works closed, was given to the Central Library, and they can be viewed on the library website.

From bricks and tiles we move to boatbuilding by the Thames. Arthur East was by no means the only builder of pleasure craft in Reading. Among the others were William Moss, Cawston's, and Maynard's, who built some of the steamers which could carry over a hundred passengers on trips up and down the Thames. On a larger scale still was Talbot's, who built Thames barges on the Reading bank of the river, downstream of Caversham Bridge, in the second half of the nineteenth century.

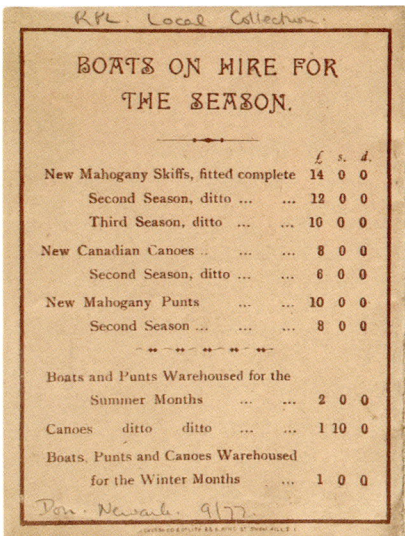

Mr East established an enviable reputation for boatbuilding, and secured contracts from overseas and from the aristocracy at home, from a boathouse at Kennet Mouth. He built and maintained a fleet of small boats in the grounds of the Royal Military Academy at Sandhurst, cadets and officers patronised his Reading establishment, and their Sandhurst band played for his special occasions. For the Princess Eugenie, he built and maintained her small boats on the lake at Chislehurst. (She was the wife of Napoleon III, living in exile in Kent.)

With the opening of the new boathouse in 1890, illustrated here, East was expanding his leisure business. It had a viewing balcony at first-floor level, and a viewing platform above the roof. Inside were refreshments, club rooms, and changing rooms where gentlemen could slip into their boating outfits, and there was a tennis court outside. The situation was handy for the stations and the town centre. It was adjacent to where Reading Bridge was to be opened in 1923, and the Thames Water offices, Clearwater Court, must be about where it stood.

Along with other boat proprietors, in the warmer part of the year he organised evening entertainments, with lanterns hanging in the trees. Prizes were offered for the best illuminated boats, bands played, and the Reading Swimming Club, who met at the new boathouse, played water polo by lamp-light. The evenings ended with a firework display.

Inside the brochure is a price list. You could take a private boat trip to Henley for 10s., or go all the way to Richmond and back for £2 5s. You could hire a boat, a steam launch or an electric launch, a skiff, a canoe or a punt, by the day or for the season, and for a fee you could have your boat warehoused for the winter, and you could hire a houseboat.

A photograph in the library's collection from around 1902 shows a second boathouse to the right of the one in the picture, in the same style but with two gables rather than three. This was something of a golden age for leisure on the Thames, but the gilt faded as the twentieth century went on. East's are listed in directories at Thames Side until 1925, and their other sites had closed before the 1932 directory was compiled.

VI. Transport

When you say you come from Reading, the response is sometimes, 'Oh, yes. It's a very good place to get away from.' And its geographical position does indeed give it good transport links. The major roads that had once converged on Silchester when the Romans were there were, over time, replaced by roads which converged on Reading. It was near a major crossing of the river Thames, and where the navigable Thames was joined by the navigable Kennet. Both river valleys carry busy railways. Many changes have occurred within living memory: older Redingensians can recall the time before the M4 motorway, when Broad Street seemed to be always clogged with traffic. Recently, Green Park railway station, just south of the town, opened on 27 May 2023. The Elizabeth Line opened throughout, from Reading to Abbey Wood, via Pa ddington and Liverpool Street Stations, on 6 November 2022. The Elizabeth Line (formerly called Crossrail) is a railway route, part of it new and underground, across central London. This will cause the value of houses in Reading to increase, so we are told, and even more high-rise flats to be built round Reading Station – not good news for everyone.

Perversely, perhaps, we consider the most recent piece of transport ephemera first – but it represents one of the oldest forms of transport. Opinion seems divided over whether the Danes mentioned in the *Anglo-Saxon Chronicle* for 871 arrived in Reading by water or over land. It is of course more romantic to picture them in their longships, coming up the Thames, but the likelihood is that they arrived over land. The navigation of the Thames was improved over time, using weirs and flash locks, and in the eighteenth century with pound locks. The navigation of the Kennet as far as Newbury had been improved by 1723, and the Kennet and Avon Canal was completed in 1810, connecting Reading with Bath, and via the Rivers Thames and Avon, connected London with Bristol, giving a continuous navigation across southern England.

Some idea of the importance of the waterways to the economy of Reading may be gained by the remark of John Doran, in his 1835 history of the town, that at the time, of its export trade, 50,000 tons went by water a year, and 100 tons by road. The promoters of the K. & A. could not have foreseen the effects of the railway on their enterprise. The Great Western Railway opened to Reading in 1840,

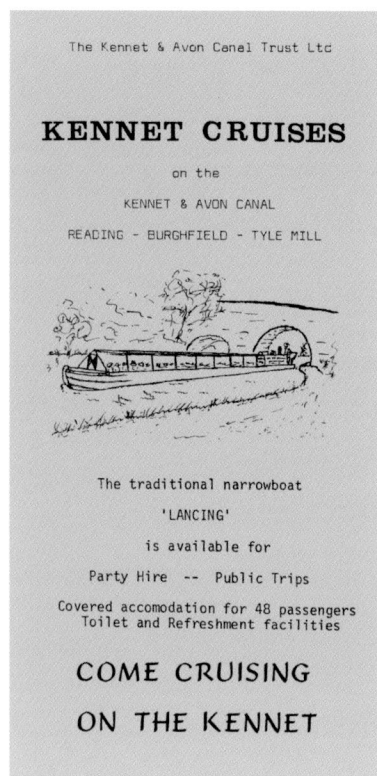

54. Leaflet from 1979, when navigation was possible only as far as Tyle Mill, with plan of the route on the page opposite

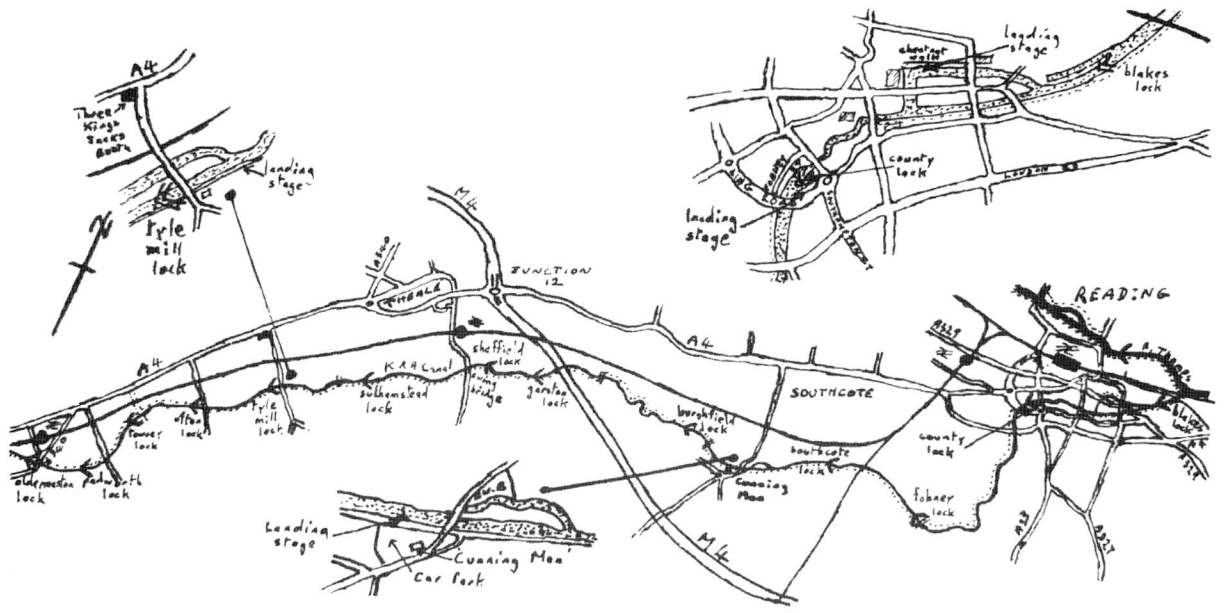

and in 1851 the canal was no longer so profitable, and was sold to the railway. A long, slow decline set in, and by the end of the Second World War, stretches of it were no longer navigable. In 1955, the Kennet and Avon Canal Association (now the K. & A. Canal Trust) was formed to reverse this trend. Attitudes towards inland waterways were changing, and using government resources and a lot of volunteer labour, the navigation was eventually restored throughout. The formal re-opening, by the Queen, came in 1990.

There was a time in the 1970s when there were regular public trips on the Kennet and Avon Canal from Reading, between May and September, on the narrowboat 'Lancing,' run by Norman Briggs and his crew. They started at County Lock, above the notoriously narrow 'Brewery Gut' which could not be navigated after heavy rain. This is the narrow stretch of fast-flowing water which now has The Oracle shopping centre on either hand, rather than the brewery.

When the leaflet was published, the upper limit of navigation from Reading was Tyle Mill, near Sulhamstead. The trips on Saturdays and Sundays went only as far as Burghfield, with the Saturday trip giving passengers a couple of hours at Burghfield, and the opportunity for lunch at the Cunning Man pub. The May and August Bank Holiday Mondays brought the opportunity to go to Tyle Mill, and stay on the boat for the short stretch to Ufton, where the boat turned round. There was a chance to stretch your legs before the return trip – the whole adventure starting at 10 am, and ending at 7 pm.

When the present author tried it, someone had forgotten to tell the people working on restoring the canal that the 'Lancing' would be coming through, and the Tyle Mill Lock was padlocked shut. Undeterred, the man in charge of the boat found a hacksaw, and proceeded to saw through the fastening, so Ufton Lock was reached after a short delay. I was impressed by his determination.

For around 150 years the town's position where the turnpike roads from Oxford, Winchester, Aldershot, Wokingham and Henley met the Great West Road between London, Bath and Bristol, meant that many stage coach services called here. Many must have been employed in the inns and stables, and as drivers, blacksmiths, wheelwrights and coachbuilders.

The coaching inns included the Angel (Broad Street), the Bear (Bridge Street), the Castle (Castle Street), the Crown (Crown Street), the George (King Street), the King's Arms (Castle Hill), the Mitre (in its original position in Friar Street near St Laurence's Church), the Ship (Duke Street) and the Turk's Head (London Road, formerly Albion Street).

The 'original' coach office of S. and T. Williams and Company was at 7 King Street, across the road from his rival, William Hone, whose office was next to the gateway of the George Inn. In 1838 something like a price war was in progress, with Hone advertising reduced fares to London of 10s. inside, and 5s. outside and on top, for travel in one direction.

In 1814, Williams 'Marquis of Wellington' is described here as 'a new and elegant post-coach' and carried only four passengers. Ordinary stage coaches took six or eight passengers, so this service must have been particularly expensive. Stage-coach travel was always expensive, and for the better-off. Compared with the railway it was slow, taking around four hours to reach London, whereas the railway, when it arrived, took around an hour and a half.

55. In 1814, the Marquis of Wellington coach set off from Reading at 6am, and would have reached London around 10am.

56. This ticket was issued in 1867 at the Whitley toll gate on Basingstoke Road.

Hatchett's White Horse Cellar, mentioned on the card, was in Piccadilly, where the Ritz Hotel now stands, and the Belle Sauvage was on Ludgate Hill, near St Paul's.

It now seems unbelievable that if you wanted to drive animals along main roads, or to take a horse-drawn vehicle along them, you had to pay towards the upkeep of the road, every time you travelled. Tolls were also collected when you crossed some of the more important bridges. On Caversham Bridge they were applied until 1869, when the new iron bridge opened. Tolls on highways were abolished in 1870.

Tickets like the one illustrated here must have been issued in their thousands, and thrown away once the journey was completed, so this scrap of blue paper is a rare survival. It was issued at the Whitley toll-gate, which at the time was on Basingstoke Road, near the junction with the present-day Bourne Avenue, but it allowed you to pass through the Whiteknights and Shinfield Gates as well, on the Shinfield Road. The toll paid was 3d., though there is no indication of the class of traffic. Different rates were charged for waggons, timber carriages, carts, chaises, coaches, carriages, gigs, horses and mules, asses, beasts (i.e. cattle), and pigs, sheep and calves.

Great Western Railway.
LONDON to READING.

On and after the **30th of March, 1840**, the Line will be FURTHER EXTENDED TO READING, for the conveyance of Passengers, Carriages, Horses, Goods, and Parcels.

Horses and Carriages being at the Paddington, Reading, Maidenhead, or Twyford Stations 10 minutes before the time specified for the departure of a Train, will be conveyed on the Railway, at the following Charges.

	CARRIAGES		HORSES	
	4-WHEEL	2-WHEEL	EACH	PER PAIR, being the same Property
PADDINGTON and READING	20s.	15s.	16s.	28s.
BETWEEN PADDINGTON and TWYFORD	16s.	12s.	14s.	24s.
PADDINGTON and MAIDENHEAD	12s.	8s.	10s.	16s.

POST HORSES are kept in readiness at the above Stations; and upon sufficient notice being given at Paddington, or the Bull and Mouth Office St. Martin's-le-Grand, would be sent to bring Carriages from any part of London to the Station at a moderate charge.

TRAINS, (Daily, excepting Sundays,)

DOWN TO

	Hour.	CALLING AT							
Reading	8				(Southall on Wednesday Mornings only)	Slough	Maidenhead	Twyford	Reading
Reading	9					Slough		Twyford	Reading
West Drayton	9.30	Ealing	Hanwell	Southall	West Drayton				
Reading	10				West Drayton	Slough	Maidenhead	Twyford	Reading
Reading	12				West Drayton	Slough	Maidenhead	Twyford	Reading
West Drayton	1.30	Ealing	Hanwell	Southall	West Drayton				
Reading	2				West Drayton	Slough	Maidenhead	Twyford	Reading
Reading	4					Slough	Maidenhead	Twyford	Reading
Maidenhead	4.30	Ealing	Hanwell	Southall	West Drayton	Slough	Maidenhead		
Reading	5					Slough	Maidenhead	Twyford	Reading
West Drayton	5.30	Ealing	Hanwell	Southall	West Drayton				
Reading	6	Ealing	Hanwell	Southall	West Drayton	Slough	Maidenhead	Twyford	Reading
Reading	7					Slough		Twyford	Reading
Maidenhead	8	Ealing	Hanwell	Southall	West Drayton	Slough	Maidenhead		
(Mail.) Twyford	8.55				West Drayton	Slough	Maidenhead	Twyford	
(Goods.) Reading	9.30						Maidenhead	Twyford	Reading

UP FROM

	Hour.	CALLING AT							
(Mail.) Twyford	3.45	Twyford	Maidenhead	Slough	West Drayton				Paddington
Reading	6	Twyford	Maidenhead	Slough					Paddington
Reading	7.30	Twyford	Maidenhead	Slough	West Drayton	(Southall on Wednesday Mornings only)	Hanwell	Ealing	Paddington
Maidenhead	8.30		Maidenhead	Slough	West Drayton	Southall	Hanwell	Ealing	Paddington
Reading	9	Twyford	Maidenhead	Slough	West Drayton				Paddington
Reading	10	Twyford	Maidenhead	Slough	West Drayton				Paddington
West Drayton	11				West Drayton	Southall	Hanwell	Ealing	Paddington
Reading	12	Twyford	Maidenhead	Slough	West Drayton				Paddington
Reading	2	Twyford	Maidenhead	Slough					Paddington
West Drayton	3				West Drayton	Southall	Hanwell	Ealing	Paddington
Reading	4.30	Twyford	Maidenhead	Slough					Paddington
Maidenhead	6		Maidenhead	Slough	West Drayton	Southall	Hanwell	Ealing	Paddington
West Drayton	7				West Drayton	Southall	Hanwell	Ealing	Paddington
Reading	8		Maidenhead	Slough					Paddington
(Goods.) Reading	11.30	Twyford	Maidenhead						Paddington

DOWN TO — ON SUNDAYS,

	Hour.	CALLING AT							
Reading	8	Ealing				Slough	Maidenhead	Twyford	Reading
Maidenhead	8.30			Southall	West Drayton	Slough	Maidenhead		
Reading	9					Slough	Maidenhead	Twyford	Reading
Maidenhead	9.30	Ealing	Hanwell	Southall	West Drayton	Slough	Maidenhead		
Reading	5		Hanwell		West Drayton	Slough	Maidenhead	Twyford	Reading
Maidenhead	6	Ealing	Hanwell	Southall	West Drayton	Slough	Maidenhead		
Reading	7					Slough	Maidenhead	Twyford	Reading
Maidenhead	8	Ealing	Hanwell	Southall	West Drayton	Slough	Maidenhead		
(Mail.) Twyford	8.55				West Drayton	Slough	Maidenhead	Twyford	

UP FROM

	Hour.	CALLING AT							
(Mail.) Twyford	3.45	Twyford	Maidenhead	Slough	West Drayton				Paddington
Reading	6	Twyford	Maidenhead	Slough	West Drayton				Paddington
Maidenhead	8		Maidenhead	Slough	West Drayton				Paddington
Reading	9	Twyford	Maidenhead	Slough	West Drayton	Southall		Ealing	Paddington
Reading	5	Twyford	Maidenhead	Slough	West Drayton			Ealing	Paddington
Maidenhead	6		Maidenhead	Slough	West Drayton	Southall	Hanwell		Paddington
Maidenhead	6.40		Maidenhead	Slough	West Drayton			Ealing	Paddington
Reading	7	Twyford	Maidenhead	Slough					Paddington
Maidenhead	8		Maidenhead	Slough	West Drayton	Southall	Hanwell	Ealing	Paddington

Passengers and Parcels, between the long and short Stations, can proceed in either direction to West Drayton, and be taken on by the succeeding Train.

PADDINGTON	1st Class	2nd Class Open Carriage		READING	1st Class	2nd Class Open Carriage
To Ealing	1 6	0 9		To Twyford	1 6	1 0
" Hanwell	2 0	1 0		" Maidenhead	3 0	2 0
" Southall	2 6	1 3		" Slough	4 6	3 0
" West Drayton	3 0	1 6		" West Drayton	5 6	4 0
" Slough	4 6	3 0		" Southall		
" Maidenhead	5 6	3 6		" Hanwell	6 6	4 6
" Twyford	7 0	5 0		" Ealing	7 6	5 0
" Reading	8 0	5 6		" Paddington	8 0	5 6

GOODS' TRAIN PASSENGERS Will be conveyed in uncovered Trucks by the Goods Trains ONLY.

Fares:— s. d.
Between Paddington and Maidenhead .. 2 0
 " Twyford .. 2 6
 " Reading .. 3 0

Fourteen lbs. of Luggage only, allowed. The charge for Goods between Paddington & the town of Reading, is 15s. 6d. per Ton, including loading, unloading, and delivery there.

Conveyances run between the Twyford Station and Henley, Maidenhead and Marlow and Wycombe. Windsor Omnibuses meet every Train at Slough. Conveyances to Uxbridge from the West Drayton Station.

Omnibuses & Coaches start:—from Princes Street, Bank, one hour before the departure of each Train, calling at the Angel Inn, Islington; Bull Inn, Holborn; Moore's Green Man and Still; Griffin's Green Man and Still; Oxford Street; Golden Cross, Charing Cross; Chaplin's Universal Office, and Bull and Mouth, Regent Circus; and Gloucester Warehouse, Oxford Street, to the Paddington Station. Fare 6d. without Luggage.

Parcels may be booked at the Railway Offices, Princes-street, Bank; at all the London Parcels Delivery Company's Receiving Houses; the above established Booking Offices; the Railway Stations; and the authorized Offices in the adjacent Places. Four Daily Deliveries will be made in Town, as well as in the Country, at the following Rate:—1s. for Parcels not exceeding 28-lbs. weight; 1s. 6d. for 56-lbs. weight; and so on, 6d. for every additional Quarter of Cwt., including all Charges for Carriage, Porterage, and Delivery.

W. Snell, Printer, Paddington.

Opposite page:
57. The first scheduled public passenger train to leave Reading, on Monday 30 March 1840, was drawn by the broad gauge locomotive, 'Fire Fly'.

The coming of railways meant the slow demise of stage-coach travel, though for places away from the tracks, horse-drawn traffic continued to be important. And with the decline of the coach trade came the decline in the importance of coaching inns. At Reading the building which was once the King's Arms, and The George still stand, together with the Malmaison, formerly the Great Western Hotel, one of the earliest railway hotels (see p. 104–5).

This rather battered timetable shows the earliest public train services from Reading. In 1840, the Great Western company's line was extended from Twyford to the town, and trains for the conveyance of passengers, carriages, horses, goods and parcels would commence 'on or after 30th March'. The intermediate stations were Twyford, Maidenhead, Slough, West Drayton, Southall, Hanwell, and Ealing. Commuting to and from work in London, or spending an evening at a West End theatre and returning the same evening were obviously some years in the future.

On weekdays, ten trains left Reading for Paddington, but on Sundays only four. The first-class fare was 8s. each way, and the fare in a second-class open carriage was 5s. 6d. The first train of the day left at 6am, and the last train coming back was at 7pm – unless you were prepared to travel on the goods train that left at 9.30pm, in an uncovered truck. At the time, mail trains went only as far as Twyford. There is no indication of the journey time on this timetable, but according to contemporary accounts it was an hour and a half between Reading and London, and probably much longer still on the goods train.

The well-off could take their carriages and horses to London for 46s. or they had the option of taking their carriages only, and having their hired horses waiting for them at Paddington. In the 1840s, a worker at Huntley & Palmers was earning 12s 6d. a week.

We now turn to consider transport within the town itself, in the early days provided by private enterprise, with Reading Corporation joining in later. Suburbs arose from the 1840s onwards, as the town expanded – New Town, Redlands, areas of Caversham and Tilehurst, then Whitley and Southcote.

The tattered letter pictured overleaf, addressed to the Mayor as Chairman of the Watch Committee, asks that the bus service between Caversham and Reading, run by Mr Barrow, should not be stopped. John Barrow, the driver, and William Barrow, the proprietor, had been in trouble a number of times

Opposite page:
58. Barrow's horse bus between Reading and Caversham ran until 1911 at least.

during the 1890s, for using horses which were unfit for work on their journeys to and from Caversham. Then in May 1899, the Borough Council decreed that all drivers and conductors of cabs, trams and buses had to re-apply for their licences, and the vehicles had to be inspected. Apparently, William Barrow's vehicle, or vehicles, had failed the test, and John Barrow had been refused a licence. The petitioners say:

> In view of the establishment of a line of Trams on this route the proprietor of the 'Busses cannot be expected to purchase new vehicles for so short a period, and we trust therefore that they may be allowed to continue.

It is hard to know how extensive Mr Barrow's operation was, if as stated in the letter the buses on the Caversham route were numbered 77 and 43 – maybe there were just two. And also, 1899 seems rather early for anyone to claim that tram lines would soon be crossing the Thames into Caversham. After the Corporation had taken over the Reading Tramways Company in 1901, this was certainly contemplated, but the Caversham Urban District Council was unwilling to pay for the modification of the road pattern, and in any case, Caversham Bridge – still the 1860s iron bridge – was too narrow to accommodate the electric cars, and certain notables living in Caversham had objected to the proposals. The Corporation Tramways therefore stopped at the Reading end of Caversham Bridge.

The letter is signed by Francis Cooksey, an estate agent, and Joseph and S. A. Bobin, all of Caversham. Joseph Bobin was the Registrar of Births and Deaths, the School Attendance Officer, and the Relieving Officer of the Henley Board of Guardians, who lived in Prospect Street.

One wonders how many copies of the letter were printed and returned, and how many signatories there were in total. Whether or not they managed to sway the members of the Watch Committee is unclear: at their July meeting it was reported that the Committee had carefully considered the letters asking that 'the licences for the omnibuses formerly licensed for plying between Reading and Caversham should be renewed, and also that a driver's licence which had been refused should be renewed', but they saw no reason to reverse their previous decisions. On the other hand, in the local papers we find John Barrow still driving the Caversham bus and getting into trouble with the law on a number of occasions in 1900 and 1901.

To His Worship The Mayor of Reading,

Chairman of the Watch Committee.

Sir,

We understand that your Officer has reported that the 'Busses (Nos. 77 and 43) the property of Mr. W. Barrow, are not up to the standard required by the new regulations. As Regular Riders on these 'Busses we beg most respectfully to express our opinion that these Vehicles are quite safe and comfortable for the traffic, and we view with alarm the probability of them being taken off the road.

The traffic to Caversham is considerable, and is daily increasing. For the past ten months, or thereabouts, Mr. Barrow has successfully and punctually catered for that traffic, and his absence from the road will be a serious inconvenience to Residents in Reading and Caversham.

In view of the establishment of a line of Trams on this route the proprietor of the 'Busses cannot be expected to purchase new vehicles for so short a period, and we trust therefore they may be allowed to continue.

Trusting you will kindly bring this petition before the Watch Committee at the earliest possible date.

We are,

Sir,

Your Obedient Servants.

20th May, 1899.

Frank Woolley Caversham

Joseph Bobin

S. A. Bobin Caversham

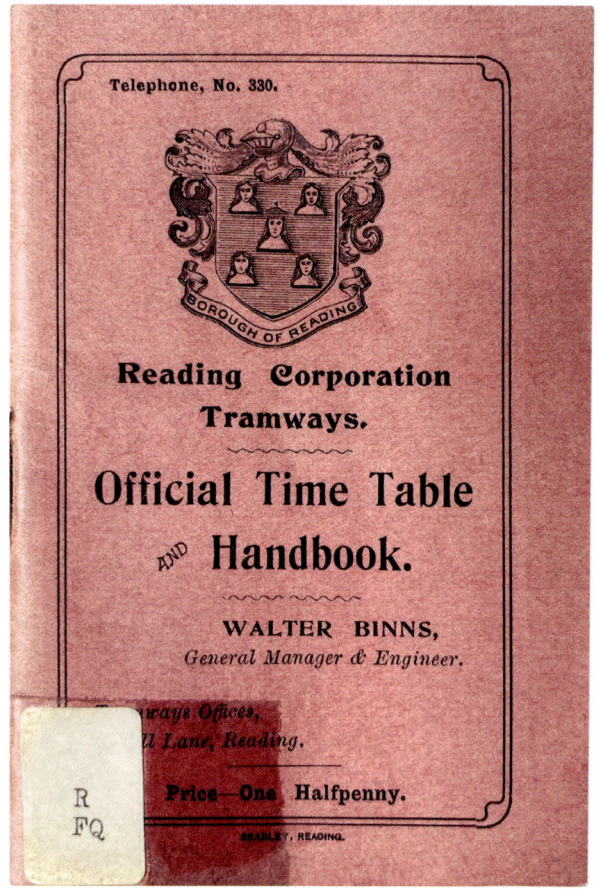

59. Tram timetable from 1906

The tramway system opened in 1879. It was horse-drawn, and operated by the Reading Tramways Company, which was bought out by Reading Corporation in 1901, extended slightly, and converted to electric traction. The electric cars entered public service on 22 July 1903.

The timetable book includes a folding map and dates from 1906. It contains 128 pages, and at the time cost ½d.

From the town centre, the rails ran out to Caversham Bridge, to the borough boundary in London Road, the junction of Wokingham Road and St Peter's Road, the junction of Erleigh Road and Addington Road, Whitley Pump, Bath Road just beyond Coley Avenue and Russell Street, and the Pond House on Oxford Road.

On the Oxford Road to Wokingham Road route, on weekdays, services started at 5.30 am, and the last service across town left at 10.58 pm. Throughout the day, cars arrived at five-minute intervals, and from the post office in Broad Street (on the site of the Lakeland store, formerly Burton's on the corner of Chain Street) the fare was one penny to any terminus.

The Corporation Tramways also ran a parcels service, using shops along the routes as agents. For 1d. you could send a parcel weighing up to 28 lb. from one agent to another, and for 2d. you could take the parcel to an agent, and have it delivered to any address within half a mile of an agent.

Besides the tram timetables, the booklet contains a wealth of information about the town – such as interesting buildings along the routes, pleasant walks from the termini, markets, hospitals, theatres, schools, parks, bathing places (open air), and the times of trains to London.

Equally fascinating are the many advertisements for old Reading businesses – such as Targett's for horses and carriages for sale or hire; Butler & Sons' Old Reading Abbey whisky; John Cox, the 'original' Reading umbrella manufacturer (see p. 65–7); and F. Hubner, 'corsets and belts for corpulency a speciality.'

The corporation began to consider using trolley-buses in 1912, seeing them at first as a way of extending the tramways, from Oxford Road up to Tilehurst and from over the water in Caversham up to Emmer Green. Then they changed their mind and obtained an Act of Parliament in 1914 which would have enabled them to run trolley-buses along Bath Road as far as Liebenrood Road, and over the new Caversham Bridge up to the Heights.

War intervened, the 1914 route was never constructed, and the new bridge did not open until 1926. The first trolley-bus route did not venture into Caversham, but ran from the Reading end of Caversham Bridge, through the town and up to Whitley Pump.

On the day of the inauguration, 18 July 1936, the invited guests were conveyed by bus to the Caversham Bridge Hotel, on the site of the present-day Crowne

60. When the trolley bus service started, some people living along the route found that they were being late for work – they had relied on the rumbling of the trams to wake them up.

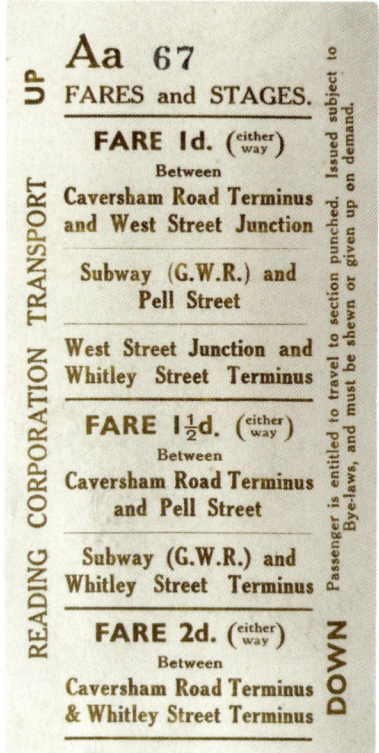

Plaza Hotel, where they could board the trolley-bus for a ride to the Pump and back. The mayor, Councillor W. H. Bale, drove the bus for part of the way. On their return, light refreshments were served at the Hotel.

Gradually, the trolley-bus network was extended, taking over some of the tramways, with the last tramcar in public service running on 20 May 1939. The new trolley-bus routes ran to Tilehurst and the Whitley Estate, the final extension being opened in 1963.

It was not many years later that the corporation was considering abandoning trolley-buses. They were coming to be seen as old-fashioned, and as other authorities stopped using them, it became difficult to obtain spare parts and equipment. The last trolley-buses ran in Reading in 1968 – though some of them continue to run at the Trolley-bus Museum at Sandtoft, near Doncaster, which has five Reading vehicles.

Motor bus services in Reading had been started in 1915, by the British Automobile Traction Company, a precursor of the Thames Valley Traction Company. Development was held back during the war, but in 1919, the Corporation Tramways Department also started bus services, running within the borough boundary. The first of the corporation routes ran between Caversham Heights and the Plough Inn at Tilehurst, via the stations and town centre.

The handbill illustrated overleaf, dating from 1930, advertises what is probably the first bus service to go along Hemdean Road in Caversham. It was to start on 1 September, 'and continuing experimentally until further notice.' The experiment must have been a success, because buses on routes 23 and 24 still go along Hemdean Road.

The buses left from the junction with Oakley Road and Grove Hill – Rotherfield Way was not yet constructed. At Church Street they turned left, and proceeded along Gosbrook Street and Gosbrook Road (which are now one and the same) to George Street. They crossed Reading Bridge, called at the stations (Great Western and Southern), and proceeded to the Broad Street terminus, opposite Cross Street. On weekdays there were 15 departures a day from Hemdean Road, and 12 on Sundays, and the fare was 2d. all the way, or 1d. to George Street.

These days, when we expect buses to depart at so many minutes past the hour through much of the day, the timetable is surprising. From Mondays to Saturdays there were gaps in the middle of the morning and the middle of the afternoon: from Hemdean Road there was nothing between 9.35 and 12.20, or between 2.50 and 5.20. The first bus from the Caversham end left at 8.05, and from Broad Street, the last departure for Hemdean Road left at 7.20. On Sundays, things were totally different. The buses didn't start till the afternoon, but they ran into the evening, with the last departure from Broad Street being at 9.30 pm.

For some years in the 1990s, there was a bus that ran right to the far end of Hemdean Road, run by a company called Reading Mainline. Their Route H went from Lower Earley (Kilnsea Drive) to Caversham (Hemdean Road) via the town centre. They had obviously worked out which areas in Reading were not

READING CORPORATION MOTORS.

NEW OMNIBUS SERVICE
BETWEEN
Hemdean Road & Broad Street

COMMENCING MONDAY, 1st SEPTEMBER, 1930, and continuing experimentally until further notice, a New Motor Omnibus Service will be operated on Week-days and Sundays between Hemdean Road (Junction of Oakley Road) and Broad Street (opposite Cross Street).

The Route will be as follows:—Hemdean Rd., Gosbrook St., Gosbrook Rd., George St., Reading Bridge, Railway Stations to Broad St. (opposite Cross St.) and vice versa.

TIME TABLE.

WEEK-DAYS.

	a.m.	a.m.	a.m.	a.m.	p.m.	p.m.	p.m.
Leave Broad St.	7.50	8.20	8.50	9.20	12.5	12.35	1.5
	p.m.	p.m.	p.m.	p.m.	p.m.	p.m.	p.m.
	1.35	2.5	2.35	5.5	5.35	6.5	6.35	7.5

	a.m.	a.m.	a.m.	a.m.	p.m.	p.m.	p.m.
Leave Hemdean Rd.	8.5	8.35	9.5	9.35	12.20	12.50	1.20
	p.m.	p.m.	p.m.	p.m.	p.m.	p.m.	p.m.
	1.50	2.20	2.50	5.20	5.50	6.20	6.50	7.20

SUNDAYS.

	p.m.	p.m.	p.m.	p.m.	p.m.	p.m.	p.m.
Leave Broad St.	2.20	2.50	3.20	3.50	4.20	4.50	5.20
			p.m.	p.m.	p.m.	p.m.	p.m.
			5.50	6.20	7.20	8.20	9.20

	p.m.	p.m.	p.m.	p.m.	p.m.	p.m.	p.m.
Leave Hemdean Rd.	2.35	3.5	3.35	4.5	4.35	5.5	5.35
			p.m.	p.m.	p.m.	p.m.	p.m.
			6.5	6.35	7.35	8.35	9.35

FARE STAGES (Fare either way)

Fare Stage Number.		
1	Between Hemdean Rd. Terminus and George St. (Caversham).	**1D.**
2	,, George St. (Caversham) ,, Railway Stations.	
3	,, Kings Meadow Rd. ,, Broad St. (Opp. Cross St.)	

Between Hemdean Rd. Terminus and Broad St. (Opp. Cross St.) **2D.**

TRAMWAY OFFICES,
READING.

J. M. CALDER,
General Manager and Engineer.

BRASLEY & SON, LTD., PRINTERS, READING

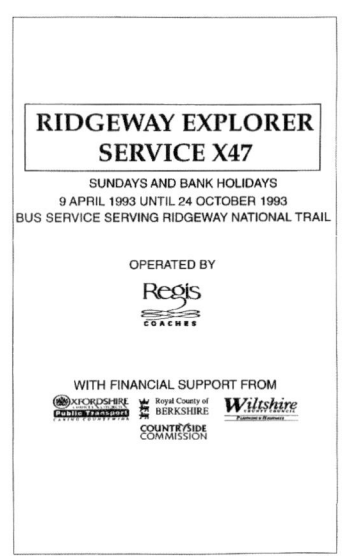
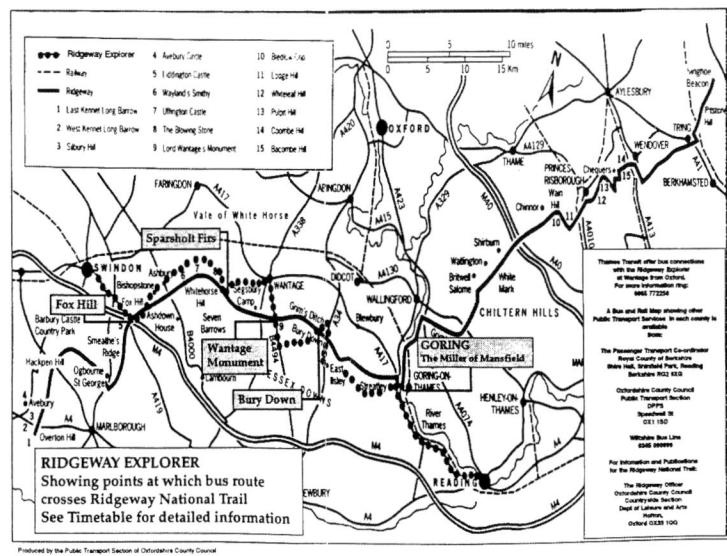

Opposite page:
61. The start of a new 'experimental' bus route in 1930

62. The Ridgeway Explorer gave ramblers easy access to the Vale of White Horse.

particularly near the routes operated by Reading Transport, and filled in the gaps. Their buses were former London Transport 'Routemaster' double-decked vehicles, with open platforms at the rear for getting on and off. They had conductors to sell tickets on board, and to help passengers mounting and alighting. The fares were cheaper, the vehicles were clean and comfortable, and got away from the stops quicker than corporation buses because the driver didn't sell the tickets. And in fact, they had conductors on the pavements as well, patrolling the bus queues in the town centre, selling tickets that could only be used on the Mainline buses. It really was a most interesting period in the history of transport in Reading, and in the end, in 1998, Reading Transport had to pay a handsome sum to buy their upstart rivals out – resulting in them making a loss on the year for the first time ever. It's a pity that no leaflets from Reading Mainline have so far found their way into the collections used for this book.

The Ridgeway Explorer bus ran for only a few seasons, between April and October, in the 1990s, on Sundays and bank holidays. It ran between Reading and Swindon,

Opposite page:
63. Smith's always ran 'luxury' coaches: one of their rivals ran 'comfy' coaches, and another one had 'cushy' coaches.

taking about 2 hours and 20 minutes for the journey, following a route parallel to The Ridgeway. Passengers from Oxford could pick up the bus by taking a train to Goring, or a bus to Wantage. The operator was Regis Coaches, who were supported financially by the County Councils of Berkshire, Oxfordshire and Wiltshire, and by the Countryside Commission.

From this timetable, it appears that two vehicles would have been needed to run the service, each making two round trips a day, between 8.30 in the morning, and 7.40 in the evening.

The purpose of the service was not, of course, to convey people between Reading and Swindon, which could have been achieved by train in half an hour or so. Rather, it was to allow them to take a walk along the prehistoric trackway, The Ridgeway, to enjoy the views over the White Horse Vale and Thames Valley, and to visit the old market town of Wantage, and the attractive Berkshire Downland villages of Aldworth, Compton Beauchamp, the Ilsleys, the Letcombes, or Woolstone. The prehistoric monuments of Wayland's Smithy, Uffington Castle and the Uffington White Horse were within a short walk of the bus stop.

For many years, Smith's were the leading coach operators in Reading. Their full story is told and illustrated in the book by Paul Lacey. Alf Smith had learned how to drive and maintain motor vehicles whilst in the Army during the First World War. On his return, with a loan from his mother-in-law and a former Army Thornycroft lorry, re-bodied as a charabanc, he set up in business in 1922. In time, he was able to take over rival firms, and to win valuable contracts, taking people to work at Aldermaston and Harwell, while continuing to run public trips to the seaside and visitor attractions, and to do private hire work.

The Berkshire A.E.C. mentioned in this letter was the Berkshire Agricultural Executive Committee of the National Agricultural Advisory Service, a branch of the Ministry of Agriculture. In Berkshire, their events were held at the Abbey Hall in Reading, or on farms. The Hall belonged to Sutton and Sons, the seedsmen (see p. 53–5). It was in Abbey Square, almost opposite where the Central Library is now, and in the old days was used for worship by Suttons employees, before the start of the working day. The cost of hiring a Smith's Luxury Coach to Ripley and back varied, from £5 16s. 6d. for 25 seats, to £8 3s. 6d. for 35 seats. Ripley is a village on the A3 Portsmouth Road, about 34 miles from Reading – presumably the venue was a farm.

At the time of this estimate, Smith's had several garages around the town, but were in the process of building a large new garage in Rose Kiln Lane, which was to open in 1950. The head office and booking office was at 20 Mill Lane, originally the mill house for St Giles' Mill. Until Mill Lane was widened to go over the top of the mill stream the house was on an island between the River Kennet and the mill stream and was reached by a bridge. By 1949, it was beside Mill Lane, with a tarred strip for coaches to pull in in front where the garden had been. The site has now disappeared under the Inner Distribution Road.

From the 1960s, the booking office was in a terrapin building on the Queens Road Car Park – which was then just a flat open-air car park.

The firm did not long survive the death of Alf Smith in 1976. His family sold the business in 1979.

SMITH'S LUXURY COACHES (Reading) Ltd.

Directors:— A. E. SMITH; B. A. M. SMITH; J. J. C. MILLS

20 MILL LANE, READING

Tel.: Reading 3247 (3 lines)

March 22nd 1949.

To Mrs. Bate,

Berks. A.A.C.

Abbey Hall, Kings Road. Rdg.

Quotation No.: 9/337/JF.

Dear Sir/Madam,

We thank you for your enquiry for the hire of .... seater Coaches to convey your party from Reading direct to Ripley, Surrey. on date to be decided

and have much pleasure in quoting you the sum of:—

£8. 3. 6.   35-seater Coach   £6. 15. 6.   29-seater Coach

£7. 10. 0.   32-seater Coach   £5. 16. 6.   25-seater Coach

via   direct.

VII. Restaurants, hotels, pubs and breweries

As in other towns, opportunities for eating out in Reading have proliferated in the twenty-first century, and the same can be said of coffee houses. The number of pubs, on the other hand, has declined greatly since the nineteenth century, a process which has been accelerated by the COVID-19 pandemic in the twenty-first. The large breweries have gone, but some smaller 'microbreweries' have sprung up, in the town and just outside. This chapter has reminders of just a few of these establishments from the past.

We begin with Colleys Supper Rooms, on Wokingham Road. The inside of the leaflet illustrated here does not contain a menu, as you might expect, but instead explains what you could expect from a visit to Colleys. You were there for the whole evening, arriving at 7.45 for 8, with 'carriages at 11.30'.

Indeed, the great innovation was that there was no printed menu. The different dishes were brought round to your table, the hot dishes straight from the oven by the waiting staff in Victorian dress with oven gloves, so that you could relish the appearance and aromas of what was on offer before deciding what to order.

There were other Supper Rooms at Bristol and Southampton, the creation of Robert Colley. As the leaflet said, 'one doesn't come here merely to eat and drink, but to enjoy an evening in the atmosphere of a private dinner party, where time itself doesn't matter, but good food does.'

The Reading supper rooms were on the corner of Wokingham Road and St Bartholomew's Road, opposite Palmer Park. In many ways they were the antithesis of today's fast food outlets, and perhaps we should not be surprised that they have not survived up to the present day. Colleys opened in 1980, and closed in 2010. Since then, the building has been Bart's Grill and Restaurant, Smokey's House, and a Portuguese restaurant, O Portugues.

Reading's position on the Great West Road meant that during the stage coach era, large inns were needed. The Great Western Hotel, where the illustrated bill originated, was very much an enterprise of the railway era, and has some claim to being the oldest railway hotel in the world, opening in 1842. It is now the Malmaison Hotel.

64. Colleys – the restaurant with no printed menu

65. Bill from the Great Western Hotel (now the Malmaison) from around 1850. One wonders how many dinners with wine and ale could have been bought for 10s. 3d.

George Bailey, mentioned on the bill, was the second manager, 1843–1855, and the bill-head extols the advantages of his hotel. On the original document, the words are tiny and barely legible, but 'Choicest Wines and Spirits' are promised, together with 'Strict Attention to the Sleeping Department.' Across the front of the hotel, the words 'For Private Families and Gentlemen' appear, and there must have been a large area for stabling and vehicles, because 'Flys, Phaetons, Gigs' and 'Posting with Expedition' are promised.

Listed on the bill are 'dinners' at 7s., 'wine' at 2s. 6d. and 'ale' at 9d., totalling 10s. 3d.

Over the years, the building has played host to many famous visitors, and has been the venue for happenings throughout the day, such as meeting for morning coffee, lunches, property sales in early evenings, and dinners and

dances – a single-storey ballroom was added onto the Station Road end. The hotel was acquired by the Trust House Forte chain in 1954, and when the route of the M4 motorway beyond Maidenhead Thicket was decided, they decided to build a new hotel by the site of the Grenadier public house and by the motorway junction, and to close their old hotel.

It closed in 1972, and became a postal sorting office, then offices for the West Berkshire Health Authority, and then offices for Clark's, the solicitors, in 1989. For a time it was unoccupied, and the building seemed likely to be demolished, despite its Grade II listing. Then the Malmaison hotel group took it on, opening in 2007, with an extra floor added on top, and an extension over the site of the former ballroom.

The Great Western Hotel Tap was across the road, under the same management as the hotel, from around 1882 to around 1956, when the name changed to The Jolly Porter. This was a comparatively down-market drinking establishment, which was replaced by a new public house in 1973, because the site was needed for the Foster Wheeler building – now the Thames Tower. The new Jolly Porter closed and became a shop selling computer games, before this building was in turn demolished when the redevelopment of Station Hill began in 2015. The redevelopment was still on-going in 2023.

Opinion is still divided as to who designed the 1842 Great Western Hotel, some favouring I. K. Brunel, and some favouring others working for the Great Western Railway Company.

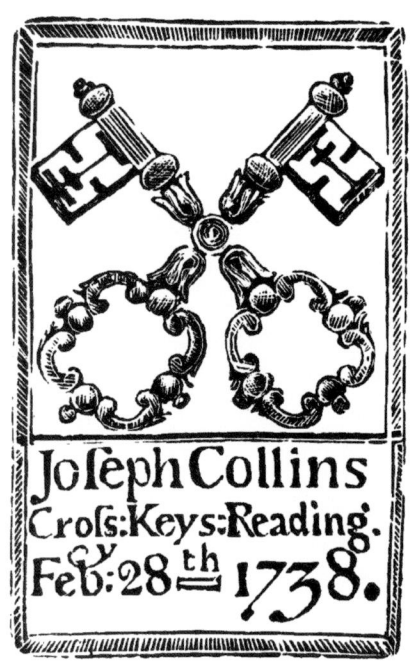

66. The significance of the date, 28 February 1738, is not known.

The recent publication on the pubs and breweries of Reading, by John Dearing, Evelyn Williams, and the present author, found around 500 inns, hotels, alehouses, beerhouses and pubs that have existed in the town over the centuries.

The exact date of this advertising card from the Cross Keys is hard to judge, and the significance of the date on it, 1738. It somehow found its way into the Central Library's collection. Maybe the original pub was built in that year, and it is possible that the card may date from then, or soon after.

It stood on the corner of Gun Street and Bridge Street, with the address 1 Gun Street. It, and replacement buildings, stood opposite St Mary's churchyard, though crossed keys are the emblem of St Peter rather than St Mary.

The inn was rebuilt in 1877, probably to the designs of architects Brown and Albury; they were certainly the architects of the club room which was added in 1884. The 'new Pevsner' describes the building as 'Reading's Best Victorian Pub' (in the bibliography, under Tyack). The authors should have seen it a few decades earlier, when it still had its Victorian interior, with a large clock set over the bar. But the 1877 exterior is intact, with tile-hanging and pargeting which has the cross keys motif moulded into it.

Over the years, ownership changed several times. In 1903, when it belonged to Whitbread's, it could boast five bars, a bar parlour, a billiard room, three bedrooms for travellers, and stabling for five horses. It served 'breakfast, chops, steaks and tea, or anything else,' and was frequented by principal tradesmen, artisans, and the labouring classes.

Whitbread's sold it to Reading brewer, J. Dymore Brown, whose business was taken over by Morland's, the Abingdon brewers. It appeared in the first edition of *The Good Beer Guide* in 1974, when it showed 'a strong Irish influence.' Morland's sold it on in 1989, after which its character changed completely. It was Bukowski's, then J.W's, then Sahara, and is now Be at One. Apparently the current name is not a reference to its address in Gun Street, but is the name of the chain of bars which owns it.

The name of The Alfred's Head pub may be connected with King Alfred the Great, who was born in Berkshire. On the other hand it may be named after the lawyer and property developer, Alfred Compigne, who is supposed to have given his name to nearby Alfred Street. The Alfred's Head was at 148 Chatham Street, on the corner of Bedford Road.

The pub does not seem to have been recorded before the 1870s, and by 1903 it was owned by the Marlow brewers, Thomas Wethered and Sons. At that time it was licensed to sell beer only, and it had one bar, and a bottle-and-jug department for those wishing to drink their beer at home. It closed around 2005, and the building is now a Romanian restaurant.

The envelope illustrated here has its flap across the top, and was presumably designed to hold one or more of the Crown Seal Cigars, described as 'the best threepenny cigar in town' in the advertising on the front.

The humorous illustration shows Pierrot, with a large ruff round his neck, being offered a threepenny cigar by Columbine. She is dressed in black, and looks away from Pierrot with a saucy grin on her face and a cigar in her mouth, with her head in a cloud of smoke.

67. Francis Henry Hooper was landlord at The Alfred's Head between 1887 and *c.* 1917.

68. A matchbox cover. Many were disappointed when The Greyhound closed in November 1995.

Back in the 1970s, and for decades before that, many people habitually carried a matchbox in their pockets, and kept a box handy at home as well. This was a time when many smoked tobacco, and you also needed matches to light coal fires and gas appliances.

Some brands of match were distributed across the land – such as Swan Vestas, Puck, Punch, and Captain Webb. Other matchboxes were distributed locally, advertising shops, tourist destinations, clubs, and pubs.

Around the year 2000 the present author was kindly allowed by Alan Bosher to borrow his collection of local matchbox labels, to scan and catalogue them, and make them viewable on the Reading Libraries website – as they still are.

The advertisement under scrutiny here is for The Greyhound pub, now no more, which for some centuries had stood in Mount Pleasant (formerly a part of Silver Street) until demolition in 2000. It was on the right-hand side, going up the hill, and was distinctive on account of the lean-to buildings at each end. One of them had been a forge, and the other a shop.

In *The Hop Leaf Gazette*, the house journal of the Reading brewers, H. & G. Simonds, it was claimed that the building had been an inn since 1512, though historians have said that it was built in the following century, on the site of buildings which had been destroyed during the Civil War.

69. This bill is for timber rather than beer, and has been initialled by Blackall Simonds himself.

For 125 years, through the nineteenth and into the early twentieth century, it was run by the Scearce family, who were the blacksmiths. The matchbox label, probably dating from the 1970s, advertises Courage ales (which succeeded Simonds ales), their hot and cold snacks, and their seafood. But in the 1990s, Beazer Homes had their eyes on the site, and the brewers were presumably willing to relinquish it for a price. There was a public outcry, which was ultimately unsuccessful. English Heritage decided that the building had been too much altered to be worth listing, and the borough planners were unwilling or unable to stop the sale.

We now turn to Reading's brewers. By the time this scrap of paper was signed, the Simonds brewery, founded by William Simonds in 1774, was by far the largest in town, producing twice as many barrels per annum as anyone else. The business started in Broad Street. William Simonds had married a Mary Blackall, and it was

Opposite page:
70. This label was probably intended to be pasted onto the end of a barrel.

their son, William Blackall Simonds, who moved the business to a site by the River Kennet in Bridge Street around 1785. The brewery was known as the Bridge Street, or Seven Bridges Brewery, and the firm, always run by the family, became H. & G. Simonds in 1885.

When W. B. Simonds retired, in 1816, his son Blackall Simonds took over, and it is he who has initialled this receipt. Previous writers do not seem to have mentioned that Blackall Simonds was a timber merchant as well as a brewer. At the time, and for a century and more afterwards, there were several timber yards along the Kennet as it made its way through Reading.

The back of the bill has the words 'J. Blagrave Esqr. Mr. B. Simonds for Deals, £2.6.4.' Perhaps the Mr F. Hawkes, mentioned on the front, made the actual purchase, on behalf of Mr Blagrave, who paid for it. Between January and March, five lengths of deal were bought, three of them 12 feet long, one 18 feet and one 20 feet, and all of them 3 × 11 inches.

The brewery came to occupy land on both sides of Bridge Street, and after around 1909 had its own railway siding which branched off the Reading central goods line, otherwise known as the Coley goods branch. H. & G. Simonds merged with Courage, Barclay and Company in 1960, and the company lost its identity, with brewing ceasing on this site in 1979. After many years of false starts, the land downstream of Bridge Street was redeveloped as The Oracle shopping centre, which opened in 1999.

The Brinns were another of Reading's brewing families. They seem to have been preceded in the trade by the Justins family. In 1844, we find Thomas Justins taking over a small brewery in London Street, on the corner of South Street. Then in 1860, we find him taking over a brewery in Castle Street – after which, presumably, brewing in the London Street premises stopped, but they were kept on as a beer house. On the 1871 census return, we find Sarah Brinn and William James Justins Brinn, both still at school, living in London Street with their great uncle, Thomas Justins. William later joined Thomas at the brewery and the firm became Justins and Brinn. Thomas died in 1876, and William Brinn continued the enterprise.

He had been born in Truro, where the new cathedral was consecrated in 1887. By the following year, the beer shop in London Street had become The Cathedral, and the Castle Street Brewery was the Truro Brewery.

This circular label must date from the time between around 1888 and 1900, when W. J. J. Brinn sold the brewery to Fergusons (see p. 18).

At the time of the sale, the brewery had 30 tied houses. These included the Bear, Bridge Street; the Foresters Arms, Brunswick Street; the George and Dragon, Bath Road; the Millers Arms, Caversham; the Roebuck, Auckland Road; the Sportsman, Shinfield Road; the Spread Eagle, Norfolk Road; and the York House, Kings Road. Fergusons no longer needed the brewing capacity, and the buildings, on the corner of Castle Street and Boarded Lane, were demolished, to be replaced by a large and impressive inn, The Truro. Fergusons were eventually taken over by Morland's, the Abingdon brewers, and The Truro lasted into the 1960s, when the Inner Distribution Road was under construction. It must have been where the police station now stands.

Opposite page:
71. Announcement of the publication of a controversial new book, 1835

VIII. Churches and religion

The dissolution of Reading Abbey in 1539 left the town with the three parish churches of St Mary, St Laurence and St Giles, and King Henry VIII as head of the Church of England. By the end of the Tudor period, things had stabilised to some extent, but meetings of other Christian denominations were not allowed. Naturally, many were unhappy at this. Catholics worshipped secretly, and 'conventicles' of other sects were held. The Quakers were active in Reading from the 1650s, and were greatly persecuted. The Toleration Act, passed in 1689, allowed Protestant nonconformists to worship, under certain conditions, but its provisions did not extend to Catholics. The eighteenth century saw the rise of the Congregationalists (or Independents), the Baptists, and the Methodists, but it was 1791 before the Catholics were allowed to meet, in licensed buildings.

Our earliest piece of ephemera for this chapter dates from 1835, a handbill advertising the publication of a book, by Robert and John Snare of Minster Street. It contained 42 pages and cost one shilling.

The full title was *A Reply to the Dissenters in their Attacks on the Established Church; addressed to the People of England, by a Gentleman of Reading*. Who that gentleman might have been does not seem to be known, and it may just be that no copies of it exist in Reading any more. The online catalogues of Reading Borough Libraries and Reading University Library do not list it, and the nearest copies today may be those in the Bodleian Library in Oxford. In fact, the Bodleian has copies of the first and third editions, so the book must have aroused some interest, and their catalogue advises us of a review, published in *The Christian Remembrancer* of November 1835. This suggests that it had attracted national attention.

In these days of ecumenism and 'Churches Together' organisations, it seems incredible that there should have been such antipathy between Anglicans and protestant dissenters. One wonders whether, in the book itself, Catholics were mentioned, or whether they were considered to be beyond hope.

According to the advertising blurb, the Gentleman of Reading 'has shown that a National Institution of Public Worship is not only just and necessary in a religious sense, but that it is also politically and morally best. He has also shown

JUST PUBLISHED!

A

REPLY

TO THE

DISSENTERS

IN

THEIR ATTACKS

ON THE

ESTABLISHED

CHURCH;

Addressed to the People of England,

BY A GENTLEMAN OF READING.

This Work embraces all the great questions of Law, Policy, Religion, Morality, and Religious Liberty, at issue between the Dissenters and the Church; and will be found to open and explain them in a way in which few persons have but little previous conception. The writer has shown on what ground a National Institution of Religion is established, and on what principle it is supported; and by a comparative view of the Clergy and the Church, and the Dissenting Preachers and their Institutions, which is the most liberal, and who is the most likely to be influenced by interest. He has shown that a National Institution of Public Worship is not only just and necessary in a religious sense, but that it is also politically and morally best. He has shown also that the Dissenters, by establishing so many New Institutions, and creating so many New Orders of Priesthood, have brought an immense and unnecessary burden on the country, and that vice and depravity among the people at large have increased from the period of their commencement; that the Dissenting Preachers have departed from the pure worship of God, and substituted their preaching for devotion; that they have infused a proud, and conceited, and pernicious feeling into domestic life; and that their proceedings and their doctrines have an injurious an a demoralizing effect on the nation.

As the Dissenters have long made it a merit to revile and denounce the Clergy and the Church, it is hoped, that if they love the truth, they will now hear *both sides of the question.*

Reading:
**Printed by R. & J. SNARE, 16, Minster-st. and
Sold by all Booksellers.**
PRICE ONE SHILLING.

72. Today, the building looks much the same, but with an external staircase with ornamental iron balustrade under the little projecting roof to the right.

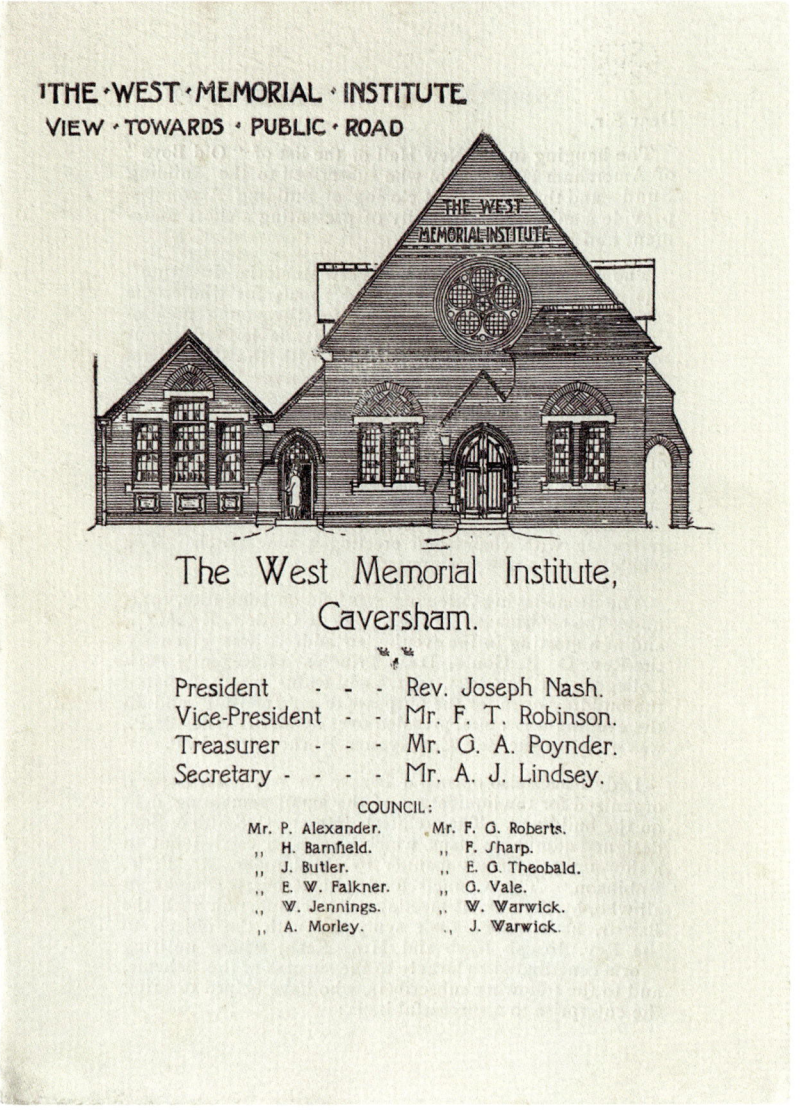

that the Dissenters, by establishing so many New Institutions and creating so many Orders of Priesthood, have brought an immense and unnecessary burden on the Country, and that vice and depravity among the people at large have increased from the period of their commencement.' Presumably these extreme views were those of a small, if vociferous, minority!

They can be partly explained because, at the time, the Anglicans were concerned that they were being 'overtaken' by the nonconformists. Their fears were to some extent borne out when in 1851 the government conducted a Census of Religion, and it was found that of those attending a place of worship in Reading, almost half went to non-Anglican churches.

Moving onwards, Caversham, across the river, had developed rapidly from the 1860s onwards, and the Caversham Free (Baptist) Church opened in 1866, mainly paid for by Ebenezer West, who ran the Amersham Hall boys' school up the hill. The architect was Alfred Waterhouse, one of the country's leading architects.

So popular was the Free Church that only eleven years later a larger church was needed. Alfred Waterhouse was again called in to design it, and like the first church, it had a large, circular window. It is now the Caversham Baptist Church.

Its predecessor, in Gosbrook Road, became a British School during the week, and a Sunday school on Sundays. It was quite separate from the National School, or Parish School, in School Lane behind it.

The British School must have closed by 1911, when the Baptists decided that it should become 'rooms for the wholesome recreation and moral improvement for the young men of Caversham, and to increase the space available for religious teaching on Sundays in connection with the Caversham Free Church.' It was named in honour of Ebenezer West, whose son, Alfred Slater West, was a major subscriber to the fund for the conversion of the building. This folding leaflet shows that a billiard table, games equipment and scout uniforms were bought.

It was published at Christmas, 1913, when all the expenses arising from the conversion of the building had been paid off. It has a list of the subscribers, and the income and expenditure accounts. Its 'artistic' style strongly suggests that it was printed by Poynders – especially since G. A. Poynder was the treasurer of the Institute (see p. 60–2).

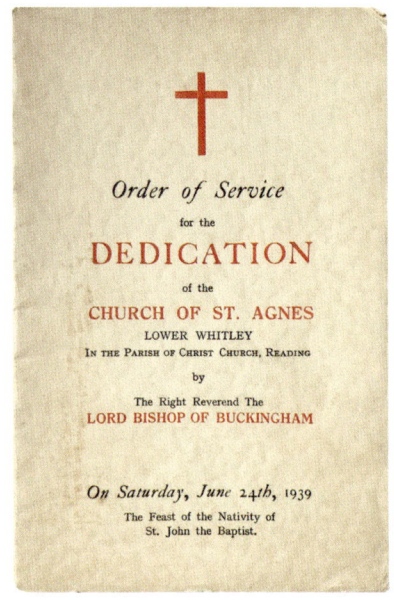
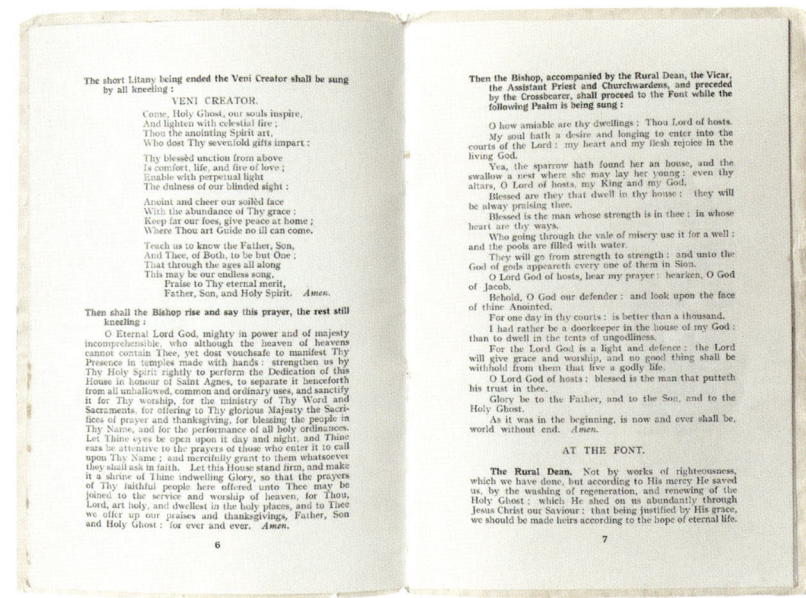

73. The dedication of the new church took place on the Feast Day of the Nativity of St John the Baptist, rather than the Feast Day of St Agnes, 21 January.

In the 1950s, the buildings, or part of them, were being used as a school clinic, and they later became a dance school. In 1999 they were bought by a developer, and divided into ten apartments, named The Waterhouse in honour of the architect, as they are to this day.

At the opposite end of town, the council's Whitley Housing Estate was well under way in the 1930s. It gained a public library in 1935, a Savoy Cinema in 1936, and a new church in 1939. St Agnes is perhaps an unusual patron saint for an Anglican church. Agnes was martyred in Rome at the age of 12 or 13, and is the patron saint of young girls, chastity and survivors of rape.

The first St Agnes' Church in Reading was in Silver Street, designed by the local architect Spencer Slingsby Stallwood, and opened in 1904. It was on the right going up the hill, just above what is now the Rising Sun Arts Centre. Although less than five minutes' walk from St Giles' Church in Southampton Street, it was a mission church of St Giles', in an area of poor housing, which had begun as an 'iron room' in 1899.

When a church for the new Whitley Housing Estate was planned, the new church was to have been dedicated to St Francis of Assisi, but then it was decided that it should be a new St Agnes' Church. The church furnishings were moved from Silver Street to Northumberland Avenue. The old Silver Street building was kept by the church for some years, and in 1946 was being used for 'occasional social and educational work,' but later it became a factory.

The dedication of the new church was conducted by the Bishop of Buckingham, which might seem unexpected. Between 1909 and 1942 there was no Suffragan Bishop of Reading, and though in 1939 the Rt. Rev. Kenneth Kirk was Bishop of Oxford, another Suffragan Bishop, the Rt. Rev. Philip Eliot, was chosen for the occasion.

From this order of service, it can be seen that the ceremony must have been impressive. It involved a procession from the vestries by the south east door, which included the architect, Ernest Ravenscroft, the builder, Mr L. A. Walden, and the builder's foreman, Mr V. Pitt. Psalm 122, *I Was Glad*, was sung during the procession. Then, arrived at the main north west entrance, the Bishop was to knock three times on the door with his pastoral staff. The door was to be opened wide, and the keys were to be delivered to the Bishop. Then the Bishop, the Rural Dean, the Vicar, the Assistant Priest and the Churchwardens were to go round the church, and prayers were to be said at various stations – the font, the chancel step, the lectern, the stalls of the clergy, the choir stalls, and the chapel. The Bishop then consecrated the altar.

By the late 1970s, the future of St Agnes' Church, together with smaller churches in Whitley Wood Lane and Elm Road, was being re-assessed, leading to the creation of a new parish. The church on Northumberland Avenue is now the Whitley Parish Church of St Agnes with St Paul and St Barnabas, large and impressive, looking more like a church somewhere in Catholic Italy than a church on the Whitley Estate. The parish retains all three church buildings for worship.

Opposite page:
74. The Masonic Hall was designed by J. B. Clacy and J. E. Danks; Clacy was the first Worshipful Master of the Lodge, in 1860, and Danks in 1878.

IX. Clubs and societies

This chapter looks at local societies, which include friendly societies, and professional and political associations.

The Freemasons trace their origins back to the building of Solomon's Temple in Jerusalem. They certainly existed in this country in the Middle Ages as a confraternity of stonemasons who recognised one another by secret words, signs and tests. By the seventeenth century honorary, 'Accepted' Masons were allowed to join, and the system of provincial confraternities, or 'lodges,' began to spread outwards from London in the eighteenth. As will be seen, some of the friendly societies which arrived later organised themselves along similar lines.

Inside this card is the menu for the four-course dinner, and the order of proceedings for the Installation of the Worshipful Brother Harold Frank Butler as Worshipful Master of the Aldworth Lodge at the Masonic Hall. Presumably the design on the front represents the interior of this building, which was in Greyfriars Road, just behind and a little below Greyfriars Church and School. It was built in 1859, and demolished in the 1960s.

On the back, we have the list of officers, with titles such as the Worshipful Master, the Senior and Junior Wardens, the Chaplain, the Director of Ceremonies, the Senior of Junior Deacons, Almoner, Inner Guard, Stewards and the Tyler, and an Organist. Some of them are referred to as Brothers, and some as Worshipful Brothers, and some have letters after their names – P.G., P.G.Purs., P.M., P.P.A.G.D.C., P.P.G.T., and P.P.G.W.

The toasts were to the Queen and the Craft, the Most Worshipful the Grand Master, the Right Worshipful Deputy Grand Master, etc. At the end of the proceedings, after the Installation of the Master, Past Masters and officials, came the Tyler's Toast. He was the door-keeper, whose job it was to keep out the uninitiated.

The next document is a share prospectus to help raise money for the building of a hall in West Street, for the use of members of the Ancient Order of Foresters. They were a men's friendly society, whose legendary past went back to the days of Robin Hood, but it had in reality begun as the Royal Foresters' Society in the

ALDWORTH LODGE, No. 5191

INSTALLATION

at THE MASONIC HALL, READING
on SATURDAY, DECEMBER, 3rd, 1955

W.Bro. HAROLD FRANK BUTLER
Worshipful Master.

early eighteenth century, and became the A.O.F. in 1834. The local branches were known as Courts, and its officers as Rangers. They are now called the Foresters' Friendly Society.

The proposed building was to include offices, court rooms and other conveniences, including a reading room. 'Amusing games (under certain regulations) will also be introduced, so that members may derive both moral and intellectual improvement.' No mention is made of refreshments or a bar. It was 'confidently submitted' that a good income would be realised from letting the premises, and they would be a source of profit for the shareholders.

It appears that the venture was successful, though the fundraising may have taken some years. John Read, printer of the document, was at the *Berkshire Telegraph* office only until 1873, and the Foresters' Hall was erected in West Street in 1878–79. The Ancient Order seems to have abandoned the hall in or before 1902, when they were meeting in the Friendly Societies' Assembly Rooms in Bridge Street. Between 1909 and 1916, the West Street building was a cinema, West's Picture Palace. In October 1916 the *Reading Mercury* announced that 'the Foresters' Hall Picture Palace' had been acquired by a sporting syndicate, and was to be known as the Reading Stadium. This was short-lived, and by 1918 the premises had become the Palm Lodge – a baker's shop and restaurant run by Mr G. G. Parslow (see p. 20–1). The Reading Co-op eventually bought the site and extended their central premises over it.

Reading had a second Foresters' Hall above 110–112 London Street, which first appears in directories in 1924, and lasted until around 1980.

The Ancient Order of Druids was another men's friendly society with a name suggesting a long existence – though in fact its origins went back only to 1880. The original Druids had been the priests of the Celtic peoples in what are now parts of France, England and Wales, who were notorious for sacrificing people to their pagan gods. In their later incarnation they were benign, but considered the ancient Druids to be forerunners of the Christians, full of wisdom and knowledge. They raised money for good causes, went to special church services, and apparently knew how to enjoy themselves. On formal occasions they dressed in white flowing robes, some of them carrying staves with sickles on the top – presumably for cutting down bunches of their sacred plant, mistletoe.

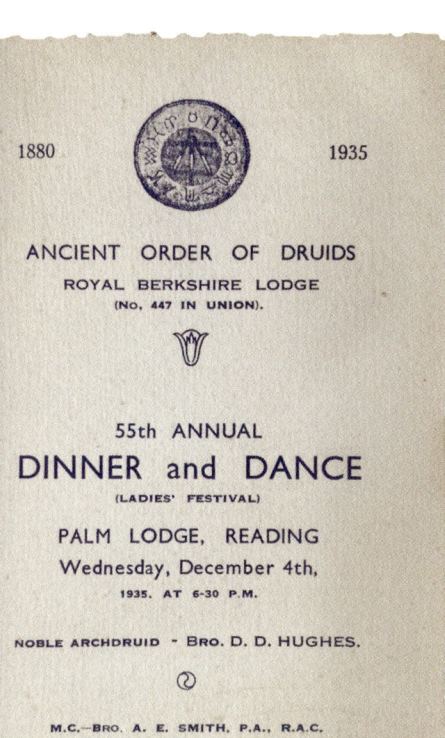

At their headquarters in Bloomsbury, a 'sacred fire' was kept burning, and they held meetings at Stonehenge.

Like the Freemasons, they were organised in Lodges, and their officers had strange titles – such as the Noble Arch Druid, the I.P.N. Arch Druid, the Vice Arch Druid, the Guardian, the Senior Bards, the Junior Bards, and there was an Organist. On the back of the card, after their names, some of them had letters denoting other offices – F.S.C., P.A., P.G.O., R.V.G.A. and R.A.C.

Their 1935 Annual Dinner and Dance was held at the Palm Lodge in West Street – the building that had been built by another friendly society, the Foresters (see p. 118–20). Presumably, in view of its name and the prevailing fashion, the Palm Lodge would have been decorated with potted palms. After the four-course dinner came the toasts – to the King, the Ancient Order of Druids, the Mayor and Corporation, the ladies and visitors, and the Noble Arch Druid.

The evening was rounded off with the singing of this song:

> Now let your voices ring
> The joys we feel each heart can tell
> While in concord loud we sing:
> Brothers all, farewell!
> Loyal Druids we,
> Enemies to care,
> Friends around we see,
> And harmony we share.

Opposite page:
75. The temporary address given on the prospectus is that of Mr. G. F. Callas, the Secretary of the Foresters' Hall Company.

76. At the time, the Druids were raising money to endow yet another bed at the Royal Berkshire Hospital.

Reading, for much of the nineteenth century, had several gentlemen's clubs in the town centre, where men of business and professional men could meet for refreshments or a game of billiards. The history of the Athenaeum Club can be traced back to around 1807.

The Berkshire Club was a comparative latecomer. It was a club for all magistrates of the county, and for other gentlemen who had to be elected by the existing members, and re-elected annually. The non-magistrates should not outnumber the magistrates, and all members had to pay a joining fee of one guinea (£1.05), plus an annual subscription of a guinea. The Lord Lieutenant

Opposite page:

77. The author has memories of the Berkshire Athenaeum Club from around 1980, when the steward was Tommy Tomlinson, assisted by his wife, Zena.

78. Among the dignitaries attending were representatives of various Habitations – Abingdon, Binfield, Burghfield and Sulhamstead, Caversham, Englefield, Maidenhead, Mortimer, Queen's Arbour, Purley, Sunningdale, Wargrave, Winchcombe, Windsor, Wokingham … and Reading, the organisers.

of the county, and the Chairman of the Berkshire Quarter Sessions were to be, respectively, the ex-officio President and Vice-President of the Club.

There appears to have been a club room, with books, newspapers and journals, where smoking was not permitted, and another room where it was. Meals and refreshments were available. Since all communications to the Club were to be addressed to the Committee of the Berkshire Club at the Queen's Hotel, this is presumably where the club rooms were. The hotel was in Friar Street, and was to be demolished and replaced by the Head Post Office around 1921. This building is presently a branch of a bar and restaurant, The Slug and Lettuce. By 1912, however, the Club had moved into a building of its own, in Blagrave Street.

In 1972 it merged with the Athenaeum Club, to become the Berkshire Athenaeum Club, which occupied the Blagrave Street building until around 1995. It is now a public house called the Oakford Social Club.

Our next item is the programme for an evening of music and speeches at the Large Town Hall (now the Concert Hall). Around that time, 1893, the Primrose League was at the height of its popularity and influence, and there would have been other social events at different times of year.

The primrose was said to be the favourite flower of the Tory politician, Benjamin Disraeli. He was a friend of Queen Victoria, who sent a wreath of primroses to his funeral in 1881. On the anniversary of his death, 19 April, it became customary for Tory Members of Parliament to wear primroses in their buttonholes. The Primrose League was founded at a meeting at the Carlton Club in 1883. Subscriptions were at two different rates – Full Members (knights and dames) at half a crown, and Associate Members at a few pence only. 'Ordinary' people were welcome to join, including women, and all could take part in the administration. Its hierarchy began with a Grand Master at the top, and the country was divided into 'Habitations,' each with its Ruling Councillor. Popularity declined after the First World War, though it was not officially wound up until 2004.

It stood for 'the maintenance of religion,' for 'the imperial ascendancy of the Empire,' and 'allegiance to the Sovereign of these realms.' It opposed home rule in Ireland.

This programme, printed on appropriate primrose paper, has a long list of Patrons and Ruling Councillors. The main speaker was Mr J. A. Rentoul MP, and the vote of thanks was proposed by Mr C. T. Murdoch, and seconded by Sir George Russell. Mr Murdoch, a banker, had been Conservative MP for Reading between 1885 and 1892, and was to regain his seat in 1895.

RULES
FOR
"THE BERKSHIRE CLUB."

1. The Club shall be called "The Berkshire Club," and shall consist of such Magistrates of the County as, from time to time, shall signify their desire to become Members of the Club; and of other gentlemen, not being Magistrates, to be elected as hereinafter provided; but not to exceed in number, at any one time

2. The Management of the Club shall be placed in the hands of a Committee of Members, to be appointed at a General Annual Meeting, on the first day of the Michaelmas Quarter Sessions. One of the Committee, in rotation, shall act as Secretary for the year thence ensuing. The Lord Lieutenant of the County and the Chairman of the Quarter Sessions shall be, respectively, the President and Vice-President of the Club, and *ex-officio* Members of the Committee.

3. In the event of a vacancy occurring in the Committee at any time previous to the General Annual Meeting, the Committee shall have the power of appointing a Member to fill the vacancy for the remainder of the year.

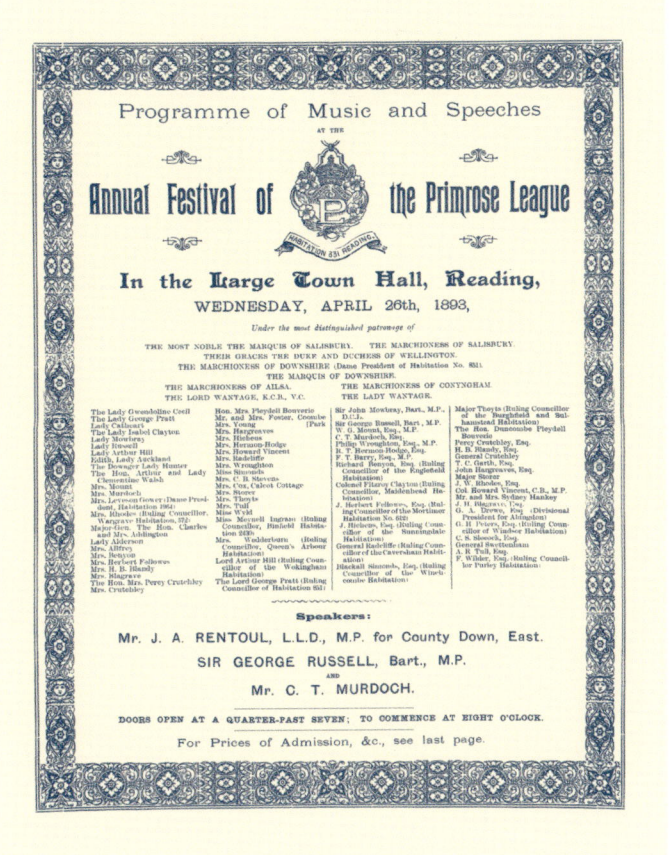

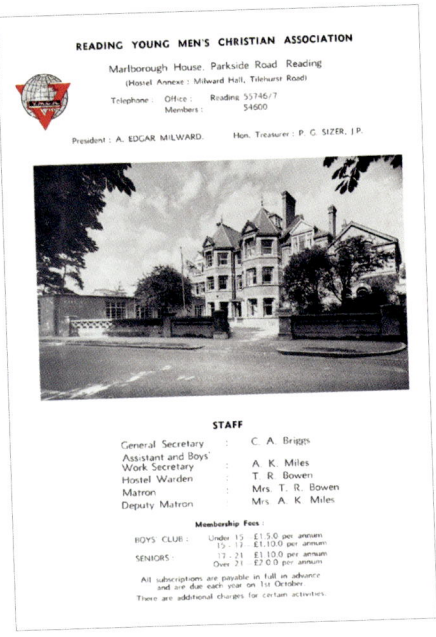 

79. As remembered by the author, in 1969 the hostel seemed to be mainly populated by young men who had arrived, some of them from other countries, to start jobs or to find work.

The music was provided by the Primrose League Choir and the Ladies' Amateur String Band. Mr E. K. Deacon accompanied, on the 'Grand Organ' and the piano. Charles Phillips conducted the choir and sang solo sections in the National Anthem, and in a song called 'For Union and for Queen'.

The Young Men's Christian Association (YMCA) was founded in London in 1844, and a Reading branch was formed in 1846. Initially the membership was 'composed principally of Sunday School teachers from the three parishes' and other members of the Church of England. The major activities were organising lectures, and fund-raising. As the century wore on, it became non-denominational, and part of an international organisation. Its first premises, including a gymnasium, in Valpy Street, opened in 1893, but money was being

raised for much grander and more extensive premises, on the corner of Friar Street and Merchants Place, which opened in 1897. The decision to move out to Tilehurst Road/Parkside Road was implemented in 1959, and the ground floor of the town centre site is now a Nando's restaurant in a new building.

A branch of the Young Women's Christian Association (YWCA) opened in 1872, meeting at first in rooms by St Mary's churchyard, and in 1881 moving to Devonshire House in Castle Street (now the College of Integrated Chinese Medicine).

This brochure was published just a few years before the present author arrived in Reading. Not having much money, much idea of the layout of the town, and knowing no-one, it was somewhere you could stay until you could find a place of your own. For me it was ideal.

There will be many who grew up in Reading who must also be grateful for what the YMCA had to offer. The list of facilities and activities listed here is impressive. There was the gymnasium, the Boys' Hall, the Games Court, the Marlborough House Lounge, the Milward Hall Lounge, a buffet, and of course a chapel, open till 10pm. The activities included chess, billiards, snooker, table tennis, weight-lifting, hockey, and football. There were Cubs and Sea Scouts, and there was a choir. On Tuesday evenings there were lectures on different faiths, different parts of the world, and about life in Reading. These last were given by Borough officials, including the Town Clerk, the Chief Constable, the Borough Treasurer, and the Chief Education Officer.

The Reading YMCA went through difficult times in the 1970s. Financial problems forced it to sell off Milward Hall, and then there was a fire at Marlborough House, but it always managed to bounce back, and to move with the times in serving the community. A glance at the website will show that the Reading YMCA now has a different emphasis. It offers sheltered accommodation to vulnerable young men who would otherwise be homeless, and in its workshop offers alternative learning for those who have difficulties in a traditional classroom environment. It still has its sports facilities, and now a pre-school, the Parkside Café (advertised as a resource for the local community and families), and an Outdoor Activity Centre in the countryside at Padworth.

Opposite page:
80. The burial place of Frances Kendrick, the heroine of this ballad, has a folklore of its own, involving a gold coffin, and a tunnel leading to its vault under Prospect Park.

X. People

This short chapter concerns just four pieces of ephemera which say something about the lives of four notable Reading characters of the eighteenth and nineteenth centuries, which didn't seem to fit in any other chapter.

Firstly, we have an eighteenth-century broadside, printed in London, now much crumpled but perfectly readable. The events described are supposed to have happened in 1706. In real life, the Kendrick family were at the time wealthy landowners, and their eldest daughter, Frances, inherited the estates at the age of 13. At some stage she married Benjamin Child, a young lawyer, who was probably not as poor as the ballad suggests. They lived together at the family home, Calcot Park, and their marriage, though happy, was a short one, with Frances dying in 1721. Benjamin was heartbroken, and around 1760 moved to a small house on Prospect Hill. The small house was greatly enlarged by John Engelbert Liebenrood around 1800, and became the present-day Prospect Park Mansion, occupied by a Harvester restaurant.

In the ballad, addressed to 'Batchelors of every station,' we learn of a wealthy heiress with an income of £5,000 a year. She has many suitors, but rejects all of them. Then, at a wedding, she comes upon a young lawyer, and her heart and passions are stirred. It is not made clear in the ballad whether words are exchanged between them. She finds out where he lives, and returns home. Then she decides to send him an anonymous letter, challenging him to a duel. The reason for this challenge is not stated, but she says:

> He has caused me such distraction
> And I will have satisfaction,
> Which if he denies to give,
> One of us shall cease to live.

Benjamin accepts the challenge and arrives at the stipulated grove with a companion. Frances is masked, and does not reveal her identity. Presumably it is obvious that she is female, if for no other reason that she says:

> It was I that did invite you,
> You shall wed me, or I'll fight you.

The Berkshire Lady.

In Four Parts.

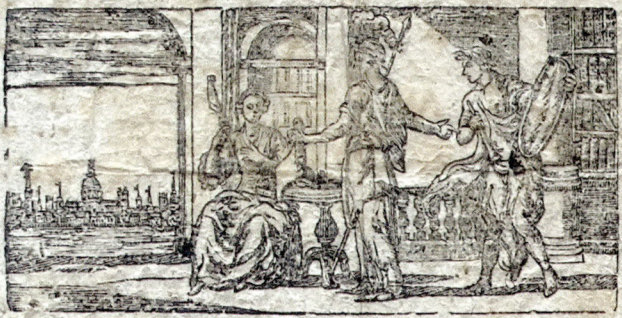

PART I.

BATCHELORS of every station
Mark this strange but true relation,
Which in brief to you I bring,
Never was a stranger thing.

You shall find it worth your hearing,
Loyal love is most endearing,
When it takes the deepest root,
Wielding gold and charms to boot.

Some will wed for store of treasure
But the greatest joy and pleasure,
Is in faithful love, you'll find,
Grac'd with a noble mind.

Such a noble disposition
Had the lady, with submission,
Of whom I this sonnet write:
Store of wealth, and beauty bright.

She had left by an old grannum
Full five thousand pounds per annum,
Which she held without controul:
Thus she did in riches roll.

Tho' she had vast store of riches
Which some persons much bewitches,
Yet she bore a courteous mind,
Not the least to pride inclin'd

Many noble persons courted
This young lady, 'tis reported,
But their labour proved in vain,
They could not her love obtain.

Tho' she made a strong resistance
Yet by Cupid's kind assistance,
She was conquer'd after all,
How it was, declare I shall.

Being at a noble wedding,
Near the famous town of Reading,
A young gentleman she saw,
Who belonged to the law.

As she view'd his sweet behaviour
Every courteous carriage gave her,
New addition to her grief,
Forc'd she was to seek relief.

Privately she then enquir'd
About him she so admir'd,
Both his name and where he dwelt,
Such very hot flames she felt.

Then at night this youthful lady
Call'd her coach, which being ready,
Homewards then she did return,
But her heart with flames did burn.

PART II.

Night and morning for a season,
In her closet she would reason
With herself, and often said,
He has my poor heart betray'd.

I that have so many slighted,
Am at length as well requited,
For my griefs are not a few,
Now I find what love can do.

He that has my heart in keeping
Tho' I for his sake lie weeping,
Little knows what grief I feel,
But I'll try it out with steel.

For I will a challenge send him,
And appoint where I'll attend him:
In a grove without delay,
By the dawning of the day.

He shan't in the least discover,
That I am a wounded lover:
By the challenge which I send,
But for justice I contend.

He has caused such distraction,
And I will have satisfaction,
Which if he denies to give,
One of us shall cease to live.

Having thus her mind revealed,
She a letter signed and sealed;
Which when it came to his hands
The young man was at a stand.

In the letter she conju'd him,
For to meet, and well assur'd him,
Recompence he must afford,
Or dispute it with his sword.

Having read this strange Relation
He was in a Consternation;
But advising with a friend,
He persuades him to attend.

Be of courage, and make ready,
Faint Heart never won a fair Lady,
In regard it must be so,
I along with you will go.

PART III.

Early on a Summer's morning
When bright Phœbus was adorning,
Every bower with his beams;
This young lady came it seems.

At the bottom of a mountain
Near a pleasant chrystal fountain,
There she left her gilded coach,
While she did the grove approach.

Cover'd with a Mask and walking,
There she met her lover talking,
With a Friend that he had brought,
So she asked whom he sought.

I am challeng'd by a Gallant,
And resolve to show my talent,
Who he is I cannot say,
But resolve to shew him play.

(Lady) It was I that did invite you,
You shall wed me or I'll fight you,

Underneath these spreading trees,
Therefore choose you which you please.
You shall find I don't despair,
For I have a trusty rapier,
So now take your choice said she,
Either fight or marry me.

Said he, Madam, what pray mean ye?
In my life I ne'er have seen ye,
Pray unmask, your visage show,
Then I'll tell you ay or no.

(Lady) I will not my face uncover
Till the marriage Rites are over,
Therefore take you which you will,
Wed me, Sir, or try your skill.

Step within this pleasant bower,
With your friend one single hour,
Strive your mind to reconcile,
I will wander here the while.

While the beauteous lady waited,
The young Batchelor debated,
What was best for to be done.
Said his friend the hazard run,

If my judgment may be trusted,
Wed her, Sir, you can't be worsted,
If she's rich, you rise to fame
If she's poor, you're the same.

He consented to be Married,
All three in a coach were carried,
Unto the Church without delay,
Where he weds the lady gay.

Those sweet little Cupids hover'd,
Round her eyes, her face was cover'd
With a mask. He took her thus
Just for better or for worse.

What a courteous kind behaviour,
She presents his friend a favour,
Then she did dismiss him strait,
That he might no longer wait.

PART IV.

As the gilded coach stood ready,
The young lawyer and the lady,
Rode together till they came,
Unto a house of state and fame.

Which appear'd like a castle,
Where you might behold a parcel
Of young cedars tall and strait.
Just before the Palace-gate.

Hand-in-Hand they walk'd together,
To a hall, or parlour rather,
Which was beautiful and fair,
All alone she left him there.

Two long hours he waited
Her return, at length he fretted,

Printed and Sold by J. Davenport, 6, George's Court, St. John's La
Where may be had the greatest variety of Slips, Collection

Opposite page:
81. The exact purpose of this notice is uncertain: it may be a funeral eulogy.

This is not to be a duel with pistols: she carries a rapier. But Benjamin's companion sensibly advises him:

> If my judgement may be trusted,
> Wed her, Sir, you can't be worsted,
> If she's rich you rise to fame,
> If she's poor, you're the same.

So marriage is decided upon, and they leave for the church in a waiting gilded coach, then make their way to the Berkshire Lady's palace.

Neither Frances nor Benjamin is named in the ballad, though we are told that they met at a wedding 'near the famous town of Reading.' The illustration on the broadsheet seems to have been chosen from stock, and does not appear to relate to the story of the Berkshire Lady in any way.

Next we have a small sheet of paper which has at some time been pasted onto card. It lists the good works of Edward Simeon during the last eight years of his life. Its purpose is not obvious; it may have been distributed to mourners at his funeral, which took place on 22 December, 1812.

He became a wealthy London merchant, but gave many gifts to his native town of Reading. On the document we see listed clothing for 1,600 Sunday school children, and a legacy for the charity to continue after his death. To the poor of Reading he gave clothing, blankets, and five tons of salt fish. We see a gift of £500 'towards reducing the price of bread, and a legacy for the reduction of the price of bread annually.' These charities were to be administered by Reading Corporation.

He also paid for the obelisk which still stands in the middle of the Market Place, and merits a chapter in Malcolm Summers' book, *Signs of the Times*. The architect he chose to design it came to be better remembered than Simeon was: it is usually referred to as the Soane Monument. Simeon was a director of the Bank of England, and John Soane (later Sir John) was architect to the Bank of England, and he is thought to have been born at Goring and was educated at Reading. Simeon offered to pay for an obelisk with four lamps, and to leave funds to pay for them to be illuminated in perpetuity. Soane designed a triangular column with three sets of lamps. There were seven oil lamps in

AN EPITOME
OF THE
BENEVOLENCE
OF THE LATE
EDWARD SIMEON, Esq.

TO HIS NATIVE TOWN OF READING,

Between the years 1804 and 1812.

He clothed 1600 Sunday-school Children.
To the Poor, at inclement seasons,
HE GAVE 900 blankets,
4200 yards of flannel,
1760 Guernsey waistcoats,
7120 pairs of stockings and gloves,
600 camlet cloaks,
5 tons of salt fish;

Towards reducing the price of bread
HE GAVE . . . . £ 500
to sundry Schools 1200
to the Dispensary 200
to sundry Clubs and Societies 650
to light the Obelisk in the Market-place, 3 per Cents, } 1000

To these acts, which so eminently distinguished him in his life, must be added the following bequests at his decease:

For clothing the Sunday-school Children of the Town of Reading, biennially, 3 per Cents, } £4044.
For the reduction of the price of bread, annually, 1617.

His private acts of benevolence are known to have been equally numerous, to persons who are now in the enjoyment of competence, and even independence.

The
𝕱ather's Lamentation
Over the Death of his only Son.
An ELEGY.
BY
MR. JESSE, of READING-LADIES'-SCHOOL.

'TWAS in the dead, and solemn midnight hour,
The shades of night hush'd nature to repose,
And all was still.—The pains of hell rush'd on
And seiz'd; as God denounc'd, when mortals fell.—
The dreadful storm of anguish being o'er;—
A perfect calm brings perfect ease to all.
And now's proclaim'd (with heartfelt joy) a Son.
Quick vibrates through the air this pleasing sound,
Which strikes the anxious ear of him, who, in
The antichamber, waits to be call'd Sire.

       Then

Opposite page:
82. Thomas Jesse (1763–1847), school master and property developer, was the author of this elegy.

each set, each lamp having a wick of 36 cotton threads. In time, these were replaced by gas-lamps, and around 1911, the corporation gave up on lighting them. It took almost another century for the monument to be restored and electric lamps to be installed.

In the beginning, the obelisk proved controversial, especially since Edward Simeon's brother, John, had recently lost his seat as MP for Reading, and was hoping to regain it at the next election. As well as being a Member of Parliament, John was also, at the time, Recorder of Reading – a position similar to that of Town Clerk. Edward's altruism was called into question, and the mixture of architectural styles and motifs of the monument was ridiculed. John Man, in his 1810 book, *The Stranger in Reading*, was particularly scathing, and wrote that the money would have been better spent on a piped water supply with a cistern in the Market Place.

Ironically, the printer of both this *Epitome of the Benevolence* and *The Stranger in Reading* was William Man, John's son.

Our third item in this chapter is a leaflet containing an extraordinary outpouring, and not the kind of thing that would be written today, let alone printed and distributed, following a similar family tragedy.

At the beginning, the father describes his relief, joy and delight, following his wife's birth-pangs, on the birth of his son:

> 'Twas in the dead, and solemn midnight hour
> The shades of night hushed nature to repose
> And all was still. – The pains of hell rush'd on
> And seiz'd: as God denounc'd, when mortals fell –
> The dreadful storm of anguish being o'er; –
> A perfect calm brings perfect ease to all
> And now's proclaim'd (with heartfelt joy) a Son
> Quick vibrates through the air this pleasing sound
> Which strikes the anxious ear of him who, in
> The antechamber waits to be called Sire.

The son's growing-up is described. Five years passed 'in harmony and love,' and 'obedience filial was by him observ'd.' His 'features of Apollo's mien' and 'manly

83. A remarkable survival from George Grossmith, the father of the more famous George and Weedon Grossmith.

actions' seem vaguely ludicrous when we are told that the boy died aged about five. Sadly, 'too good, for human nature long to bear,' he became ill, and 'seeing the boasted skill of physic fail,' passed away.

> He fix'd his eyes – my God! – and breath'd no more. –
> The shades of death ne'er spread his lovely face,
> As usual is; but smiles triumphant reign'd;
> As if, in dread of death more anguish be.
> Alas! He is no more. – The grave holds that,
> Which once I held – a substitute to me.

Who was intended to read this, one wonders? Perhaps copies were to be distributed at the funeral. Mr Jesse would presumably never have imagined that it could be general readers in the twenty-first century, who had probably never heard of him before.

Thomas Jesse, besides being a schoolmaster, was better known as a property developer, who lived at Castle Hill House – the former King's Arms Inn. He was responsible for Jesse Place and Upper Jesse Place – stuccoed houses on Castle Hill. Jesse Terrace was the work of his nephew, also known as Thomas Jesse. The 'only son' was Thomas Norris Jesse, who died in 1794, but there was also a daughter, Anna Maria. She married her cousin, the builder of Jesse Terrace.

Finally in this chapter comes a witty piece from George Grossmith (1821–1880). This George was the son of William Grossmith, a Reading carver, gilder and picture-frame maker of Minster Street. He was the father of the famous brothers, George and Weedon Grossmith, whose *Diary of a Nobody* appeared in book form in 1892, having been first published in the pages of *Punch* magazine.

This 'middle' George was baptised in St Mary's Church in 1821, worked for the *Reading Mercury* newspaper and became a court reporter for *The Times*, but the family's talent for acting, as well as writing, soon became apparent. He spent part of each year touring the country giving comic lectures, whilst his older brother, William Robert, baptised in 1816, was an infant theatrical prodigy.

William Robert Grossmith had been taken to the Reading Theatre in Friar Street (see p. 135–7) at a tender age, and was overcome by the experience. He

HORA FUGIT.

TIME.
"'Tis I who measure vital space,
And deal out years to human race;
Tho' little prized, and seldom sought;
Without me love and gold are nought."
GAY.

TO MY FRIENDS AND COMPANIONS, AND TO THE YOUTH OF ALL CLASSES, THIS HUMBLE SPECIMEN OF TYPOGRAPHY IS MOST RESPECTFULLY DEDICATED.

ACROSTIC.
T ime, when correctly understood,
I s the most precious earthly good;
M ay we, now young, our little share
E mploy with diligence and care.
G. G.

That the value of time is seldom duly appreciated by youth, is, unhappily, too apparent; and though we are repeatedly forewarned by experienced monitors, and see the painful results of such inadvertency EVERY day of our lives, in men whose prospects have been ruined by their fatal inordination during their minority, yet how apt are we to disregard their goodly precepts and admonitions— how heedless too of each MOMENT of this, the most precious portion of our lives—and how loath to consider, that now is the opportunity given us to lay the foundation of useful knowledge, —"to sow the seed of virtue in our hearts"—ere we are encumbered with the cares and anxieties OF life. Let not those of us who are of poor parentage, and who have nought to depend on, save the issue of our own labours, for a moment despair! or pass away our present days idly, under the idea, that—as our future TIME will be wholly spent in servitude and toil for the rich, who will not deign to encourage us because of our humility—education, to us, will be of no avail! Let us not entertain an hypothesis in every respect so palpably absurd, or offer a plea for ignorance so truly unjustifiable and unworthy; but rather let us bear in mind the words of that learned man who said, "A virtuous education IS A better inheritance than a great estate." Nor let those of us who have wealthy parents, waste our present hours in indolence and empty pleasures, because we opine we are amply provided for. For whilst "honors, MONUMENTS, and all the works of ambition, are destroyed and demolished by Time," the reputation of wisdom is transmitted to posterity: and, young men who are once steeped in the pleasures and vanities of the world, are seldom known to partake OF any other colour. If then, (to quote the words of the exemplary Benjamin Franklin) time be of all things the most valuable, wasting time must be the greatest prodigality. Let us, therefore, be no longer at the MERCY of that "thief of time" procrastination; but, by perseverance and assiduity, so expand our minds, and improve our morals, as to ensure us the respect of those whom we are in duty bound to serve and obey.

DOUBLE ACROSTIC.
E xempt from care, or aught to rack the braI N,
N eed we repine, while youth is our's? Yet, I O !
V ain, reckless, wild, the stripling time has sliD E,
Y ields but to vice; and dies!—himself his foE.

DESIGNED AND PRINTED, (WITH KIND PERMISSION,) BY GEORGE GROSSMITH, AT THE "READING MERCURY" OFFICE, READING, AUGUST, 1830.

began learning songs and speeches by heart. By the age of six, he was creating a sensation on the stages in London and his native Reading, and was nicknamed, after an actor of Roman antiquity, 'The Young Roscius'.

This piece of prose from the 'middle' George is printed on watered silk, in the shape of an hour-glass in a stand, and must have been intended as something to be framed and hung on the wall, and so should not perhaps be included in a book of ephemera. Written at the bottom are the words, 'Designed and printed (with permission) by George Grossmith at the 'Reading Mercury' office, Reading, August 1839.' The sentiments he expresses seem too sententious for present tastes. He concludes:

> If then (to quote the words of the exemplary Benjamin Franklin) time be of all things the most valuable, wasting time must be the greatest prodigality. Let us, therefore, be no longer at the MERCY of that 'thief of time' procrastination; but, by perseverance and assiduity, so expand our minds, and improve our morals, as to ensure us the respect of those whom we are in duty bound to serve and obey.

The words in capitals are printed so as to appear in the centre of every fourth line of the text: reading from top to bottom, they read: 'EVERY MOMENT OF TIME IS A MONUMENT OF MERCY,' and there are quotations and acrostics, top and bottom.

XI. Stage, screen and radio

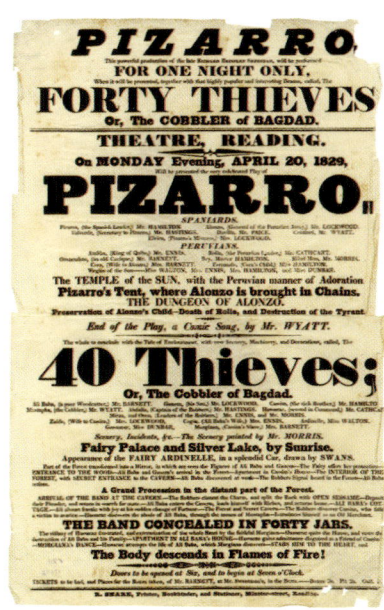

The history of drama in Reading can be traced back before the days of theatres in occasional references, here and there. The churchwardens' accounts of St Laurence's record expenditure on religious plays, before the Reformation. In 1613 there is mention of a 'gallant masque' held at Caversham Park, where Sir William Knollys entertained Queen Anne of Denmark, the wife of King James I of England, on her way to Bath, while in 1786, there was a theatre attached to the New Inn (later the Marquis of Granby) by what is now Cemetery Junction.

The Friar Street theatre of the playbill illustrated here was on the site of the first purpose-built theatre in the town. It had opened in 1788 and was rebuilt in 1801. The 1829 document comes from a collection of around 75 playbills and theatre programmes from the Benham manuscripts, kept in the Central Library – mostly from Reading, but some from Newbury and some from London. This one was chosen because it now seems so extraordinary – a double bill, with fantastic scenery and effects, performed once only, on a Monday night. *Pizarro*, by Sheridan, has a cast of Spaniards and Peruvians, with scenery representing the Temple of the Sun, Pizarro's tent, and the dungeon of Alonzo. It ends with the Destruction of the Tyrant, and is followed by a comic song by Mr Wyatt. *40 Thieves; or, the Cobbler of Bagdad* is, of course, the story of Ali Baba, with scenery painted by Mr Morris. The production seems to be a kind of pantomime,

84. This Reading theatre was in existence from 1788. It was rebuilt in 1801, and closed in 1853.

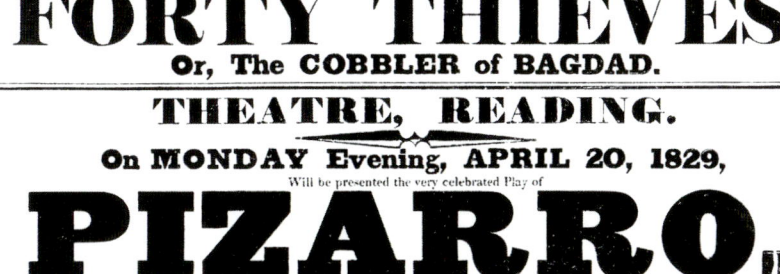

TOWN HALL, READING,
TO-NIGHT!

ADMISSION: RESERVED SEATS, 2/- SECOND SEATS, 1/- Children Half-price.

The great Original and World-famed Wizard

HERR DOBLER

First appearance in England since his most successful tour through South Africa.

There is only one DOBLER.—*Vide the London Times, June 9, 1873.*

NEW, STARTLING & INCOMPREHENSIBLE ILLUSIONS.

HERR DOBLER'S

MARVELLOUS FEATS

Can be performed by no other Conjuror in the World.

The Edinburgh Scotsman, December 25th, 1883, says:—"Unquestionably the best conjuring entertainment ever in Edinburgh."

FROST, in his "Lives of the Conjurors," says: "His illusions are of such a surprising character that they carry the mind of his audience with him throughout his performance, so inexplicable are the mysteries he practises. He is most pleasing in manner and prepossessing in appearance."

The Cape Times, October 23rd, 1888, says: "Herr Dobler is certainly an expert in his business and a Conjuror of the first water.

It is impossible to see his performances without astonishment and admiration."

The Cape Argus, October 23rd, says, re the Dark Seance: "Those who saw it on Saturday night were most profoundly impressed with the power and ability of Herr Dobler, who, in his particular profession, is unquestionably a very clever man. Seeing that Herr Dobler comes with a good reputation of twenty-five years' standing in Great Britain, it is unnecessary to tell the public that they should pay him a visit."

HERR DOBLER'S GREAT INDIAN FLOWER TRICK
AT EVERY PERFORMANCE.

A large basket is filled with beautiful flowers from an *empty paper cone*.

No Apparatus.   No Covered Tables.   No Sleeves.   No Coat Pockets.

HERR DOBLER

IS THE ONLY REAL SLEIGHT OF HAND ENTERTAINER IN THE WORLD.

ALL THE LATEST MARVELS OF THE WIZARD ART.

The Greatest, Most Refined, Most Amusing, Most Scientific, and Most Wonderful Exhibition of Conjuring in the World.

LESSONS GIVEN IN THE ART.

Doors open at ... ... at 10.

Opposite page:
85. It is amazing to think that all this must have been accomplished using gas lighting.

which includes the appearance of a fairy, 'in a splendid Car, drawn by Swans,' and at the end, the villain is stabbed through the heart and 'the body descends in Flames of Fire!' The doors of the theatre opened at 6, and the performance began at 7. One wonders what time it ended!

This Reading Theatre was one of a chain of theatres, run initially by Henry Thornton. On his retirement in 1817, the theatres were taken over by Bronsdorph and Jones, with Edward Barnett as manager. The company also owned theatres in Oxford, Henley, Newbury, Andover, Guildford and Farnham. Presumably this production would have moved on to other theatres in the chain. The Reading Theatre closed on Barnett's retirement in 1853.

In Victorian times, stage entertainments took place in various halls in Reading as well as in theatres – among them the Reading Public Rooms in London Street (1844), the Large Town Hall in Blagrave Street (1882) and the Queen's Hall in Valpy Street (1894). Herr Dobler, the magician, had performed previously, in 1865 and 1876, at the Albert Hall in Friar Street, which stood where the Lola Lo cocktail bar and club stands now, and had started out as the Assembly Rooms. After a fire and re-building, it had opened as the Theatre Royal and Albert Hall in 1871, and was to be rebuilt as the Royal County Theatre in 1887. This in turn was to burn down, in 1894, and to be replaced by the New Royal County Theatre (see p. 138–40) a few doors along the street.

But in 1884, Herr Dobler was at the Town Hall. Off the stage, he was George William Smith Buck, born at Newark-on-Trent in 1836. He was the son of 'Professor' Buck, also a stage magician, and had probably chosen his stage name on account of a famous Austrian magician of the previous generation, Ludwig Dobler, who had toured England in the 1840s.

The English Herr Dobler performed in Reading on six occasions between 1874 and 1886. He was at the Town Hall in 1878, 1881, 1884 and 1886. On the first two of these occasions he must have performed in the old Town Hall (now the Victoria Hall), but on the last two he was in the New Town Hall (now Concert Hall). The visits were usually for a week. Admission cost 2s. or 1s., children half price, with doors open at 7.30, performances starting at 8, and carriages at 10 pm.

Billed as 'The Wizard of the World', Herr Dobler advertised among his feats the Great Indian Flower Trick; the Wonderful Sovereign and Canary Bird; the

Opposite page:
86. The Royal County Theatre existed between 1895 and 1937, in Friar Street, where the Optimax Laser Eye Clinic, Playlist Live bar, Black Diamond Club, Betfred betting shop and Doner Kebab shop are now.

Extraordinary Illusion with a Borrowed Watch, Borrowed Handkerchief, and a Glass Tumbler; Printing by Magic; and Spirit Writing.

The show ended with his Dark Séance, for which audience numbers were limited, with tickets on sale during the interval. The Davenport Brothers, from the United States, had charged 10s. 6d. for their Dark Séance when visiting England, but in Reading it was only one shilling extra to attend. During the séance, Herr Dobler appeared with a length of rope. The lights went out, and when they came up two minutes later, he was securely tied to a chair. Members of the audience were invited to come up on stage and examine the knots. Then a bell and a tambourine smeared with phosphorus were placed on a small table, and the lights went out again. The bell rang and the tambourine floated through the air. During the course of the séance, the advertising promised 'Spirit Manifestations, Floating Instruments, the Flying Coat, Luminous Forms, and other Wonderful Manifestations which were and are now palmed upon the Public as Spiritualism'. At the end of the performance, when the lights came up, Herr Dobler was still tied to the chair.

As has been said, the first Royal County Theatre opened in Friar Street in 1887. Unfortunately, during a thunderstorm in 1894, lightning struck a roof ventilator, setting fire to the roof and the whole theatre.

Nearby in Friar Street, an independent chapel, the Augustine Chapel, had opened in 1877, but after ten years, the congregation had decided to amalgamate with that of the Castle Street Congregational Chapel, so in 1887, the Augustine chapel was converted into the Prince's Theatre. With the burning down of the Royal County Theatre in 1894, after extensive alterations, the Prince's Theatre became the New Royal County Theatre, and opened in 1895.

The architect responsible for these latest alterations was Frank Matcham, the leading theatre architect of the day. The new theatre boasted electric lighting, much ornamental plaster-work, and a foyer with a rockery and waterfall, ferns and palm trees, all reflected in gilt-framed mirrors.

This particular programme was for a play, *England's Flag*, presented by Vereker and Vernon's No. 1 Company. The playwrights were Harold White, C. A. Clarke, and Sydney Vereker. The star role was taken by 'the leading young actor', Sydney Vereker, and Miss Maud Vernon was also among the cast.

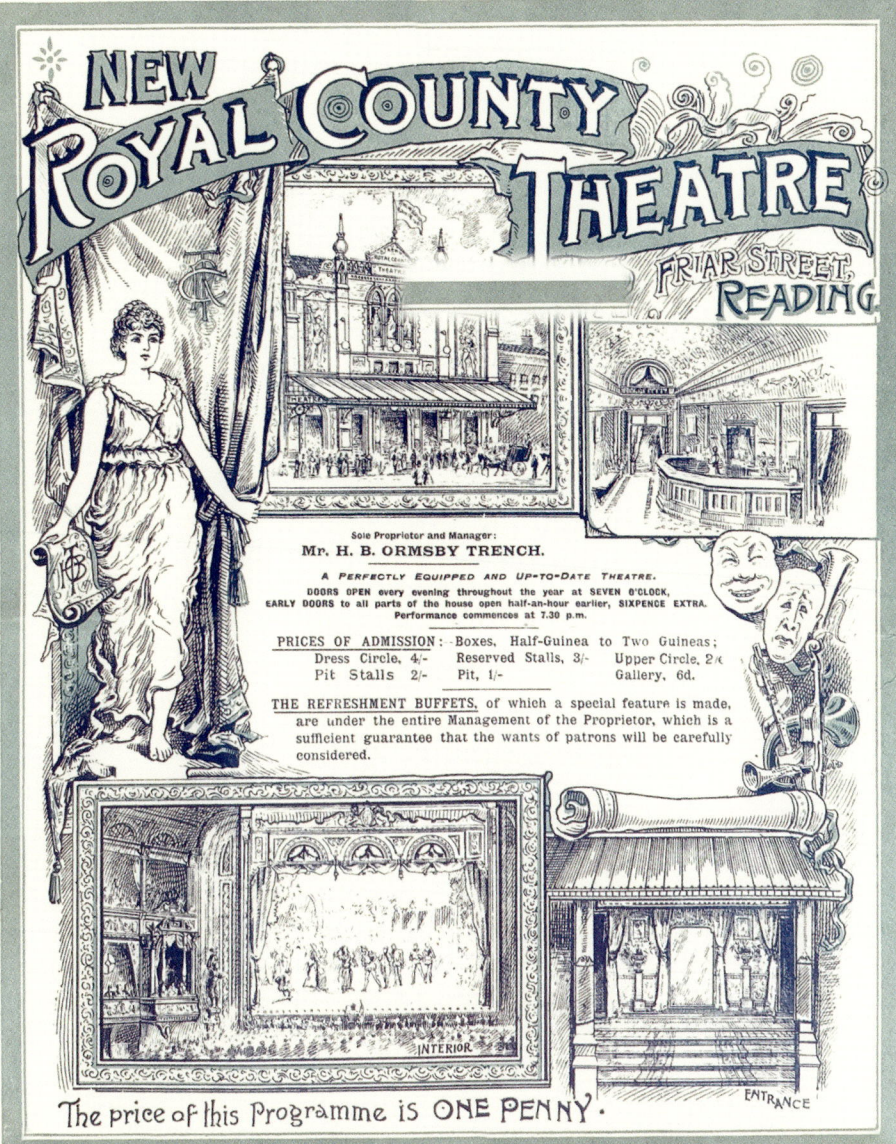

Inside, most of the programme was taken up by advertisements for Reading shops and businesses, among them Henry Bird's Weldale Brewery, Cawston's boatyard at Waterman's Cottage, Caversham (i.e. Piper's Island); Farrer's Circulating Library in Broad Street (later W. H. Smith's); and the Britannia Hotel, Caversham Road, 'patronized by all the profession'.

On the back was a notice to 'country and district patrons'. A late train left the South Eastern Railway Station every night at 10.45, for Earley and Wokingham.

The 1920s and 1930s were to bring in the cinema-going craze, and the New Royal County Theatre, by this time having dropped the 'New' from its title, installed projectors and a screen, and showed films during the summer season.

Its end came suddenly and unexpectedly during the run of the pantomime, *Robinson Crusoe*, in 1937. The theatre burned down during the night of 7–8 January, and was not rebuilt, and Woolworth's extended their store over its site, giving it an entrance in Friar Street. Photographs of the smouldering ruins show the gothic windows of the Augustine Chapel still there, under the plaster-work.

Opening in 1907 as a variety theatre, all the 'big names' of variety theatre seem to have appeared at Reading's Palace Theatre of Varieties – Marie Lloyd, Florrie Ford, G. H. Elliott, Harry Houdini, Max Miller, George Robey and Gracie Fields among them. The architect was W. G. R. Sprague, who designed other theatres in London and the provinces.

A regular feature of the varieties in the early days was the Palace Bioscope – appearing as one of the variety turns, this was one of the earliest places to show moving pictures in the town. Shows were twice nightly, and changed weekly.

On the bill for the week commencing 20 September 1937 were the Crazy Gang, the Bavero Trio, the Four Darlings, Carvey and Mac ('direct from the padded cells of Colney Hatch'), and Professor Sparks (the mad electrician). Top of the bill next week was The Great Levante, the Australian illusionist.

The proprietors of the theatre, B. & J. Theatres, had as directors Leo and Cecil E. Blush, Harry Joseph, and J. Idris Lewis. It was owned briefly by Oscar Deutsch, who was building the Odeon Cinema next door. It opened in 1937, and shortly after that, The Palace was taken on by the owners of the Royal County Theatre, which had recently burned down. This left The Palace as the only purpose-built theatre in town, but the coming of television made it ever harder to attract

86a. Advertisements in the theatre programme, among them for the Britannia Hotel and Farrer's Circulating Library

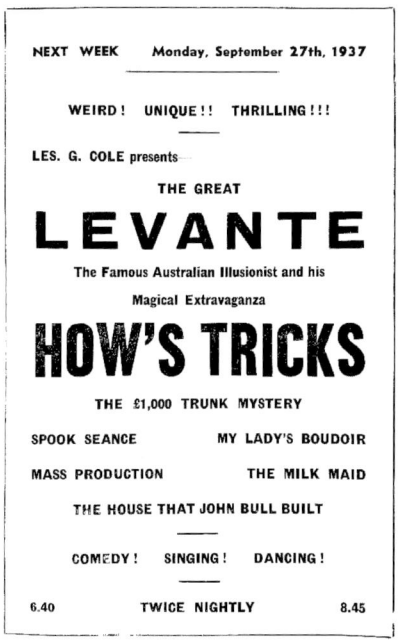

87. The Palace theatre had several different owners over the years. It closed in 1960.

audiences. In the end, its variety shows promised female nudity, with titles like *Nothing on Tonite*. It closed at the end of the pantomime season in 1960, and was demolished the following year. An office building, Liverpool Victoria House (now called Zenith House), went up on the site, with shops below.

After the Second World War, Reading had a professional repertory theatre, which opened in 1948 in the hall of the Pendragon Co-Educational Boarding School, before moving, five years later, closer to the town centre. The school was at 59 Bath Road, where they must have achieved some success because in 1953 they persuaded Reading Council to lease larger premises in London Street to them – the Everyman Theatre (p. 142–3). The short existence of the Pendragon company makes this programme a very rare survivor.

```
Pendragon Theatre
Licensee : G. D. March

The
Pendragon Company
presents

LOVE IN
A MIST

by

Kenneth Horne

Programme    Price    Threepence
```

88. The Pendragon Theatre Company, a professional company, existed for only around five years.

Kenneth Horne, who wrote *Love in a Mist*, is better remembered today for his radio comedy shows of the 1950s and 1960s – *Much-Binding-in-the-Marsh*, *Beyond our Ken*, and *Round the Horne*. The actors were Angela Wheatland, Kevin Barry, Pauline Hector, Robert Patrick, Derek Valentine and Jeanne Thompson. The furniture was lent by the Old Times Furnishing Company, and the stage dressings by McIlroy's department store (see p. 40–1). The next week's production was to be a complete contrast – *The Glass Menagerie*, by Tennessee Williams.

The Paxton House Hotel, which was next door at No. 57, advertised its after-theatre suppers. By 1950, the building was a nursing home, and by 1954, both buildings were run as the Reading Combined Hospitals Preliminary Training School. They are now offices for the National Health Service.

When the Pendragon Theatre Company moved from Bath Road to London Street in 1953, to the building with the pillars – it became the Everyman Theatre. The building had started as the Reading Public Rooms in 1843, and was later used as a Primitive Methodist Chapel. In 1998 it became the Great Expectations hotel and bar, and in 2022, following refurbishment, it became the Hotel 1843. The name 'Everyman' recalls the medieval morality play, as well as suggesting something for everyone.

Theatre audiences gradually declined. There were disagreements between the council, who owned the building, and the company over the kind of plays they should present, with the company interested in more modern and innovative productions. The councillors became less and less inclined to subsidise the theatre, which the ratepayers appeared not to want. With television sets in more and more homes, this was not perhaps the best time to be running weekly rep., and the last 'Everyman' production was in 1957.

In the 1953 production of *The Deep Blue Sea*, the heroine, Hester Collyer, was played by Elizabeth Summers. Two other members of the cast, Kevin Barry and Derek Valentine, had also appeared with the Pendragon Theatre Company. The set was furnished by Kingston's of Duke Street, the kitchen unit was lent by Joyne's, who were higher up London Street, the gas cooker and gas fire were lent by the Southern Gas Board, and the golf clubs by Blake's sports shop in Minster Street. The next week's production was to be *Surrender at Noon*, by local author and playwright Alan Wykes.

89. The Everyman Theatre, 1953. Inside the programme, ladies are requested to kindly remove their hats.

90. This programme was produced by the first Reading Repertory Company: the present-day Reading Rep. has its theatre in Kings Road, near the College.

We now move on to look at some of the amateur dramatic societies which have performed in town. There was a time when almost every church had its own society, and the local papers sent their critics to write reviews of the performances. There were annual musical festivals (and the Tilehurst Eisteddfod) where societies could compete against one another for awards. Each society performed a one-act play, or one act of a longer play, and an adjudicator awarded points, and made helpful comments.

In 2021, the professional Reading Repertory Theatre opened its new auditorium, next to the college in Kings Road. The list printed on the back of this programme shows that a previous amateur Reading Repertory Company had started in 1935. It put on a programme of three, four or five plays a year, many of them very well known in their day, such as *Mary Rose* by J. M. Barrie, *Night Must Fall* by Emlyn Williams, *Time and the Conways* by J. B. Priestley, and *Dear Octopus* by Dodie Smith. *Ladies in Retirement*, by Edward Percy and Reginald Denham, is a melodrama, based on an actual murder of the 1880s, and set in a lonely house in the marshes of the Thames Estuary. It was first produced in 1940, and was adapted as a film, 1941.

The company was run by Oliver and Linda Bridges. They were the grandparents of Kate Winslet, the present-day screen actress. Before the Second World War, the company performed in the Palmer Hall in West Street, a building which is at the time of writing a shop called Mr Bean's Barbers. In 1942 they had moved to 70 London Street, presumably because the Palmer Hall was needed for the war effort. The new venue was the '70' Theatre, which was in fact behind the dental surgery of Mr Bridges, and his wife was a member of the cast. The stone-fronted London Street building has now been turned into apartments, called London Court.

The other members of the cast were Frederick Ball, Betty Bristow, Enid Caddy, Sybil Hicks, Edna Kingston, Norah Pollard, and Freda Roberts. Bill Bristow directed the play, and built the set. For a living, he looked after the window displays in the Heelas department store. The production played for eight evenings.

In 1942, a subscription of 7s. 6d. bought two seats for each of the three following productions. Although an amateur company, they must have had an exceptionally gifted set designer in Bill Bristow, if the photographs in the local studies collection of the Central Library are anything to go by. This first Reading Rep. returned to the Palmer Hall after the war, but decided to close down in 1953.

Of the many talented amateur dramatic groups in Reading, this programme from the Earley Players was selected because of the venue – the Rainbow Hall in the Co-operative Buildings in Cheapside. The building still stands, but is currently used only for warehousing. The present author remembers the Rainbow Hall as a lunch-time rendezvous in the 1970s. In the daytime, the Hall functioned as the Co-op restaurant. It was not decorated in all the colours of the rainbow, nor did it have multi-coloured lighting, as might have been expected. But it did have the stage, with the kitchen behind it. After ordering a meal, a uniformed waitress appeared with your plates, walking across the stage and through the scenery, which was expertly painted to represent mountains and a lake. It seemed bizarre. Sadly, shortly afterwards, the hall had to be closed

91. The Rainbow Hall opened in 1959, and it played host to dinners, dances, fashion shows, competitive and brass band festivals, as well as stage plays.

THIRTY-SECOND SEASON OF PLAYS

THE
EARLEY PLAYERS

RAINBOW HALL
CO-OPERATIVE BUILDINGS
CHEAPSIDE
READING

PROGRAMME SIXPENCE

92. As is to be expected, many of the Berkshire Shakespeare Players appeared in the productions of other societies.

to the public because it was on the first floor, without adequate means of egress in case of emergency.

The Earley Players began in 1927, at first playing in the former chapel of Bulmershe Court, and also had open-air performances in the grounds. After the Second World War, the site became Bulmershe Teacher Training College, later re-named the Berkshire College of Education. The Players' emblem, a trumpet with a banner hanging below, seems to have the silhouette of a dancing bear above it, rather than the bull which might have been expected. The play is *Breath of Spring*, a farce, about the theft of fur coats and stoles, and the actors in 1960 were Esme Few, Peter Fullbrook, Jane Gleeson, Iris Lloyd-Davies, Brian Lowe, James Platt and Elsie Short. The producer was Eric Few, and costumes were supervised by Vi Bowman, who is remembered by the present author doing much the same kind of thing in the 1970s.

Most of the pages in the programme are taken up with advertising, which for present-day readers is probably just as interesting as the information about the play. Among the advertisers are Blake's, the sports outfitters in Minster Street, Hobbs the dry cleaners with three branches, Langston's of West Street Corner, suppliers of shoes for ballet, tap and character dancing (see p. 21–3), and Vinden's the florists in Friar Street. The Reading Fine Art Gallery (successors to J. P. Ballard deceased) was then in Cross Street: ten years later it was in London Street.

From the back of the next programme under consideration, we can see that the first production of the Berkshire Shakespeare Players was *A Midsummer Night's Dream*, in 1951. After that, there had been 20 productions over 22 years, most of them Shakespeare plays. However, in 1960, they had done *Tobias and the Angel*, and a pageant, *Player King*, in 1964.

The productions were in the open air and floodlit, sometimes in the Abbey Ruins, and sometimes in the gardens of Caversham Court. For this production, specially tiered seating was erected in the ruins, and performances did not start until 8 pm Mondays to Thursdays, and 9 pm on Fridays and Saturdays. This meant that for audiences, as daylight faded, the experience became more and more intense – though it was occasionally shattered by a particularly noisy train,

THE BERKSHIRE SHAKESPEARE PLAYERS

present

MEASURE FOR MEASURE

by

William Shakespeare

A Floodlit Production in
THE ABBEY RUINS, READING
4th — 9th JUNE, 1973
Monday to Thursday at 8 p.m.   Friday and Saturday at 9 p.m.

since Reading General and Southern Stations were nearby. A small orchestra played in between the scenes.

In *Measure for Measure*, Peter Cockman played Duke Vincentio, and Michael Evans was Angelo, his deputy and the villain of the piece. Notable among the many names on the programme are those of the Aburrow family – Leslie who was on the stage, his wife Marjorie who was 'front of house' and Secretary of the Players, and their son Geoffrey, who, together with Olive Hall, looked after the floodlighting.

The Royal Berkshire Archives has a collection of minutes, accounts, programmes and press cutting for the Players up to 2003, after which they seem to have disbanded, but the tradition of open-air drama has been continued to the present day by the Progress Theatre, and by Rabble Theatre.

For many years, the Progress Theatre in The Mount, off Christchurch Road, has enjoyed an enviable reputation for its adventurousness, versatility and the consistently high standard of its productions. Founded in 1946, it performed at first in the Palmer Hall in West Street, before moving up to The Mount and renting the Mildmay Hall from the Reading Industrial Co-operative Society.

The Philanthropist, an early play by Christopher Hampton, must have been a risky undertaking. A review of the first night at the Royal Court Theatre in London in 1978 described a dinner party for six, in the rooms of a university lecturer.

> After pairing off … the six mix and meld. The next morning they reap the aftermath of the previous night's sexual activity, or even inactivity.

A review of a revival in 2017 described the play as 'a memorable portrait, not only of academic insularity, but also of the destructive nature of reflex niceness'. So, hardly surprising that the programme has 'not suitable for children' in large letters. Later in the season, they were to have their fun at a pantomime version of *Treasure Island*.

For an amateur group, the long runs must have demanded a great deal of dedication. *The Philanthropist* had nine performances, followed by a discussion of the play on the Sunday afternoon following. *Treasure Island* had 14 evening performances and four matinees!

93. This Progress Theatre production of *The Philanthropist* had a young Ken Branagh playing John, a student.

94. A Sainsbury Singers programme from 1972. The company has no connection to the supermarket chain.

Such was its reputation that Progress Theatre attracted actors and directors from across the area – many of them drama teachers, former professional actors, and aspiring professional actors.

Newcomers to Reading might assume that the Sainsbury Singers were connected with Sainsbury's supermarket, in Friar Street, where it has been for the last 60 years or so. In fact the group was founded by Frank Sainsbury, a well-known baritone singer and teacher of music. Their first production was *H.M.S. Pinafore*, at the Palmer Hall in West Street, in January 1939, with Mr Sainsbury conducting. The story is told in the book, *Airs & Places*.

The company struggled during the war years when most of the men were serving in the forces, but a fresh start was made in 1947, with a move to the Town Hall. This was a much larger auditorium, but was far from ideal. For each production, the stage and proscenium arch had to be built from scratch, and

because of the immovable 'Father' Willis organ, it was impossible to get from one side of the stage to the other behind the scenery without going up and down steps. The present author well remembers the length of time it took to change the scenery during their production of *My Fair Lady* in 1976.

Nevertheless, the Sainsburys have tackled Gilbert and Sullivan, Viennese operettas, Broadway musicals, and in 1972, grand opera. On Monday and Tuesday nights, Pixie Denzey was Carmen; on Thursday, Friday and Saturday, Gwyneth Havard. The role of Don José was similarly split between Morley Alexander, and Graham Clark who at the time was making a name for himself at the Royal Opera House. His website lists his three appearances at Reading – and after that, performances across the world.

The availability of The Hexagon from 1977 must have made things much easier! Their production of *Chess*, the musical, in May 2020 had unfortunately to be postponed because of the COVID-19 restrictions, but was presented in May 2022.

Turning our attention now to the silver screen, the present author found over twenty Reading cinemas when researching his 2017 book on the subject. They were not, of course, all operating at the same time. Here we shall look at one cinema, and one cinema club.

The Vaudeville, popularly known as 'The Vaudy', opened in Broad Street in 1909, in what had been the menswear department of A. H. Bull's department store (see p. 43–4). There were 450 seats. By 1914 it claimed to be 'the most successful picture theatre in the provinces', and it survived the First World War, whereas several other Reading cinemas – the Howard, the Paragon, the Standard Electric and West's Picture Palace – did not. It went through a number of extensions, the last of them in 1921, all of them accomplished without the cinema having to close. In the end there were 1,457 seats in the auditorium, and there was a café, a tea lounge and a soda fountain. The films had orchestral accompaniment until 'talking pictures' arrived around 1930. This programme, for June and July 1920, lists the pieces the orchestra was to play, and on request to Mr Lionel Falkman, patrons could request additional pieces, if they were suitable for the film being shown.

95. The building which was 'The Vaudy' is still there, with a new frontage, now a branch of Boots on the corner of Broad Street and Union Street ('Smelly Alley').

By 1953, the Vaudeville was owned by the Rank Organisation, which re-named the cinema, giving it one of the names the company 'owned', the Gaumont. A few years later, it was proposed to install a wide screen, until it was discovered that the building was not strong enough to take the weight of the big screen and its supporting frame. So the Gaumont was closed in 1957 – and the Pavilion Cinema on the corner of Oxford Road and Russell Street was re-named the

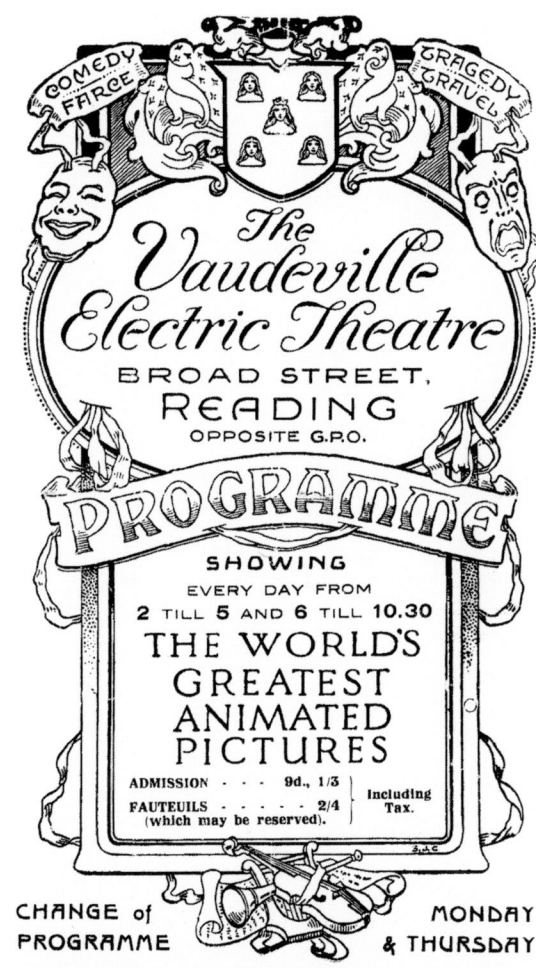

96. The first programme of the Reading Film Theatre

Gaumont a few days later. The Broad Street cinema became a branch of Timothy Whites, the chemists. A completely new front was put on the building, but the top part of the auditorium remains above the present-day shop, though it can't be seen by shoppers: it is now a branch of Boots.

The Reading Film Theatre was opened on 12 January 1970, by Mai Zetterling, the Swedish actress and director, and this is its first programme. The first film to be shown, *The Girls*, was partly written by her, and was directed by her.

The RFT was supported by the British Film Institute, the University of Reading, and the County Borough of Reading. All seats cost four shillings.

For most of the time, the RFT has operated from the Whiteknights Campus of the University, and its screenings have happened only in term time, but it has always been open to members of the public.

It began in the Palmer Building, but in the 1990s, there were suggestions that it might move into one of the large town centre cinemas, which were to close as the new multiplex in The Oracle shopping centre opened, but this was not to be. The cost of refurbishing and then running one of these buildings would have been prohibitive, and presumably the university location suited many of the existing audience members who lived, worked or studied in the area.

For a year or so, for films likely to attract smaller audiences, the university's cinema in Minghella Building was used, but then in 2020, the COVID-19 restrictions brought conventional screenings to a halt. Nevertheless, they continued on line. Then in 2022 came a complete change, as 'live' screenings returned, and did indeed move to the town centre, to the new Biscuit Factory cinema in the Broad Street Mall shopping centre.

Incidentally, the cinema's name has nothing to do with Huntley & Palmers. It is one of a chain, the first of which had opened in Crawford's old biscuit factory in Edinburgh.

Finally in this chapter on entertainment, we turn to radio. In theory, until 1972, the BBC held the monopoly on public radio broadcasting in this country. Radio Luxembourg, a commercial station broadcasting from the Continent, had from the 1930s provided an alternative, and in the 1960s, pirate radio broad-

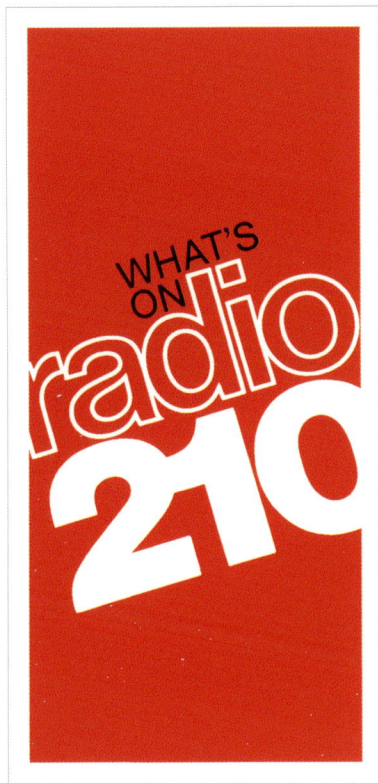

97. A leaflet from Reading's first independent local radio station

casters had operated from ships anchored offshore. Both aimed to give younger people the kind of music they wanted. In closing down the pirates the government had made itself unpopular in some quarters, and an Act of Parliament was brought in to allow what was called Independent Local Radio, controlled by the Independent Broadcasting Authority.

Radio 210 (pronounced two-one-oh) started in 1976, with studios off the Bath Road in Calcot, and a transmitter on the roof of The Butts Centre – the shopping centre which is now called the Broad Street Mall. It later used the transmitter at Hannington, and so was able to cover North Hampshire as well as the Thames Valley.

This leaflet, from six years later, contains a programme guide, photographs of the presenters, and details of branded merchandise for sale. There were T-shirts, aprons, bags and pens on offer.

The variety in the programming is impressive. There were news bulletins every hour, and traffic bulletins every half-hour during the morning and evening rush hours. Children's programmes featured, and of course sports programmes on Saturday afternoons. Specialist programmes included rock, soul, big band, jazz, folk, country and western, black, Asian and classical music. There were information programmes for black and Asian listeners, there was a hospital link, and a programme for farmers.

As time went by, the local radio scene became ever more complex, with new stations and changes of name and ownership. This tended to mean that local radio was not so local as it had been in the beginning. AM and FM channels were split, with Radio 210 becoming 2-Ten FM, and in 2009 it became part of the Heart Network. Then it was merged with Heart Oxfordshire to become Heart Thames Valley. Since then we have had 107 Jack FM, The Breeze (Reading), and SAM FM.

Meanwhile, the BBC had launched Radio Berkshire in 1992, with studios in the former chapel at Caversham Park, which was also the site of its monitoring station. With the move of the monitoring station to London in 2016, the studios have moved to Thames Valley Park.

98. The bazaar was to raise money for the enlargement of the Town Hall organ.

Opposite page:
99. The English Chamber Orchestra, one of the leading ensembles in the land, was similar in size to orchestras of Mozart's time, and in 1976 was playing Mozart in Reading.

XII. Music and dance

The importance of the organ in the Town Hall – now the Concert Hall – is now established beyond dispute. It represents the rare survival of a typical Victorian town hall organ built by one of the most famous exponents of his day – 'Father' Henry Willis – in more-or-less original condition. The proposals of the 1970s and 1980s, which would have meant the loss of the organ, and the hall with its fine acoustic, now seem incredible (see p. 209).

This pinkish card advertises a bazaar, to be held over three days in the Town Hall in 1881, in order to raise the £800 necessary to move and enlarge the organ.

The instrument had been presented to the town by the Reading Philharmonic Society in 1864. It stood in what was then the Town Hall – which was later known as the Small Town Hall and is now the Victoria Hall. When plans were taking shape for the adjacent Large Town Hall, it was decided that the organ should be moved to the new hall, and enlarged to suit the acoustics of its new setting. The cost was to be shared between the Philharmonic Society and the Borough Council.

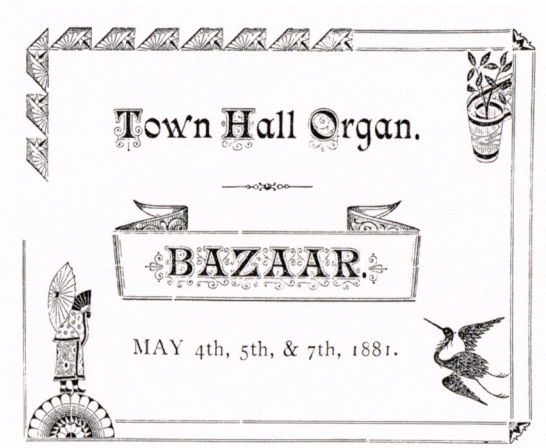

The John Lewis Partnership Music Society
and Heelas of Reading

THE ENGLISH
CHAMBER
ORCHESTRA

Kenneth Sillito   *Violin*
Jose-Luis Garcia   *Violin*
Neil Black   *Oboe*

Director : Kenneth Sillito

Friday the 2nd July
Town Hall Reading

So here we have the Society setting about raising the necessary funds – the £800 did not include the case, which was designed by the architect of the new hall, Thomas Lainson, or the hydraulic pumping apparatus. In the old hall, the organ had been pumped by hand.

Inside the leaflet it is apparent that the bazaar was a sale of work, run by the ladies of the Society. The names of the stallholders are listed, and the name and address of the treasurer. Supporters are asked to send their 'contributions of work, &c.' to the stallholders, and their contributions in cash to the treasurer. This means that the stalls would be selling needlework, embroidery, crochet work, knitting, etc., and in addition to the eight stalls, there was a refreshment stall, run by Mrs H. B. Blandy, and a flower stall, run by the Misses Phippen.

No fewer than sixteen ladies are named as patrons of the event, beginning with the Countess of Carnarvon, the Lady Emma Purey-Cust, the Lady Constance Shaw-Lefevre, and the Lady Mowbray, and their names are followed by those of ladies without titles, such as Mrs Alfred Palmer and Mrs Herbert Sutton.

The enlarged organ in the new hall was opened on 31 May 1882.

We remain, for the time being, in the Town Hall, with the programme for the Heelas Concert in 1976, though later the Heelas Concerts were to move to The Hexagon. Something of the history of the department store of Heelas, Sons and Company is given in the account of item 24 (see p. 38–41). The business has been run by the John Lewis Partnership since 1953, and 'John Lewis and Partners' is now on the front of the shop. It is managed rather differently from other retailers. The employees are partners and share in the profits, and they have a holiday scheme which eases them into retirement by increasing their holiday entitlement according to their years of service.

The Partnership, in order to give something back to the community, promoted concerts in the towns and cities where they had a presence, starting in London in 1951. Heelas of Reading had an annual concert. It was advertised to account holders, and to obtain tickets you had to go to the carpet department on a particular morning – but anyone could go, and the tickets were free.

As a young person on a low salary and in rented accommodation, an account where you paid over a monthly sum to a shop was out of the question. In addition, I had to be at work most mornings, and the concerts should have

PRICE ONE PENNY.

Official Programme
OF
Mr. Frank Attwells' Baden Baden Concerts
IN THE
ABBEY RUINS & FORBURY GARDENS, READING,
ON
Wednesday & Thursday, August 26 & 27, 1891.
✥ FIREWORKS & FANCY COSTUME CARNIVAL. ✥

Competitors should assemble under the Lime-lights in the Abbey Ruins,
By 9 p.m. each Evening, when the Prizes will be given.
Lime-lights by Professor Lewis.
JUDGES:—A. HEWETT, Esq., Southampton, Mons. P. D. COLLIER, (*Ex-member of the Nice Carnival Committee*).
DANCING AL FRESCO, on a specially laid floor in the Banqueting Hall, 6.30 to 9.30.
PEA RIFLE SALOON in the Ruins, by Messrs. Randa. REFRESHMENTS by Mr. Marchant.
Inclusive Admission:—ONE SHILLING. Packets of 25 Tickets, One Guinea.
GATES OPEN FROM 2 TILL 5, AND FROM 6 TILL 10.

For HOT and COLD LUNCHEONS, TEAS, ICES, &c.

Victoria Cafe Restaurant, Broad Street, Reading.
Private Saloon for Ladies. Upstairs Saloon for Teas. Smoking Saloon.

MUSICAL INSTRUMENTS for SALE or HIRE
FITTINGS and REPAIRS of every description at

Frank Attwells'

Piano, Organ and Music Warehouse,
162, 163, Friar Street,
Reading.

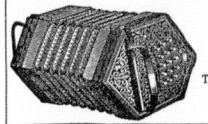

Tuners sent to all parts. Uniform charge regardless of distance.

BEECROFT AND SON, PRINTERS, READING.

100. The front cover (*left*) mentions a pea rifle saloon, where round bullets the size of peas were shot at targets.

been impossible – but since I worked in the Municipal Buildings, I could hear the rehearsals in the distance. I often had to work until 7 pm, and discovered that if I asked nicely after work, whoever was on the door would find me a seat, and give me a programme. And so it was that in the 1970s I got to six concerts and heard some of the best musicians in the land, for nothing.

In 1976, the English Chamber Orchestra gave us a concerto grosso and an oboe concerto by Handel, the double violin concerto of J. S. Bach, an arrangement of Tchaikovsky's *Andante Cantabile*, and a divertimento by Mozart. Not everyone's cup of tea, but for me, an interloper, this was musical entertainment as good as it gets, this side of heaven.

From the classical, we move on to popular music of different kinds – and music for dancing. It is a pity that no pieces of ephemera seem to have survived, at least in the library and university collections, from the golden age of ballroom dancing, and Reading's dance-halls, among them the Oxford Ballrooms, and the Olympia.

But from before that time, in 1891, we have the programme for an outdoor event, in the Forbury Gardens and the Abbey Ruins. The 'Baden-Baden' title suggests that music would have been of the kind you would expect to hear at a fashionable Continental spa resort – popular overtures, waltzes, polkas and selections from operas and operettas. On each of the two days, there were afternoon and evening sessions. In the afternoons, there was music from the Band of the Grenadier Guards in the Forbury gardens, with a display of Japanese Daylight Fireworks during the interval. In the evenings, the Grenadier Guards were again in the gardens, and the Band of the Royal Military College was in the Abbey Ruins. After the concerts came a fancy dress competition, under the limelight in the ruins, where there was also a banqueting hall with a specially laid al fresco dance floor, and a pea rifle saloon. The evening was rounded off by another firework display.

Frank Attwells must have been a man of action. His father was a hairdresser and his mother ran a servants' registry, in the shop in High Street above which they lived. Frank was apprenticed to a London piano manufacturer, and became himself an accomplished musician. He returned to Reading in 1870 to take over the family shop, by now in Friar Street, as a music shop. In time he was to take over the music shop run by the Binfield family, and to have a new 3-storey shop

157

ST. ANDREW'S SCOTTISH DANCERS AND PIPE BAND

MONDAYS JUNE 14th and 21st

FORBURY GARDENS

7 pm – 9 pm

101. This event is remembered by the present author as a pleasant way to spend a summer's evening.

built on the site of 162 –163 Friar Street. The County Court building now occupies its space. He organised the Town Hall promenade concerts, and at the other end of Friar Street, he took over the lease of the Theatre Royal, and supervised its rebuilding. It re-opened in 1887, as the Royal County Theatre (see p. 137).

He was an accomplished swimmer, and ran the Reading Amphibious Club, which entertained the public with water polo matches, and raised money for good causes. Mr Attwells himself is said to have saved several people from drowning in Reading's waterways. He must also have saved lives as the Deputy-Captain of the Reading Volunteer Fire Brigade.

He had been a councillor since 1884, and he became Mayor in 1891. Sadly, he was in poor health at the time, and died the following year, whilst still in office, aged 46. He and his wife are commemorated on a drinking fountain, originally by the Reading end of Caversham Bridge, and now by the Thames Side Promenade off Richfield Avenue.

Perhaps Reading is not the kind of town where you would expect to come across a bagpipe band and a team of Scottish dancers – but then you wouldn't have expected the Ukrainian dancers who were performing in Reading around the same time.

The Presbyterians in Reading opened their iron church, on the corner of London Road and Craven Road, and next to the Royal Berkshire Hospital in 1876. By 1880 they were able to build the substantial Victorian church, which was replaced by the present modern building in 1972–73. The Presbyterian movement was particularly strong in Scotland, and so St Andrew's, dedicated to the patron saint of Scotland, attracted exiled Scots from across the Reading area.

The St Andrew's Scottish Dancers were formed in 1949, and the pipe band followed in 1957. The story of the band is told in the book, *Airs & Places*. It built up a good reputation and was called upon to march and to play at ceremonies and celebrations across the area, and it has also performed in many European countries, and in Japan. Both the band and the dancers are still active.

On this occasion in 1973, I believe the bystanders were invited to join in with the better-known dances – *The Gay Gordons* and *Dashing White Sergeant*, which some of us remembered from school days. The Pipe Band gave us some

102. The Kennet Morris Men performed dances from Cotswold villages, from Lichfield, and a stick dance from Upton-on-Severn.

airs with intriguing titles, some of them romantic, and others distinctly unromantic – *Mairi's Wedding*, *The Rowan Tree*, *The Skye Boat Song* – but also *Cockney Jocks* and *The Muckin' o' Geordie's Byre*!

For music and dance of a different kind, we have a programme from the Kennet Morris Men. The earliest record of morris dancing found by the compilers of the *Oxford English Dictionary* dates from 1458. The origins of morris dancing are enigmatic, and there are many theories, including fertility rituals, or a connection with Moorish people from North Africa.

The earliest record of morris dancing in Reading dates from 1513, when the churchwardens of St Laurence's Church paid threepence 'for ale to the moreys dawncers on the dedication day'. The day would have been the patronal festival of the church – St Laurence's Day falls on 10 August. Later in the century we find the churchwardens spending thirty shillings on 'certain apparells of

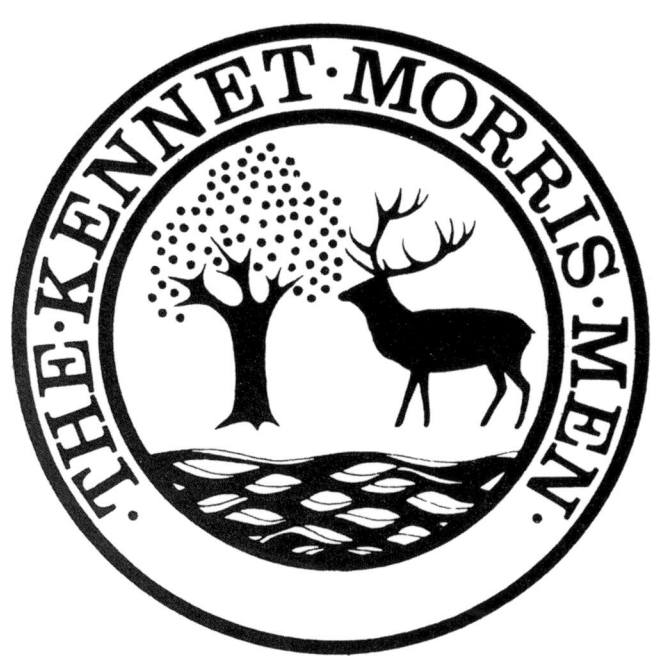

SALSA DANCE AND STRETCHING BODY & MIND in AlleyCat

COMPLEX

mores dawncers belongyning to the Churche', which seems a very large sum, considering that around the same time, 3s. 3d. was paid to two workmen for three days' work.

Morris dancing enjoyed something of a revival, together with in interest in folk songs, around the turn of the 19th–20th centuries. The Kennet Morris Men came along rather later, in 1957, to dance in the Kennet Valley, around Reading and Newbury. The 1991 programme on which this emblem appears shows that they also performed in south Oxfordshire and north Hampshire. Sometimes they danced at an inn, for one evening, sometimes at two or three inns, sometimes they had a whole day touring round, and occasionally they travelled farther afield, to perform with other morris sides.

One of their annual events around the time of this programme was the Reading Walking Tour, remembered by the present author. In June 1991 they were at the County Arms in Watlington Street at 8 pm (now no longer an inn, though the building is still there), at The Retreat in St John's Street at 8.45, and at The Eldon Arms in Eldon Terrace (later a pub called The Weather Station, which closed in 2022) at 9.30. The last two were in narrow back streets without yards or gardens, so the dancing was in the streets, and any motor traffic just had to wait until there was a pause in the dancing.

The COVID-19 pandemic curtailed their public appearances, but they resumed in July 2022. Their informative website includes an account of their celebration of the 500th anniversary of the mention of morris dancing in the records of St Laurence's Church. On 10 August 2013, 500 years to the day, their 'Redding Moreys Dawncers' gave a demonstration of 'reconstructed' dances from Tudor times, in costumes of the period. They danced outside the church, and at various other town centre locations, and refreshed themselves with beer at the George Hotel – Reading's longest-surviving inn.

We end this chapter with the Alley Cat Complex, an ambitious concept which unfortunately lasted for only two years. The leaflet lists evening dance sessions – merengue, salsa, bolero, chachacha, mambo and cumbia, for beginners and intermediates. There were also 'Stretching Body and Mind' sessions with Diana Perez from Colombia, sessions for toddlers in the mornings, and afternoon sessions for young people in the long school holidays.

Opposite page:
103. The Alley Cat, during its short existence, offered a wide variety of facilities and activities for adults and young people.

Jamie Roberts founded the complex. He had been the drummer with the band Mungo Jerry, and was the Alley Cat Musical Director. Sarah-Jane Bullock was the Principal of Dance, and Beryl Jarvis, her mother, was the artistic director, who also ran the Beryl Jarvis School of Theatre and Dance. The complex included two recording studios, four rehearsal and practice rooms, a drum rehearsal room, a large dance studio, changing and shower facilities, a refreshment bar, etc. It was also home to Reading Theatre Arts and the Generation Theatre Group.

The buildings were on Hodsoll Road, on the north side of Great Knollys Street, which today has the former Queen's Arms public house on one corner, and the Civitas Academy on the other. The land at the end of this short road, up to the railway, was a large yard and buildings belonging to the corporation. The Cattle Market, also belonging to the corporation, was to the east of the yard. In the 1970s, a new road, the Cross Town Route, was planned to come through here, joining the Scours Lane roundabout on Oxford Road with the Suttons Seeds roundabout on London Road, but this never materialised. The main use of the yard was as a civic amenity site, but the buildings were used for all kinds of purposes – among them the headquarters of Civil Defence, a day nursery, and council offices for refuse collectors, road sweepers, and public lavatory attendants.

Changes came in the 1990s when the corporation had to find a new site for the bus garage, since the Mill Lane site was needed for The Oracle shopping centre. The new bus depot was built on part of the yard, and from 1996 onwards, residents had to take their rubbish to Smallmead rather than Hodsoll Road. The rest of it became the site of the new school, which opened in 2017.

That was not the end of the ambitions of Jamie Roberts, however: his complex had to close in late 1993, but in 1995 he opened a dance venue called Alley Cat Live in Gun Street. This lasted until 1999. The building, after several changes of name, became the Cocktail Club in 2022.

Opposite page:
104. More disreputable pastimes would have been available on race-days, such as watching and betting on prize fighting and cock fighting.

XIII. Sport

Considering the widespread popularity of sporting events, not much has survived of the ephemera emanating from them. This probably says something about the collectors whose material has been gone through to produce this book.

The earliest sporting item dates from 1783. The whereabouts of the original race-card are unknown, but fortunately someone thought to give a photograph of it, stained and damaged as it is, to the library.

The first mention of racing on Bulmershe Heath found by Nigel Sutcliffe, for his book on racing in Reading, comes in 1705. In 1783, the races were still taking place on the Heath, and continued there until 1814. (After a lull, racing started again on King's Meadow in 1843.) The races were held over three days, with one race a day, in three heats, starting at 4.30. The *Reading Mercury* announced that 'On Tuesday next the races begin here, when we expect a very numerous and genteel company'. The stewards promised that 'the course will be put into very fine order. It is ordered and expected that no-one shall erect a booth or stall or sell liquors without subscribing half a guinea towards the plates'.

Perhaps for us today, more interesting than the racing is what people did before and after the races. For the evenings, the stewards promised 'the assemblies as usual', in the town hall, which would have involved music and dancing, for the well-to-do. The 'ordinaries' mentioned on the race-card were for the moderately well-off. They were public dinners at a set price. On the first day the venue was the Bear Inn, Bridge Street, on the second day the Crown in Crown Street, and on the last day the King's Arms in Castle Hill. Then, rather more down-market and mentioned at the end, there was cock-fighting at The Cross Keys, on the corner of Gun Street and Bridge Street (see p. 106–7).

The Reading Theatre in Friar Street was not to open until 1788: when it did, it was always open at the time of the races. One can't help wondering about the 'genteel company' that was promised. It seems that like race-meetings everywhere at the time, the races would also have attracted dishonest bookmakers, people passing on forged money, pickpockets, prostitutes and the drunk and disorderly.

READING RACES, 1783.

TUESDAY, AUGUST 5, 50l. Weight for Age.

Mr. Richardson's b. h. *Pantloon*, 5 yrs. old, 8ft. 5lb. J. Braffit, white.	1	3	4	3
Cpt. Bertie's br. h. *Sharp*, 5 years old, 8ft. 8lb. S. Cheffney, blue.	4	2	2	ds
Mr. Temb's ch. g. *Brush*, aged, 9ft. 3lb. William Price, striped.	6	5	3	dr
Mr. Compton's br. h. *Cottager*, 5 years old, (a mare) 8ft. 11lb. Gem. Dilly, black.	5	1	6	1
Mr. Turner's ch. h. *Girandole*, aged (1 plate) 9ft. 3lb. R. Goodison, red.	3	6	5	dr
Mr. Thornton's b. h. *Copper Bottom* aged, 9ft. 5lb. Rider unkown.	2	4	1	2

WEDNESDAY the 6th, 50l. Give-and-Take.

Mr. Thornton's b. h. *Copper Bottom*, aged, 14h. 1-8th.—8ft. 7lb. 14oz. S. Arnold, str.
Captain Hoare's bay n. *Freeholder*, aged 14h. 1in. 1-8th.—9ft. 14oz. Rider unknown.
Mr. Eccles's bay m. *Omea*, aged, 14h. 1in. 2-8ths.—9ft. 1lb. 12oz. Rider unknown.
Mr. Watt's gr. h. *Medley*, aged, J. Talbot, yellow.

THURSDAY the 7th, 50l. for Four-Year-Olds.

To Start each Day at Half past Four.
☞ Ordinaries the first Day at the Bear, the second Day at the Crown and the last Day at the King's Arms.—Balls, as usual.
⁂ Cocking each Day of the Races at the Cross-Keys.

Reading and District Motor Club

CALIFORNIA SPEEDWAY

Fixtures Season 1939

Opposite page:

105. Despite the cheap railway excursion fares, and not helped by the poor weather, the attendance was disappointingly poor, at 4,000.

106. According to their website, the Reading Racers are still hoping to bring speedway back to the town.

Reading Football Club was founded in 1871, one of the oldest professional clubs in the country. It moved to its new purpose-built ground, Elm Park, in 1896. This handbill was produced by the Great Western Railway to advertise cheap half-day tickets from the Bristol and London areas to watch Bristol Rovers play Reading at Elm Park in 1905. They were playing in the Southern League.

From the Bristol area, the half-day return cost 3s. 9d. third class, and passengers from Clifton Down, Redland and Montpelier Stations must change at Stapleton Road. From the London area, the situation looks distinctly complicated. Those travelling from many of the underground stations

> must travel via Paddington (or via Westbourne Park if the Train stops at Westbourne Park) by Ordinary Trains, and returning by Trains shown on other side to Bishop's Road to join the return Excursion Train from Paddington Station. Paddington terminus is connected to Bishop's Road station by a covered way.

Bishop's Road Underground Station was at the western end of Paddington Station, on the northern side, once the terminus of the Metropolitan Railway. It was rebuilt in 1933, and today is the Paddington Station where you can join the Hammersmith and City Line. The other Paddington Underground Station was at the time called Praed Street. The reason for having to use Bishop's Road probably lies in the fact that the underground railways were run by different companies in 1905, and the London Passenger Transport Board, which brought together the Underground, the trams and the buses, was not established until 1933.

On the day in question, 18 November, the weather was 'unfavourable.' Bristol Rovers had scored by half time, and Reading were yet to score. The second half began with a determined Reading side putting on the pressure, 'and following a dashing attack by the Reading right, Garbutt got the ball into the centre, and Leonard neatly drove the ball home, out of the reach of Cartlidge. It was a pretty and well worked-for goal, and it sent the hitherto despondent Reading folk into ecstasies. Reading now pressed with great spirit, and were somewhat unlucky not to secure a lead.' So the result was a 1-1 draw.

The 1939 fixture list for the California Speedway has found a place in a book of Reading ephemera because it was issued by the Reading and District Motor Club,

Opposite page:
107. Today, we have the Amateur Regatta, the Town Regatta, and a little downstream, the Thames Valley Park Regatta.

though the track where they were racing was around eight miles from the town. This was at California in England, to the south of Wokingham, which is now the California Country Park.

The area had been a brickworks on the Bearwood Estate. Presumably the works was named after the California Gold Rush of the 1840s and 1850s – the name is recorded on the 1872 Ordnance Survey. The resulting clay pit had become filled with water, which was called Longmoor Lake. The land was sold off in the late 1920s to a London coach proprietor, Alf Cartlidge. He had the idea of turning it into a destination for day-trippers, and bringing Londoners out into the countryside by charabanc. So part of the lake became an outdoor swimming-pool, the narrow-gauge railway which had been used to transport the clay became a miniature railway for the visitors, there was a small zoo, and there were fairground rides. A pavilion was built, with a bar, and a large ballroom with a 'glass floor' – which sounds decidedly dangerous.

The speedway track, opened in 1933, had a surface of cinders, and refreshments were provided for the spectators. This 1939 programme shows that the Reading club met there fortnightly from May to the end of October – or would have done if the Second World War had not intervened. During the war, California was used for troop training. The track re-opened in 1948, and closed for the last time in 1958.

That was by no means the end of speedway in Reading. Many will remember the Reading Racers, who started in 1968 at the Tilehurst Stadium, and then moved to the Smallmead Stadium. The Racers achieved many successes in the 1970s, 80s and 90s, and drew in the crowds. When they had to move from Smallmead there were plans in 2008 for a new stadium on Island Road, to the south of Reading, but these came to nothing. Currently, the Reading Racers are in exile, competing in other towns.

Turning now to watersports, various regattas have been held on the Thames over the years. The Reading Rowing Club Regatta normally took place upstream of Caversham Bridge, with spectators in the meadow, by the Thames Side Promenade. It seems that in 1948, the year of this programme, a shorter course was used, upstream of Reading Bridge (see Gillian Clark, *Down by the River*). Other regattas used Dreadnought Reach, downstream of Kennet Mouth.

READING ROWING CLUB

Annual Regatta

Saturday, Sept. 25th, 1948

President:
Col. G. S. Field, o.b.e., t.d., j.p.

Umpires:
Dr. T. R. M. Bristow
Dr. E. C. Huddy
E. James Carter, Esq.
Major J. Gibbon

Judges:
A. L. Meads, Esq.
H. R. Simmonds. Esq.
Capt. R. H. Langham, m.c., t.d.
H. W. Rushmere, Esq.

Chief Steward:
R. Hemmings, Esq.

Programmes:
Mrs. H. J. Hughes

Colonel the Rt. Hon. Sir Leslie Wilson, G.C.I.E., G.C.S.I., D.S.O., has kindly consented to present the prizes immediately after the last race.

PROGRAMME - ONE SHILLING

Opposite page:
108. This piece of paper, which bears the marks of safety pins in the corners, must have been round the course about 1986.

Their story is a complex one, beginning in 1842. In 1843, the Reading Regatta became the Reading and Caversham Regatta, but then it lapsed, to be revived in 1877. The Reading Rowing Club had begun in 1867 at the Griffin Inn, Caversham, which had a garden running down to the Thames. In 1894 it took on the running of the Reading and Caversham Regatta.

The club had adopted the rules of the Amateur Rowing Association, but the word 'amateur' had a different connotation from what we would now expect. Clubs which were part of the Association could not have anyone who worked on the river as a boatman or lock-keeper as a member, and nor could they accept anyone who had been 'in trade or employment for wages, as a mechanic, artisan or labourer engaged in any manual duty.'

Not surprisingly, other regattas started in Reading where these restrictions did not apply – the Reading Working Men's Regatta (now called the Town Regatta), and the Reading Tradesmen's Regatta. The A.R.A. rules came in for much criticism, and with the return of men who had fought together in the First World War, were eventually changed.

This programme lists the races – the Junior Fours, Rum-Tum Sculls, Maiden Fours, Junior Pairs, Keyser Fours, Senior Pairs, Senior Sculls, Challenge Fours, and Scratch Fours. Thanks were expressed to the Caversham Bridge Hotel, to Mr A. Cawston for the use of his boathouse, and to the officers of the Royal Military Academy Boat Club and the President of the Reading University Boat Club for the loan of boats.

After the races came the presentation of prizes by Col. The Rt. Hon. Sir Leslie Wilson, and after that, for ticket-holders, there was dancing from eight till midnight at the Grosvenor Hotel (later to become the Caversham Rose, and in 2022 changing into a Miller and Carter steak house), in Kidmore Road, Caversham. The tickets cost five shillings, including refreshments.

In later years the headquarters of the Reading Rowing Club were on Fry's Island, but then in the 1970s and 80s they were based at several different boathouses, before settling in 1989 at their new premises upstream of Caversham Bridge.

Over 500 half marathons are now run in the United Kingdom. The first Reading race was held on 13 March 1983, and it has continued to be held, usually in March or early April, on most subsequent years. On account of the COVID-19 pandemic, there was no race in 2020, and the 2021 event was postponed until the autumn.

digital

561

READING
HALF MARATHON

JIP • Tel ; Windsor (07535) 62527

Like all such events, as well as winning, part of the joy of taking part is the raising of money for charity.

The course of the Reading Half Marathon is by definition a little over 13 miles in length, and is run on paved roads, closed to traffic, to the town centre and back. Starting and ending points have included the University's Whiteknights Campus, the South Reading Leisure Centre, the Rivermead Sports Centre, and the Madejski Stadium (now the Select Car Leasing Stadium).

The sponsors have been Digital (computer services), Asics (sports goods), Mizuno (sports shoes), Vitality (insurance), and, from 2018, Sage (suppliers of accounting software).

The Digital Equipment Corporation sponsored the first six races, 1983–1988. At the time it was expanding its operations in Reading. It had arrived in the town in 1964, had opened its U.K. headquarters at Worton Grange in 1981, and had built new headquarters on Thames Valley Park (the site of the old Earley Power Station) in 1988, with Worton Grange becoming its research facility. By the time it was sponsoring the Half Marathon, it employed around 3,000 people in Reading.

XIV. Royalty, festivals and processions

Processions through the streets have been a part of public life for centuries – sometimes heading to a church for the mayor-making or some other special service, sometimes to a celebration in a park or one of the riverside meadows, sometimes to collect money for the Royal Berkshire Hospital or some other good cause. Others were held as a mark of dissatisfaction with an employer or with government. Such events could, of course, give rise to public disorder, and had to be regulated by the police, as we shall see, and as still happens. Inevitably, the arrival of television changed things to some extent.

Our first example of processions outlines the festivities planned to celebrate the recovery of King George III from a debilitating mental illness. He was King for 60 years, 1760–1820, but suffered bouts of illness in the latter half of his reign, for the last ten years of which, his son acted as Regent. The cause of his indisposition is uncertain: it may have been porphyria, a hereditary disease, or it may have been bipolar disorder. The course of the illness was the subject of a play by Alan Bennett, *The Madness of George III*, first produced in 1991, which was turned into a film, released in 1994.

When the king became ill in 1788, one of the leading experts on mental disorders in the land was called in – none other than Anthony Addington, by this time in retirement at Reading, where he had a private asylum next to his house in London Street. Addington predicted the king's recovery, and by March 1789, this had happened. The king was well enough for a national day of rejoicing to be held, set for Thursday 19 March.

The notice overleaf, from Richard Maul, the Mayor, informed the towns-people of the celebrations in The Forbury, involving a bonfire and firework display. It does not mention the barrels of beer, which were usually laid on for such occasions, but doubtless they would have been provided.

The Mayor was writing from the Council Chamber, presumably in the new Town Hall which had opened a few years earlier. With the opening of an even newer and larger Town Hall in 1882, the old hall became known as the Small Town Hall, and is now the Victoria Hall. This was to be the scene of a public dinner for 283 people, starting at 3 in the afternoon. With tickets at 10/6 each,

Opposite page:
109. The local paper had a lengthy list of the buildings which were illuminated for the occasion, and reported on the magistrates allowing prisoners in the gaol and the bridewell to be 'regaled'.

110. The procession which did not go quite according to plan

it was only for the wealthy. It was advertised on a separate sheet – the Library's collection has a copy.

When the Mayor proposed the toast, 'God bless the King,' there was a royal salute from 21 cannons on Forbury Hill. Then at 8 pm, there was a procession from the Town Hall to The Forbury, headed by 'a band of music,' and the fireworks began.

The leaflet warns people against setting off their own fireworks in the street. They could do so in The Forbury near the bonfire, but should not 'cast or fire any squibs, rockets, serpents, or other fireworks in the Market-Place, of any of the streets of the Borough,' on pain of prosecution. Constables and officers would be patrolling the streets.

There was another day of national rejoicing in 1863, to mark the wedding of the Prince of Wales – Albert Edward, eldest son of Queen Victoria and Prince Albert, later to become King Edward VII. Among his family he was known as Bertie. His marriage to Princess Alexandra of Denmark had been arranged between the royal families, and took place on Tuesday 10 March, in St George's Chapel, Windsor.

In Reading, the celebrations included a morning procession for the mayor and corporation, fire brigade, various friendly societies and the Temperance Society. There were the 'usual rustic sports', and in the Corn Exchange (see p. 4–6) 1,300 poor people sat down to lunch.

The afternoon children's procession advertised here was not quite as planned, because a few days before the wedding it was announced that the royal train, carrying the Prince and Princess to their honeymoon destination, would pause at the 'upper' station of the Great Western Railway in Reading, to receive an address from the mayor. The local papers commented on the crowds trying to gain access to the platform, and even more people lining the railway tracks. However, space had been allocated for the children, and afterwards, with some difficulty, the children's procession re-formed and completed its route.

In the original plan the schoolchildren were to assemble in the Market Place at 2 pm, and from there to walk, four abreast and accompanied by four bands, through the Butter Market, Minster Street, Gun Street, Bridge Street, Horn Street (now Southampton Street), Crown Street, London Street, Queens Road,

Borough of READING.

TO-MORROW being the Day fixed for the Commemoration of his MAJESTY's happy Recovery from his late Indispofition, A DISPLAY OF FIREWORKS will be exhibited in the FORBURY; after which a BONFIRE will be made in the fame Place: It is much my Wifh, both out of Refpect to the very joyful Occafion, and that Perfons of both Sexes may with Safety, and without the leaft Alarm, fee the Fireworks and the Illuminations, that the ftricteft Order be obferved and kept in the FORBURY and all the Streets; I therefore requeft that the Inhabitants will not begin to illuminate until the Fireworks are nearly over; that fuch Perfons who are defirous of exhibiting any Fireworks of their own Conftruction, will content themfelves with doing it in the FORBURY, *after the Exhibition*, near the Fire; and that no Perfon will caft or fire any Squibs, Rockets, Serpents, or other Firework, in the Market-Place, or any of the Streets of this Borough: and I give this public Notice, that if any Perfon fhall, contrary to this reafonable Requeft, *prefume* to caft a Firework, or be aiding in cafting or firing any Kind of Firework in the Market-Place or any of the Streets, they will be profecuted, fined, and punifhed as the Law directs.— I have directed the Conftables and Officers to patrole the Streets; but I hope and truft no Diforder will be committed.

Council-Chamber,
18th March, 1789. **Richard Maul, Mayor.**

MARRIAGE
OF HIS ROYAL HIGHNESS THE
PRINCE OF WALES.
PROGRAMME
OF THE
SCHOOLS' PROCESSION,
TUESDAY, 10th of MARCH, 1863.

The Schools to meet in the Market Place at 2 o'clock, from whence they proceed in the following order:—

BANNER.	Ragged School, Silver Street.	Broad Street Sunday School.
Reading Blue Coat School.	Silver Street Sunday School.	Castle St. Congregational Sunday School.
Band of Music.	Trinity Chapel Sunday School.	Coley Street Ragged School.
Reading Green School.	**Band of Music.**	Hosier Street Sunday School.
Reading School of Industry.	St. Lawrence's Parochial School.	St. Mary's Episcopal Chapel School.
St. Giles' Parochial Schools.	St. James' Sunday School.	Minster Street Sunday School.
St. Giles' Ragged School.	King's Road Sunday School.	Oxford Road Sunday School.
Church St. Sunday School.	**Band of Music.**	Trinity Church School.
St. John's School.	St. Mary's Parochial School.	**Band of Music.**

The Schools to enter the Market Place as follows:—The Blue Coat School, Green Girls' School, and School of Industry, with the Schools in St. Giles' Parish, by way of High Street.

The Schools in St. Lawrence's Parish, by way of King's Road and High Street.

The Schools in St. Mary's Parish, by way of Friar Street.

The ROUTE of the PROCESSION to be through—
Minster Street, Gun Street, Bridge Street, Horn Street, Crown Street, London Street, Queen's Road, King's Road, King Street, Broad Street, West Street, Friar Street,
Returning to the Market Place.

The Children to walk four abreast. Upon the return of the procession to the Market Place, the Children to sing

THE NATIONAL ANTHEM.

God save our gracious Queen,	Thy choicest gifts in store	God save our future King,
Long live our noble Queen,	On her be pleased to pour	Be Thou to him the Spring,
God save the Queen!	Long may she reign;	Of Joy and Peace;
Send her victorious,	May she defend our laws,	Bless, too, his Royal Bride,
Happy and glorious,	And ever give us cause,	Be Thou their Heavenly Guide,
Long to reign over us,	To sing with heart and voice	O'er all their life preside,
God save the Queen!	God save the Queen!	God save the Queen.

After which the Schools to proceed to their several School Rooms, where each child will be presented with a Cake and an Orange.

S. BRADLEY, PRINTER, MARKET PLACE, READING.

Opposite page:
111. The jubilee fountain, with cascades of water, is pictured in the centre, at the bottom of the programme cover.

Kings Road, King Street, Broad Street, West Street, Friar Street, and back to the Market Place. This notice gives the order in which the various schools were to proceed – church schools, charity schools, Sunday Schools, and the Silver Street and St Giles' Ragged Schools.

Back in the Market Place, the children sang the National Anthem, omitting the verse about enemies, their politics and knavish tricks, and adding a new final verse:

> God save our future King,
> Be Thou to him the Spring
> Of Joy and Peace;
> Bless, too this Royal Bride,
> Be Thou their Heavenly Guide.
> O'er all their Life preside,
> God Save the Queen.

Then the children dispersed, and in their school rooms, received cake and an orange.

In the town centre, celebrations went on into the night, with illuminations, an ox-roast and firework display in the Forbury Gardens. By 1863, some of the town's buildings were illuminated by gas, while some still relied upon oil-lamps.

The long reign of Queen Victoria was celebrated with a Golden Jubilee in 1887, and a Diamond Jubilee in 1897. For the Golden Jubilee, nine days of events were planned, 18–26 June, starting with the 'opening' of the memorial fountain in St Mary's Butts, still there, but today containing earth and plants rather than water. From the programme it appears that there was some doubt as to whether the statue of the Queen, commissioned from George Simonds, would be ready for unveiling. In fact it wasn't, and Duke of Cambridge did the unveiling, outside the Town Hall, the following month.

One of the week's attractions was the Royal Horticultural Society's Show, in the 'Show Yard' between the London and Wokingham Roads, near St Bartholomew's Church. The land wasn't to become Palmer Park for another two years.

On the Tuesday, there was a midday salute of 50 cannons on Forbury Hill, and four bands played, in different parts of town – the Massed Band of The

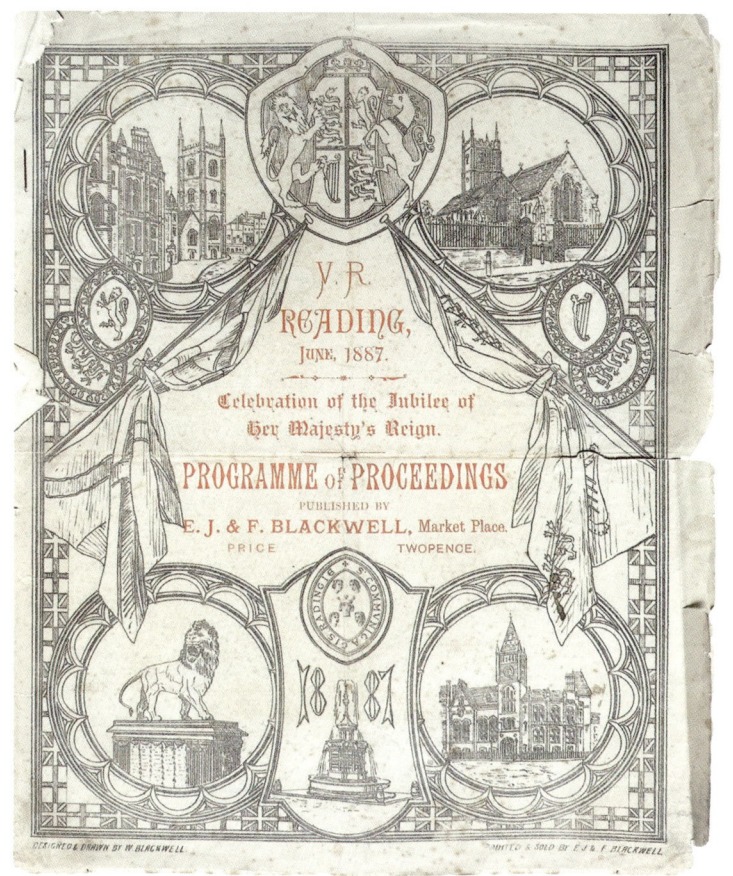

Royal Iniskilling Fusiliers, the Reading Town Band, the Mechanics' Band and the Temperance Band. At 1 pm, around 1,800 of the town's 'aged poor' and Crimean and Maiwand Veterans sat down to dinner in the 'large rooms of Messrs. Sutton and Sons.' (see p.53–5 for Sutton and Sons and p. 224–5 for Battle of Maiwand.)

The athletic sports in the afternoon included climbing the greasy pole, and wrestling on donkeys. The aquatic sports included a water tournament in canoes using mops, and swimming races wearing clothes – including shoes and 'high hats.' It would seem that no women took part. The day ended with a firework

112. Entry to the afternoon Municipal Garden Party was by invitation only.

display by James Pain of London, which included a 'colossal fire portrait of H.M. the Queen'.

The Children's Procession and Fete took place on the Wednesday on the Recreation Ground, reached via Caversham Road and New Road. The land had been given by George Palmer in 1875, and must have been what's now known as King's Meadow. The procession must have involved walking along Vastern Road, and children from no fewer than 56 schools and Sunday schools took part. It was preceded by the opening of the new children's public playground 'at the back of Great Knollys Street' by Mr Palmer.

There was a Service of Praise and Thanksgiving in St Mary's Church at the beginning of the week, involving three church choirs and the Reading Philharmonic Society. *Zadok the Priest* and the *Dettingen Te Deum* by Handel were sung, and, according to the programme, 'the alms will be presented.' This was a collection to defray the cost of the celebrations, according to the newspaper report. There was a similar service in St Laurence's Church, as the final event in the celebration.

This is just a sample of events from the programme – the amount of necessary organisation and marshalling must have been tremendous.

The 1897 Jubilee followed a pattern similar to that of ten years earlier. Once again, there was a royal salute from 50 cannons on Forbury Hill. The 'aged poor,' again 1,800 of them, were this time catered for by William McIlroy, in his 'Great Rooms' in West Street. His huge new department store was not to open for another four years (see p. 40–1). The fireworks were this time on the Wednesday, and the venue was now called King's Meadow rather than The Recreation Ground. There were free concerts in the Town Hall and the Corn Exchange (see p. 4–6 for the Corn Exchange).

The Municipal Garden Party, part of the celebrations, was held on Thursday 24 June in the Forbury Gardens and Abbey Ruins, for invited guests, and must have been a rather sedate affair. The Mr Bartlett, to whom this invitation was sent, has not so far been identified.

The designer of the invitation is also unidentified: the same person probably also designed the cover of the programme for the Garden Party, of which the Library has a copy. The invitation suggests medieval knights and jousting, but the events in the Forbury Gardens do not seem to have included anything so exciting.

The refreshment tents were on the north side of the Gardens, which had three band stands – two of which were presumably erected for the occasion. The Reading Horticultural Society had a tent in the Abbey Ruins, where the Field-Fisher Quartette and Master Caryl Field-Fisher entertained with songs, sketches, recitations and dances.

The bandstands were occupied by the Band of the 3rd King's Royal Rifles, the Band of the 3rd Battalion, Royal Berkshire Regiment, and, by way of contrast, the Royal Pierrot Banjo Team.

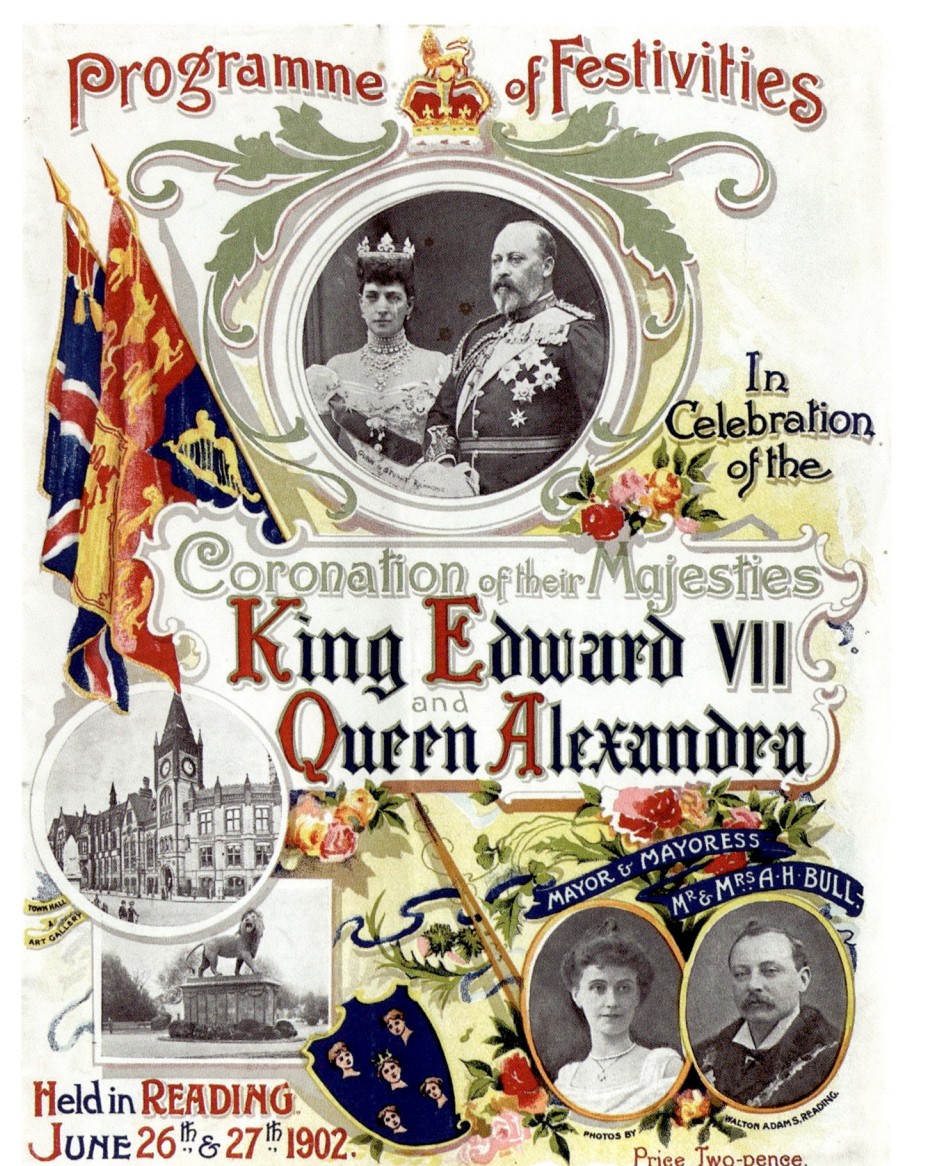

Opposite page:
113. Because of the king's indisposition, the coronation of King Edward VII and Queen Alexandra had to be postponed until August 1902.

Comparing the two Jubilee programmes, the second seems a rather more restrained than the first, though the local papers hailed it as an unqualified success – a unique occasion which 'was being celebrated in a thoroughly hearty manner.' The amount spent on the celebrations was more than the amount spent on the 1887 Jubilee.

This earlier Jubilee had given to the town a drinking fountain, a statue of the Queen, and a children's playground. For this occasion, the permanent memorial was a nursing institution for the sick poor – the Queen Victoria Institute in The Forbury. The charity, though no longer in The Forbury, is still active, now specialising in foot care for the over-60s.

Victoria died in 1901, and her eldest son, Prince Edward, was to have been crowned on Thursday 26 June 1902, but the new King was taken ill and the coronation had to be postponed at short notice until Saturday 9 August. The celebrations planned for Reading, announced in this booklet, were to have taken place over two days, but now had to be concentrated into one. Almost all of what was planned did take place, but the aquatic sports and children's events were held in advance, on 23 July. A summary of what was planned follows.

Thursday was to have started with the ringing of the bells of the three parish churches, and a service in St Laurence's Church. This was followed by a grand procession through the town. It was to go out along Kings Road, and to return via London Road, and two hours were allocated for the walk. No fewer than six bands of music marched at intervals along the procession, which included uniformed organisations, friendly societies, 'allegorical, emblematical and historical cars,' 'masqueraders,' and soldiers who had come back from the Boer War. The procession ended outside the Town Hall, where the mayor and corporation would view its arrival from a specially erected stand. After the singing of the National Anthem, the royal salute was to be fired by cannons on Forbury Hill.

The afternoon was to include the Children's Festival in Prospect Park. J. C. Fidler, who had been instrumental in acquiring the park for the Borough the year before, laid on refreshments for the teachers and helpers at the Mansion House. The sports events happened at the same time, on King's Meadow and the adjoining Biscuit Factory Recreation Ground. The 'amateur sports' took place on one, and 'non-amateur sports' on the other, with the latter including quoit

Opposite page:
114. Unusually, the 1911 coronation of King George V and Queen Mary was held on a Thursday.

competitions, a Siamese race and 'tilting the bucket.' Daylight fireworks were also promised.

There were to be variety shows and concerts on the Coley Recreation Ground and in the Forbury Gardens and Palmer Park, and the Band of the Princess Charlotte's Royal Berkshire Regiment was to play on Moss's Island (which is now Fry's Island or De Montfort Island).

On the second day there was to be a regatta on Dreadnought Reach, downstream of Kennet Mouth, where three bands accompanied the races, and the Reading Temperance Prize Band played in the Forbury Gardens, where the Mayoress planted a scarlet oak. The 'Dinner to the Aged Poor' was at Prospect Park, while at the Town Hall, the Mayor presided over a dinner for the inmates of the workhouse. In the afternoon, the aquatic sports at King's Meadow included the usual novelty races, but rather than climbing the greasy pole, the ordeal was now walking the greasy pole. Maybe it overhung the river bank?

In the evening, there was a promenade concert in the Forbury Gardens, and a water carnival by Caversham Bridge, which involved illuminated boats and pierrot troupes. The bridge itself – still the Victorian iron bridge – was also illuminated, one side by the Reading Gas Company, and the other side by the electricity company. No fireworks are mentioned.

As a King, Edward VII was popular, though his playboy lifestyle and womanising were well known at the time. He brought in the Edwardian Age. He was also rather stout, and it is interesting that when the town decided to erect a statue to his memory in Station Square, the statue turned out to be of an idealised, slim figure.

The reign of Edward VII had been comparatively short, and the celebrations for the coronation of King George V and Queen Mary were held between Thursday 22 June and Sunday 25 June 1911: the coronation itself was on the 22nd. Like the 1902 coronation, the celebrations began with the ringing of bells, but the grand procession preceded the service, this time in St Mary's Church. Three bands were involved – the Royal Artillery Mounted Band (Aldershot Command), the 4th (Territorial) Battalion, the Band of the Royal Berkshire Regiment, and the band of the 'King Alfred' Training Brig. (This sailing vessel was moored in the Thames, and trained boys in skills which would prove useful, should they decide on a

maritime career.) The usual uniformed organisations marched, along with the Board of Guardians, and representatives of the University College. In the church, Psalm 122 was sung, and a setting of the *Te Deum*, between which came 'the Recital of the Solemnities.'

The afternoon brought the aquatic sports, this time to be viewed from the Thames Side Promenade, which had been laid out in 1907. Competitions involving canoes and mopsticks were in evidence, and there were some events for ladies, including 'Graceful Diving.' There was a promenade concert in the Forbury Gardens, during which the Mayoress planted a silver birch tree.

The Children's Festival was again in Prospect Park, but on this occasion, younger children, and children from East Reading, could travel the greater part of the way by electric tram.

The dinner for the 'aged poor inhabitants' happened on Friday: their number had now risen to 2,000, and they were accommodated in the Large and Small Town Halls, the Corn Exchange and the Tramways Depot in Mill Lane. For occasions like this the trams were parked outside the sheds, and the inspection pits were covered over. For the general populace, there was music in the parks, and free entertainment at the 'Reading Palace (Theatre) of Varieties,' which had opened in 1907.

No events were planned for Saturday, but on the Sunday afternoon there was another grand procession from the Town Hall to St Mary's Church. This time, the various friendly societies took part in the procession, together with the Mayor, Sergeant-at-Mace, Deputy Mayor, aldermen, councillors, Town Clerk, and other officials. The order of service was identical to Thursday's.

For the 1937 Coronation, no programme of events has come to light among the two collections searched for this book. For the Coronation of the present Queen, there were processions, a civic service, concerts, athletics and water sports, even though many were now able to watch the events in London from the comfort of their homes on television. The 2023 coronation was marked by a children's festival in the Forbury Gardens, there were street parties, and people gathered in church halls and pubs to watch the ceremony on screens, but there were no processions with bands in the town centre.

Programme & Guide

His Royal Highness the Prince of Wales will arrive at the G W Rly. Station at 10.30 a.m. and will be received on the platform by the Lord Lieut. of Berks Mr. J H. Benyon, the Mayor of Reading Councillor L. G. Sutton, Mr. C. S. Johnson, Sir G. Stewart Abram, Mr H G. Williams, Major General T. T. Pitman, and Mr T A. Burrows.

Ex-Service men employed on the Station will form up on the arrival platform. H R.H. will inspect a guard of honour which will be furnished by the Royal Berkshire Regiment.

TIME TABLE
The table of the tour is as follows:
10.40—Arrive at Great Western Railway Station
10 45 to 11.15—Messrs. Suttons and Sons seed trial grounds
11 20 to 12.20—Messrs. Huntley and Palmers
12 30 to 12 45—Caversham Bridge by launch to Reading Bridge
1 p.m. to 1.55—Town Hall for luncheon
2. 5 to 2.15—Co-operative Bakery
2 25 to 2 50—Messrs H and G. Simmonds Ltd.
3. 0 to 3.15—Messrs Huntley, Boorne and Stevens Ltd.
3 20 to 3 35—Royal Berkshire Hospital
3.40 to 4.15—University of Reading
4.20 to 4.35—Reading School
4.40 to 5.15—Palmer Park
5.25—Great Western Railway Station

H R.H. will enter Messrs Suttons and Son's seed trial and experimental grounds by the main gate, passing up the drive flaked on either side by borders of annual flowers.

At Messrs Huntley and Palmers the Prince will be shown the production of the biscuits through its many stages

At Caversham Bridge the Prince will unveil a tablet, consisting of four plates. The centre plates contain the words Caversham Bridge and the Arms of Reading. On either side will be a plate one of which will be inscribed as follows: "Erected by the Corporation of Reading under the powers of the Reading Corporation Act 1913 and first used on the 18th day of May 1926 This tablet was unveiled on the 25th day of June, 1926, by Edward Prince of Wales who but for unforeseen circumstances would have opened the bridge for traffic. The other plate will bear the inscription 1731—1924.

The Prince will tour the building of the Co-operative Bakery and see the bread making in all its different stages

The Prince will visit H. and G. Simonds brewery and will leave by way of Gas Lane to the firms social club.

H.R.H. will visit the factory of Huntley, Boorne and Stevens, Ltd. where he will see numerous operations in the manufacture of plain and decorted tin boxes The Prince will leave by way of Southampton Street

A display on a gigantic scale is organised by the Reading Elementary Schools, including various games, country dances, and school sports

During his visit the Prince will make a number of inspections of the guards of honour etc.

115. The work-a-day appearance of this programme is probably a result of the National Strike.

The visit of the Prince of Wales in 1926 was much photographed, and some of the pictures can be seen on the Reading Libraries website. In them, the Prince is a slight figure, carrying a bowler hat. He was Edward Albert Christian George Andrew Patrick David, known among the Royal Family as David, the eldest son of King George V. Though destined to become King on the death of his father in January 1936, the coronation was cancelled at short notice, following his abdication in December. It was to have been held in May 1937. His Prime Minister refused to condone his determination to marry a divorcee, Mrs Wallis Simpson, and had the marriage gone ahead, his position as head of the Church of England would have been untenable. At the time, the Church would not marry a divorced person if the other spouse was still alive.

Opposite page:
116. The Reading Festival emblem, a helmeted head with bunting below, is that of the national Festival of Britain, but with the word 'Reading' in place of '1951'.

The Prince's visit to Reading was to have taken place on 18 May, but had to be postponed on account of the National Strike. This meant that instead of opening the new Caversham Bridge to traffic, it was already open by the time His Royal Highness arrived, and he had to be content with unveiling plaques on the bridge.

The day must have been gruelling for the Prince – between arriving at the Great Western Railway Station at 10.40 and departing at 17.45, he was to make ten visits, with a brief stop for lunch in the Town Hall in between. Many of the places he visited are no longer there. They were:

- Suttons Seed Trial Grounds (Suttons Business Park is now on the site.)
- Huntley & Palmers biscuit factory (much of the site occupied by new apartment blocks, and by Kennet Place, the 1990s office building on Kings Road)
- Caversham Bridge. Then, by launch to Reading Bridge, and from there to the Town Hall for lunch
- The Co-operative Bakery in Grovelands Road
- H. & G. Simonds' Brewery (The Oracle shopping centre is now on the site.)
- Huntley, Boorne and Stevens' tinplate works, Southampton Street, Crown Street, London Street: most of the site is now occupied by apartment blocks
- The Royal Berkshire Hospital, London Road
- The University of Reading, London Road
- Reading School, Erleigh Road
- Palmer Park, for a display of games, sports and country dancing, organised by the Reading Elementary Schools

On top of this, 'During his visit the prince will make a number of inspections of guards of honour, etc.'

After the end of the Second World War, the government planned a Festival of Britain on London's South Bank, to help lift the gloom of post-war austerity. The Royal Festival Hall is a lasting legacy. But also, as the Mayor of Reading explained in his introduction to this programme, 'every locality was encouraged to participate and add its own spontaneous and individual activity to the national events.'

Alderman A. F. Clark, J.P., Mayor, 1950 - 1

Foreword
by His Worship the Mayor

ON the morning of 3rd May the King and Queen attended a Service at St. Paul's Cathedral in connection with the opening of the Festival of Britain. The King afterwards, from the steps of the Cathedral, broadcast a message to the nation and declared the Festival officially open.

The Festival is designed to put the whole of Britain on show, both to its own people and to the world, between the months of May and September. It will be spread over the United Kingdom and every locality will be encouraged to participate and add its own spontaneous and individual activity to the national events.

In Reading we hope that we shall be able to play our part and put our town on view to visitors from home and overseas. We are proud of our loyal and ancient borough, and of its long history and traditions. We have faith in its future, and we want everyone who comes here to see its beauties and to appreciate our way of life.

The brochure contains details of the programme in Reading, and I feel sure it will be agreed that it is quite a comprehensive and worthy one, and contains items which will meet all tastes.

I take this opportunity of expressing the grateful thanks of the borough to all those who have assisted in arranging the programme, and of wishing every success to their endeavours.

ARTHUR F. CLARK,
Mayor.

About
READING

READING has contrived to build a modern industrial and administrative centre on the foundations of an ancient market town. For centuries it has provided a convenient meeting point for the people of the downs, the river valleys and the Chiltern slopes. Its industries today are still largely based on the needs of the farmer or on the manufacture of the materials he grows. It has become a considerable residential neighbourhood and has increased in popularity as an inland holiday resort.

The visitor walking through the streets today will find much evidence of the continuity of development of the town. Its medieval buildings have all suffered much. Of the Benedictine Abbey, once one of England's greatest monastic foundations, only a few broken walls remain in the Forbury Gardens to suggest something of its former grandeur. The four ancient churches—the Priory Church of St. Mary ; St. Laurence, the municipal church ; the Franciscan foundation of Greyfriars ; and St. Giles, in Southampton Street—have all been much restored or rebuilt, but all are on their medieval sites and retain something of their original character.

The domestic architecture of the town ranges from the seventeenth century Watlington House, built by a wealthy local clothier, to the elegant eighteenth century and regency buildings in the London Street and London Road area, the

Reading is indeed delightfully situated in the sumptuous valley of the Thames. The river at this point, as will be seen in part from the photograph above, has both grandeur and simplicity, and the residents in summer are able to enjoy this natural feature to the full.

The town itself, a settlement for a thousand years, has a long and honoured history. Many of its central streets are flanked by delightful eighteenth- and nineteenth-century dwellings, and their haphazard planning has left a diverting charm, particularly for the person with an eye for the beautiful or curious.

185

Opposite page:
117. The 1971 Festival of Reading was a much more professional affair than the festival of 20 years earlier, and proved to be the forerunner of the present-day Reading Festival.

In the booklet, 88 events are listed, some of them very low-key and things which would have happened without the festival. Together they shed some interesting sidelights on the social life of the town and the nation, and mention local venues and organisations which no longer exist. Below is a selection:

- Carnival Fete on Hill's Meadow, 14 May, Whit Monday
- *Let's Make an Opera*, by Benjamin Britten, school matinees at 2.30, evenings at 7.30, produced for United Children's Charities at the Palmer Hall, West Street
- *John Gabriel Borkman* by Ibsen at the Pendragon Theatre, Bath Road.
- An Evening of English Plays, presented by the St Crispin Players, at Caversham Court
- *Toad of Toad Hall*, presented by Reading Repertory Company, at Caversham Court
- *Richard of Bordeaux*, presented by the Earley Players at Park Institute
- Physical Culture and Dancing Display at the Palace Theatre, Cheapside
- Reading Horticultural Federation 11th Annual Show, Suttons Sports Ground, Cintra, Christchurch Road
- The Grand Festival Water Carnival, Thames Side Promenade – rowing, swimming, aqua sports and a parade of decorated boats
- Swimming Gala, King's Meadow Mixed Bath.
- Festival of Television, organised by the Radio and Television Retailers' Association at the Town Hall.
- The unveiling of the memorial plaque to W. H. Fox Talbot, 'The Father of Modern Photography,' at 55 Baker Street, where he had his photographic establishment

The words 'Reading' and 'Festival' today mean something that happens off Richfield Avenue on the August Bank Holiday weekend, and is run jointly with another Festival in Leeds. This 1971 festival is where it all began.

It was a more professional event than its 1951 predecessor, with its own logo, and was unconnected with any national event. It ran for four weeks in June and July, with the aim of promoting Reading, 'The Total Town,' and the brochure is glossier, with advertising. The advertising shows that around half

Opposite page:
118. The nature of West Reading Festival changed over the years. 2019 saw the last one.

the shop units in the new Butts Shopping Centre had been taken up. It's now the Broad Street Mall.

The Festival Ground was on King's Meadow, with twelve marquees containing exhibitions by the Borough and County Councils, and many local organisations, with events every day – folk dancing displays, dog shows, fashion shows, schoolchildren dancing, etc.

The University was hosting a three-day conference on 'The Environment and Health,' and a series of lectures on 'Management Development,' both signs of changing times. But there were also many popular events, like the National Jousting Championships in Prospect Park, the funfair on Christchurch Meadow, Chipperfield's Circus (with performing animals) on Hill's Meadow, the Beer Festival in Forbury Gardens, and the Festival Ball at the Top Rank Suite.

Classical music was in evidence, at the Town Halls, Large and Small, and the University's Great Hall, with some of the foremost performers of their day. Moods in Music, organised by percussionist Les Lawrence, had a children's concert, a concert in the Town Hall, and a Festival Spectacular on the Festival Ground to include the *1812 Overture* with an orchestra of 300 musicians, bells and cannon effects. The Great Western Hotel was offering dinner recitals. And there was the Jazz, Pop and Blues Festival at Richfield Avenue, held over the weekend of 25–27 June. This was the forerunner of what is now The Reading Festival held over the August Bank Holiday weekend.

Dramatic entertainment included *A Delicate Balance* at the Progress Theatre, *Curtmantle* in St Laurence's Church performed by the St Laurence Players (who included the present author), and *Macbeth* in the Abbey Ruins, performed by the Berkshire Shakespeare Players.

Sporting events included 6-a-side football, cricket, bowls, road and track cycle racing, archery, badminton, lawn tennis, table tennis, the Reading Amateur Regatta, a 24-hour canoe race, and the Thames Mile Swim – the last of them perhaps not advisable today.

The statue of Rufus Isaacs, Marquess of Reading, was unveiled in Eldon Square Gardens. The British Rail Diesel Depot in Cow Lane held open days, as did the Unified Family at Row Lane Farm House, Dunsden. The 'Family' turned out to be a local branch of 'The Moonies,' a curious religious cult – as the present author discovered by making the mistake of going there.

The West Reading Festival started in 1977, and in 1983 it was held over three weeks. The prime movers were the Reading Council for Racial Equality, and Father John Methuen of St Mark's Church in Cranbury Road, the festival chairman. As Mr Methuen wrote, the festival wasn't for raising large amounts of money for charity or a community project – it was 'FOR all the people of Reading, to celebrate this community in which we live.' The Member of Parliament for Reading North, and then for the newly formed Reading West Constituency, Tony Durant, was another active supporter.

Events took place in many different places, among which were – St Mark's Church, St George's Church, Holy Trinity Church, All Saints' Church, the Elim Pentecostal Church, Grange United Reformed Church, West Reading Methodist Church, the Salvation Army Citadel, Battle Library, Southcote Hall, Walford Hall, the Oddfellows' Hall, Brock Barracks, Prospect Park, Huntley & Palmers Sports Ground, Elm Park, Presentation College, The Hexagon, and Reading Town Hall.

The computer demonstration at Battle Library must have been an interesting sign of things to come. The Slough Microshop was demonstrating its Commodore Computers, 'with systems for business, education and personal use. Come along and see what they can do.'

The main festival event took place on the Bank Holiday Monday. The Carnival Queen, crowned during a dance at The Hexagon the previous Friday, headed the parade, which wound its way from the lorry park in Great Knollys Street, to the festival ground in Richfield Avenue, via Oxford Road and Caversham Road. There was to be music and dancing, refreshments, stalls and side shows, and the awarding of prizes for the best floats in the Carnival Parade.

Over time, the West Reading Festival became the Reading Community Carnival, with a Caribbean theme. It was held in Prospect Park, and its nature changed, to become more like the Notting Hill Carnival. It was not held in 2020 on account of the corona virus pandemic.

The Caversham Charity Folk Festival started in 1994. Its aim was to give people a good weekend, while collecting money for different charities. The brochure from 2001, with the cover pictured overleaf, states: 'We do not charge an admission fee to our Festival, but we do aim to raise money to benefit our supported charities …'

Opposite page:
119. The Caversham Charity Folk Festival was held from 1994 to 2004. Events were free to attend.

120. Have university students become more serious? The last Reading rag parade was in 1998.

Many were involved in running it, many of them representing the different folk dance and song societies in the area. This 2001 Festival was particularly ambitious. The last one was held in 2004. The main events were held on meadows near the River Thames by the Rivermead Leisure Centre – actually on the Reading side of the water. There was a main marquee, and a children's marquee with events for youngsters. There was a beer tent run by the West Berkshire Brewery, who had brewed a Festival Ale for the occasion. Salter Brothers ran boat trips up and down the river, with bands playing. There were events in the Caversham shopping precinct, and several pubs and bars welcomed performers and festival goers – the Riverside Bar (now called River Spice), Three Men in a Boat Bar (a part of the Holiday Inn, now called the Crowne Plaza Hotel), the Clifton Arms in Gosbrook Road, and the Crown in Bridge Street. Ceilidhs and barn dances were held in Our Lady and St Anne's Church Hall, Washington Road. It was a community effort, and with around 50 sessions over the three days, it must have taken a great deal of organisation.

One Caversham pub which could not open its doors in 2001 was The Millers Arms in Paddock Road. It had closed a year or two before, but had been the site of the main marquee for previous festivals, on its lawn which went down to the river. The present author has fond memories of Morland's beer, sausages, and sitting on a straw bale in the marquee, enjoying the proceedings.

Finally in this celebratory chapter, we come to *The Rattler*, the University rag mag. – a copy of the 1977 edition has survived in the present author's collection of bits and pieces.

Although the University of Reading has many students, they're not particularly noticeable in the town centre. The one day of the year when this was not the case was the Rag Day, an annual event for many years. The main event was the Rag Procession, which made its way along Broad Street on a Saturday afternoon with many floats, colourful, witty and bizarre, and people in outrageous costumes rattling collecting boxes under the noses of the onlookers, and selling copies of *The Rattler*.

Inside its pages are jokes, cartoons and advertisements. The adverts are almost as interesting as the jokes and cartoons, many of them from Reading firms which are remembered, but no longer trading. This being the 1970s, the theme of many of the cartoons is the 'hippy,' with long hair, dark glasses, duffel coat, flared jeans with patches, and a cigarette dangling from the mouth.

In the week leading up to the procession, other pranks and stunts were perpetrated, such as 'charwomen' scrubbing the tarmac in Broad Street (in the days when it was busy with traffic), seeing how many students could fit into a telephone box or mini-car, and the 'kidnap' of the Mayor of Reading, until someone arrived with the 'ransom' money. The local papers played along, giving the event publicity, and it all seemed worthwhile, good humoured, and fun.

The purpose was to collect money, which was shared between different charities – in 1977 there were twelve of them, five national, and seven local, and the organisers were the Reading University Student Appeal for Charity.

Of course, there were complaints. Not all of the stunts, or the jokes in the magazine, were in the best possible taste. And the custom of throwing flour-bombs from the floats into the crowds of onlookers in the main streets wasn't welcomed by all.

The event has a surprisingly long history: the earliest rag day was in 1927, and the last one was in 1998, when, for a variety of reasons, including bad weather, the week's events made a loss.

121. Unlike many of the 'dying words' of condemned prisoners, Joseph Edwards's protested his innocence to the last.

XV. Crime and punishment

From celebrations, we now turn to a darker aspect of life, beginning with the words of a man condemned to death by hanging at Reading Gaol. Unlike many 'dying words,' this is not a confession, with a declaration of contrition, but a protestation of innocence. Joseph Edwards forgives the man who bore false witness against him, John Feathers, a post boy living in the Bear Inn, Bridge Street, Reading. He ends with a short letter to his wife, asking that their son is brought up 'close to the Church, and in the fear and love of God,' so that he will avoid bad company.

AN EXTRACT COPY OF

JOSEPH EDWARDS'S DYING WORDS,

WHO Was EXECUTED March, 23, 1799, on the NEW DROP, at

READING, IN BERKSHIRE.

THE laſt dying words of Joſeph Edwards, a native of Wells in Somerſetſhire, this he wrote in his Cell, on the 19th day of March 1799, but by the providence of Almighty God and a falſe accuſation and a terrible falſe oath, John Feathers a Poſt-boy ſwoar a-gainſt me at the bar, upon my trial, and upon his oath only, I am brought to this untimely death which the ſame John Feathers ſwore he drank part of a pint of ale at the Globe at Wallingford, which I abſolutely deny, and declare before the Almighty God and man I never was there in my life; I further beg, if there is any good chriſtian that comes from Woodley in the pariſh of Sonning, I hope and truſt in God they will take the trouble to caution them children of Millard's how to ſwear againſt any man for the future, not that their oaths injured me, only I hope it will be a caution to others as well as them not to bring another inocent man to the ſame untimely death I am about to ſuffer. A gentleman

SENTENCES of the PRISONERS tried at the Special Assizes at Reading, began Dec. 27, ended Jan. 4, 1831.

George Arlett, Luke Brown, Thomas Brown, John Cook, Daniel Hancock, Edward Harris, Wm. Hawkins, Thomas Hicks, John Nash, John Nailor, Charles Vince, and *George Williams,* charged with having destroyed a thrashing machine at Wasing, the property of Wm. Mount, esq.—*Luke Brown, Thomas Brown, Hancock, Vince, Hicks,* and *Williams,* are also charged with violently assaulting the constables at Brimpton.—*Arlett, Harris, Hicks, Nash,* and *Williams,* 14 years' transportation; *Luke Brown, Hancock, Hawkins,* 7 years; *T. Brown, Cook, Nailor, Vince,* 18 months' imprisonment.

Thomas Arnold, Charles Bates, James Bennett, John Carter, John Cosborn, Wm. Cox, Anthony Edwards, Thomas Edwards, George Goby, Frederick Gater, Jacob Gater, George Holmes, Peter Knight, Wm. Randall, Jonathan Sandford and *James Williams,* charged with having riotously assembled and destroyed upwards of twenty thrashing machines, in the parishes of Kintbury, Hungerford, Inkpen, Hampstead Marshall, Enborne, and Beenham.—*Bates, Death recorded; J. Gater,* 9 months' imprisonment: and *Holmes,* 12 months. The others Acquitted.

Samuel Allin, Charles Horton, John Horton, and *James Simonds,* charged with having destroyed a thrashing machine the property of Richard Glasspool at Binfield.—14 years' transportation each.

Wm. Oakley, Alfred Darling, and *Wm. Smith,* alias *Winterbourne,* charged with breaking machines and robbing the person.—DEATH,—all to be hanged.

Wm. Simonds, charged with breaking a thrashing machine at Waltham St. Lawrence.—7 years transportation.

Thomas Willoughby, for forcibly demanding money of G. B. Caudell and Thos. Washborne.—Death recorded.

Wm. Gale charged with breaking a thrashing machine, at Welford, the property of John Smith.—Discharged.

Edward Everett, charged with demanding money from Richard Child, at Chilton Foliat.—Discharged.

John Cope, John Field, David Garlick, and *George Rosier,* for destroying machinery at Hungerford.—Death recorded.

Timothy May, James Watts, Joseph Turk, and *Jeremiah Dobson,* charged with breaking machinery in the manufactory of Richard Gibbons, at Hungerford.—All Death recorded.

John Aldridge and *George Whiting,* charged with destroying a thrashing machine, the property of Thos. Winkworth, at Hungerford.—*Aldridge* seven years transportation.—*Whiting* 18 months imprisonment.

Wm. Chitter, David Hawkins, Wm. Haynes, & *Israel Pullen,* for riotously assembling at Hungerford.—Death recorded.

Isaac Burton, Jason Greenaway, Giles Fidler, James Turton, Wm. Waving, George Allick, & *James Deacon,* charged with robbing John Hawkins of one sovereign, and destroying his thrashing machine, at Welford.—*Burton, Greenaway,* and *Waving,* 7 years transportation.—*Deacon,* 12 months.—The others detained on another charge, for trial at Abingdon.

Joseph Smith and *Charles Green* for forcibly demanding bread and cheese of W. Lovelock, at Kintbury.—7 years trans.

Henry Day, charged with robbing Thomas Longford of two sovereigns, at West Shefford.—Acquitted.

John Wheeler, for breaking a thrashing machine the property of Martha Davis, at Waltham St. Lawrence.—7 years.

Stephen Denton, Charles Gilham, Wm. Hamblin, and *James Wait,* charged with breaking a thrashing machine the property of Jethro Lailey, at Bradfield.—*Hamlin* is also charged with robbing the Rev. J. J. Moor of 5s. and John Reading of 5s. and breaking the machine of John Reading.—*Denton,* 12 months imprisonment: the others six months.

John Church, John Stockwell, Thomas Tailor, and *Wm. Tailor,* for robbing G. Austin of £2. at Boxford.—Acquitted.

Elijah Baker and *James Grant,* for destroying Mr. Caudell's machine, at Shalbourn.—*Baker* 12—*Grant* 6 months imp.

Wm. Ball, charged with riotously assembling, with others, at Aston Upthorpe and Blewberry.—Discharged.

Alexander Barrett, James Hutchings, John Lewis, and *Stephen Williams,* charged with destroying a thrashing machine, the property of W. Mount, esq. at Wasing.—*Barrett* 3 months—*Hutchings* 12—*Williams,* 14 years transportation.

George Liddiard, Richard Nutley, and *Wm. Pearson,* alias *Brazier,* charged with breaking thrashing machines the property of Wm. Webb, at Hampstead Marshall, and John Porter.—*Liddiard* 18, the others 12 months imprisonment.

William White, charged with riotously assembling, with others, at Kintbury.—Twelve months imprisonment.

George Sturgiss, charged with demanding 2s. 6d. from Thomas Owen, at Kintbury.—Acquitted.

Cornelius Bennett and *Henry Honey,* charged with having robbed Thomas Ward of two pounds, at West Woodhay.—*Bennett,* seven years transportation.—*Honey* Acquitted.

James Cook, charged with robbing Stephen Elliott of 1s. at Aldermaston.—Acquitted.

John Burgess, charged with having demanded 1s. from John Hutchens, at Inkpen.—Acquitted.

James Burgess, for breaking the machines of W. Keep, at Aldermaston, and W. P. Brokenbrow.—14 years trans.

John Jennaway, charged with robbing Charles Spanswick of £2 and breaking his machine at Lambourn.—12 months.

John Gater and *Daniel Bates,* charged with breaking a thrashing machine, the property of W. Webb, at Hampstead Marshall.—*Gater,* 12 months.—*Bates, Death recorded.*

John Smoker, charged with having riotously assembled with others.—Acquitted.

Edmund Price, charged with sending letters to Jn. Briginshaw of Bray, threatening to burn his premises.—Acquitted.

Francis Norris and *Charles Rosier,* for machine breaking and robbery.—Death recorded.

Wm. Page, charged with breaking the thrashing machine of John Kidgell, at Bradfield.—Twelve months imprisonment.

Joseph Quarterman and *James Fuller,* charged with breaking a thrashing machine of W. Mount, esq. and Mr. Hickman.—12 months.

George Dobson, charged with robbing Wm. Squires of 14s. at Kintbury.——Discharged.

William Page, charged with robbing Stephen Collins of one sovereign, at Hampstead Marshall.——Death recorded.

Joseph Tegg and *George Merritt,* charged with robbing James Taylor of two half-crowns.——Discharged.

Wm. Sims, and *Thomas Radborn,* charged with robbing Edwd. Webb, of one sovereign, at Kintbury.——Death recorded.

Thomas Hanson, Edward Davies, Nathaniel Cole, James Willis, James Hamblin, Robert Josey, and *Wm. Josey,* charged with robbing James Froome of 5s. and breaking his machine at Streatley.—*Davies,* 18 months.—*Hanson,* 14 years.—The others acquitted.

Thomas Bunce and *Thomas Britton,* charged with breaking the thrashing machine of Sarah Larkcom, at Stanford Dingley.—Acquitted.

Thomas Dance, charged with breaking the windows of Wm. Arming, at Hungerford.—Twelve months.

Robert Gibbs and *Thomas Goodfellow,* charged with breaking the thrashing machine of Thos. Ward, at West Woodhay.—*Gibbs,* Twelve months.—*Goodfellow,* Fourteen years.

Edmund Viccus and *Charles Milsom,* for machine breaking———Fourteen years transportation.

John Coventry, charged with breaking the machine of Mr. Hickman, of Aldermaston.—Twelve months.

John Hutchins, charged with breaking the machines of Wm. Lailey and Benjamin Matthews, at Stanford Dingley.—Six months.

Joseph Nicholas, Edmund Steel, and *Wm. Carter,* charged with robbing J. Randall of one sovereign, at Kintbury.—Death recorded.

Wm. Westell, charged with robbing the Earl of Craven of ten pounds.—Death recorded.

James West and *John Edney,* charged with destroying the thrashing machine of Jason Austin, at Basildon.—*West,* 7 years.—*Edney* 14.

John Greenaway, charged with setting fire to a stack of wheat, &c. at Shottesbrook, the property of John Webb Aldridge.—No Bill.

Robert Page, seven years' transportation.———*Charles Williams* and *William Beckett,* twelve months' imprisonment.

(Cowslade and Co. Printers.)

Opposite page:
122. The list of charges and sentences handed down at Reading Assizes, following the 'Swing' Riots of 1830–31.

According to the *Reading Mercury* of 11 March 1799, Edwards had been convicted at the Berkshire Assizes of 'breaking open the dwelling-house of W. Mabbott, Esq., at Woodley, and stealing thereout a large quantity of plate and other articles.' Edwards, from Wells in Somerset, claims that he was in a different part of the country at the time of the burglary, and that he had never been to Woodley in his life (though he was employed by Mr Mabbott), and describes the ill treatment he had received at the hands of lawyers, the Town Clerk of Reading, and those who had testified against him. He is writing these lines 'to caution the spectators in general, both old and young, male and female,' and declares that he is 'innocent as the child unborn.'

The execution took place on 23 March, on the 'new drop' at Reading. This would have been in the 'New' County Gaol, which had opened in 1793, replacing the old gaol in Castle Street, and which was demolished in turn to make way for the buildings of the 1840s.

The leaflet was published by G. Coopey, who calls himself a 'walking stationer'. He probably made an income from travelling to assize towns, collecting the words of condemned men – many of whom would not have been able to write – and printing them and selling them to the spectators on execution days.

The *Reading Mercury*, in its account of the execution, commented: 'Mercy could not be shewn to this unhappy man, it being an invariable rule not to spare any clerk, shopman or servant of any denomination whatever, who shall defraud or rob his master, whose protector he ought to be.'

Moving forward to 1830, a flimsy sheet of paper records the trial of 120 men of Berkshire, accused of taking part in disturbances, at the Special Assizes at Reading. Agricultural workers in corn-growing areas of the country were dismayed by the impact of steam threshing-machines on their livelihoods. At the time, corn was usually built into ricks in farmyards or stored in barns after harvesting, so that it could be threshed and winnowed over winter, when there was not much work to be done on the land. The new machines needed labour, but only for a short while, and the labourers were afraid of being laid off work, and having to apply for parish relief and live as paupers during the coldest part of the year.

Tempers ran high. Landowners and farmers claimed they couldn't pay higher wages to compensate, and began receiving threatening letters about the consequences of bringing in the new machines, signed by the mythical 'Captain Swing.' Scholars say that his name resulted from the name of part of a flail, the implement used to thresh corn by hand, but one cannot help feeling that there might have been the added threat of someone swinging from the end of a rope.

'Riotous assemblies' of angry men, some of them no doubt fuelled by alcohol, roamed the countryside at night, breaking the threshing-machines, burning ricks, breaking windows, and demanding money. At Hungerford they attacked the foundry of Richard Gibbons, where the machines were built, in broad daylight.

The sheet of paper records the names of those accused, the accusations, and the sentences handed down at the Special Assizes held at Reading between 27 December 1830 and 4 January 1831. Some prisoners were discharged, some acquitted, some imprisoned for between 9 and 18 months, and some were to be transported for 7 or 14 years. The words 'death recorded' appear against 20 of the 120 names, but later, according to W. S. Darter's memoirs, 17 of them must have been given lesser sentences, and three were due to hang. In Reading, great sympathy was felt for the three, and petitions were hastily got up. Darter tells how the dinner which followed the Assizes was interrupted by two Quakers demanding clemency, and the matter was laid before the Home Secretary, Lord Melbourne, and ultimately the king. In the end, only one man was hanged. Perhaps it was felt that to satisfy the government, the lawyers and the farmers, someone had to 'swing', and it fell to the lot of the unfortunate William Smith, alias Winterbourne, from Kintbury.

The County of Berkshire had two County Gaols – at Abingdon and Reading. This led to contention between the two towns and across Berkshire. Eventually it was decided that the building at Abingdon had defects which could not be put right without great expense, and it was closed 1868. In the twenty-first century it has been converted into apartments!

In 1866, the date of our next document, prisoners were divided into four classes, according to the length of the sentence – Class I for a week, Class II for up to three weeks, Class III for up to six weeks, and Class IV for more than six weeks.

Breakfast for all prisoners was a pint of gruel, made from 2 oz. 'Scotch' oats, salt, and water. This came with bread, 4 oz. for Class I prisoners, and 6 oz. for everyone else.

123. The last line of this notice states that it was approved by the Home Secretary, Spencer Horatio Walpole. One wonders what a modern-day nutritionist would make of it.

Dinner was bread only for Class I. For Classes II and III it was bread with potatoes, with the female prisoners getting a little less than the men.

Supper was bread only for Class I, and bread with gruel for Classes II and III.

Only those 'in' for six weeks or more received anything other than bread, gruel and water. The men had 2 oz. cheese and 3 oz. bacon, per week, and the women slightly less – 1¾ oz. cheese and 2½ oz. bacon. This conjures up images of people in kitchens diligently weighing things by the quarter and half ounce.

Presumably Home Secretary Walpole considered the uninteresting and inadequate diet part of the punishment: it must have led to the physical decline of many of the Class IV prisoners.

DIETARY
For the Berks County Gaols of Reading and Abingdon.

CLASS NO. I.
Convicted Prisoners confined for any term not exceeding Seven Days.

	MALE.	FEMALE.
BREAKFAST	1 pint of Oatmeal Gruel, 4 oz. of Bread	1 pint of Oatmeal Gruel, 4 oz. of Bread
DINNER	6 oz. of Bread	6 oz. of Bread
SUPPER	6 oz. of Bread	6 oz. of Bread

CLASS NO. II.
Convicted Prisoners for any term exceeding Seven Days, and not exceeding Twenty-one Days.

	MALE.	FEMALE.
BREAKFAST	1 pint of Oatmeal Gruel, 6 oz. of Bread	1 pint of Oatmeal Gruel, 6 oz. of Bread
DINNER	8 oz. of Potatoes, 4 oz. of Bread	6 oz. of Potatoes, 4 oz. of Bread
SUPPER	1 pint of Oatmeal Gruel, 6 oz. of Bread	1 pint of Oatmeal Gruel, 6 oz. of Bread

CLASS NO. III.
Convicted Prisoners for any term exceeding Twenty-one Days, and not exceeding Forty-two Days.

	MALE.	FEMALE.

Opposite page:
124. One of the candidates at the 1826 General Election was implicated in a national scandal.

XVI. Local government

The Municipal Corporations Act of 1835 meant that across the country, councillors had to be elected. It seems incredible today that councillors in many towns were a self-electing oligarchy, or that you could pay to become a councillor. Even in 1835, the electors were all male, as were the councillors. Over time, the responsibilities of town councils grew. As we saw in the opening chapter, they ran the markets. They also supervised trading standards, and eventually became responsible for roads and bridges, for the water supply and sewerage, for the electricity supply (though Reading never took over the gasworks), public transport, the police, education, libraries, museums, parks, and cemeteries. But in the nineteenth century they were not the only body with a hand in running the town's affairs – there were the Local Board of Health, the Guardians of the Poor, and the Parish Constables and Surveyors of Highways.

We begin the chapter with elections. In 1826, the election of Members of Parliament was organised by the corporation, as it is now. Unusually, this handbill results from one of the great scandals of the year, which blew up during the election campaign, and became known as the Shrigley Abduction.

Edward Gibbon Wakefield had on false pretences removed Ellen Turner, a young heiress, from her boarding school in Liverpool, and married her at Gretna on 8 March. They had then gone to Dover and crossed the Channel to France, on their way letting the English press know of the marriage. Ellen's father, William Turner, a wealthy cotton manufacturer of Shrigley Park near Macclesfield, was incensed, and determined to rescue his 15-year-old daughter from an enforced marriage. Under Scottish law the marriage was legal, but eventually the French authorities were persuaded to allow Ellen to return home to her father. The marriage had not been consummated.

Edward Wakefield, on whose behalf this handbill was issued, was parliamentary candidate for Reading, the father of Edward Gibbon Wakefield the abductor. He had no local connections, and there was already a whiff of scandal around him: he had himself eloped with the girl he made his wife, setting an example for his son. Rumours were spreading that he had aided and abetted his son in the abduction plot. In the handbill, he denies this, and denies he had any knowledge of his son's marriage until several days after the event.

TO THE ELECTORS OF Reading.

IN allusion to a Paragraph which has appeared in the Newspapers relating to the marriage of Mr. Edward Gibbon Wakefield with Miss Turner, the Electors of Reading are informed it is not true that the statement of this marriage was sent to a Newspaper Agency-office, by Mr. Edward Wakefield, as is therein stated.

The fact is, that Mr. Edward Wakefield was totally ignorant of all the circumstances attending the transaction in question, or that any acquaintance or marriage was even contemplated between Mr. E. Gibbon Wakefield and Miss Turner, until several days after the marriage had taken place. The statement of the marriage was forwarded by Mr. E. Gibbon Wakefield, from Carlisle, for insertion in the London Newspapers, unknown to, and without any communication with, Mr. Edward Wakefield.

The Electors of Reading are informed, that Mr. Edward Wakefield will return to the Borough in a few days, and fully confirm this statement.

DRYSDALE, PRINTER, READING.

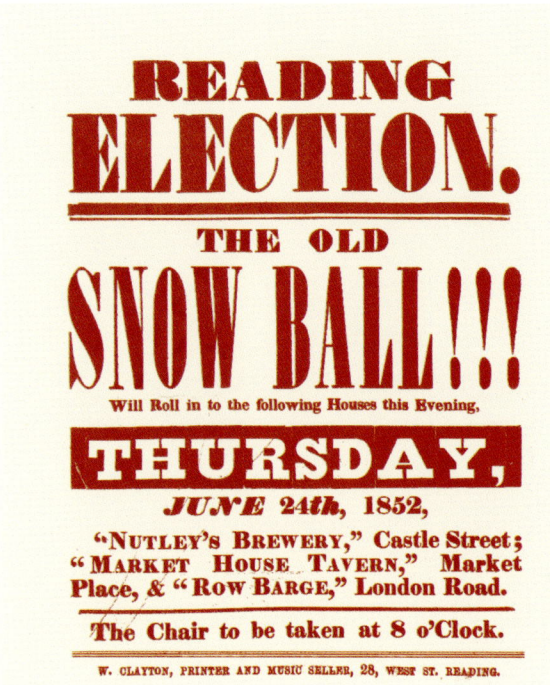

125. A 'Snow Ball' was a political meeting at an inn at election time where free drinks were dispensed to electors.

126. The exact date of this notice is not known, but it must have been some time in the 1840s.

The Tory electors of Reading appear to have believed him, and at a meeting held at the White Hart Inn (the Broad Street Mall now occupies the site) pledged their support, but when it came to the election, that was not sufficient. John Berkeley Monck (580 votes) and George Spencer (492 votes) were elected, and Charles Fysshe Palmer (488 votes) and Edward Wakefield (366 votes) were defeated. Reading had 1,061 electors, each with two votes.

Edward Gibbon Wakefield, after serving three years in gaol for the abduction, went on to enjoy a distinguished career, interested in prison reform, and colonisation, especially in South Australia – which seems somehow appropriate.

By 1852, the date of our next item, Reading had a larger electorate, thanks to the Representation of the People Act of 20 years before. They now numbered 1,399, though electors were all male and had to own or occupy premises worth £10 or more. They had over three weeks in which to cast their votes, and there was no secret ballot. Afterwards, lists of electors were published in the local papers, showing how each one had voted. This gave rise to various kinds of abuse, one of which was 'treating,' whereby drinks were freely dispensed at political meetings in public houses, to voters who would then feel obliged to vote for particular candidates. In Reading these 'Snow Balls' were run by the Liberal party, presumably so-called because they rolled on from one pub to the next, maybe getting larger as they rolled.

All of the three pubs mentioned on the poster no longer exist. Nutley's Brewery, at 71 Castle Street, went under various other names and ended its days as a pub called The Kennet, demolished to make way for the Inner Distribution Road in the 1960s. The exact position of the Market House Tavern in the Market Place is not known, but the Row Barge was on the north side of London Road, near the corner of Watlington Street. The name was changed to the Royal Berkshire Hotel, and it closed around 1962. A petrol station is now on the site.

The *Berkshire Chronicle*, Tory in its outlook, described the 'Snow Balls' as 'hole-and-corner meetings packed up in the back parlour of a dingy public house, where the minds of the deluded audience are inflamed with spirituous liquors, and then further excited by the inflammatory harangues of paid orators.'

In 1852, Reading was represented by two Members of Parliament, and the Liberals, Francis Piggott and H. S. Keating, won, and the Tory, Captain S. A. Dixon, was defeated.

As well as Members of Parliament and local councillors, the Guardians of the Poor also needed to be elected. The Poor Law Amendment Act of 1834 had set up the Poor Law Unions, and the Reading Union comprised the three parishes of St Laurence, St Mary and St Giles. Five Guardians were elected for each parish. At first, under the new system, the old parish poor-houses remained in use, and it was not until 1866 that a Union Workhouse was opened, on Oxford Road, at the time on the edge of the borough. The workhouse buildings

127. A document illustrating the complex nature of local government in 1849

BOROUGH OF READING
IN THE
COUNTY OF BERKS,
(TO WIT.)

AT THE GENERAL QUARTER SESSIONS OF THE PEACE of our Sovereign Lady the Queen, in and for the Borough of Reading, in the County of Berks, at the Guildhall there, on Friday, the Nineteenth day of October, in the thirteenth year of the reign of our Sovereign Lady Victoria by the Grace of God of the United Kingdom of Great Britain and Ireland, Queen, Defender of the Faith, and in the year of our Lord one thousand eight hundred and forty-nine, and from thence continued by adjournment until Friday, the thirtieth day of November, in the thirteenth year aforesaid, the said Session is holden by adjournment aforesaid, at the Guildhall aforesaid, before HENRY ALWORTH MEREWETHER, Serjeant-at-Law, Recorder, and one of Her Majesty's Justices of the Peace, acting in and for the said Borough.

WHEREAS, it has been presented to this Court by the Grand Jury duly impanelled at the same, that they have received Presentments from the respective Constables and Surveyors of the Highways of the Parishes of Saint Lawrence and Saint Giles, that BLAKE'S BRIDGE, situate within this Borough, and within the jurisdiction of this Court, is in a state too dangerous for passengers to pass over; and it is necessary for the safety of her Majesty's subjects that the same be immediately Closed. IT IS HEREBY ORDERED that the said Bridge be forthwith CLOSED, until the parties lawfully compellable to repair the same shall be duly indicted at the next ensuing Sessions, to be held for this Borough aforesaid.

HENRY ALWORTH MEREWETHER,
Recorder.

WE, the undersigned, Justices of the Peace for the said Borough, do hereby require the Constables and Surveyors of the said respective Parishes, and all others whom it may concern, to cause the above order to be duly executed.

HENRY ADAMS, *Mayor.*
THOS. HARRIS.

R. WELCH, PRINTER, MARKET PLACE, READING.

eventually became Battle Hospital, which closed in 2005, and the site has been redeveloped with a supermarket and car park. Only the gatehouse remains.

It has not yet proved possible to work out the exact date of this notice, but it must have been at some time in the 1840s. The elections do not seem to have been reported in the local press every year, and there are no papers relating to them in the Royal Berkshire Archives. Nevertheless, at the 1842 election, three of the five Guardians elected by St Laurence's parish were the same as those listed here, and in 1845, four of the five were the same. All of them were active around this time: Henry Portsmouth of Friar Street was Chairman of the Reading Union Gas Company; there were two tradesmen in the Market Place named William Harris, one a confectioner and the other a linen draper; William Ferguson was a wine merchant in the Market Place (see p. 18), Charles Hewitt was a grocer in Broad Street; and John Copeland Maggs was a pawnbroker in Broad Street, and also a town councillor.

Nor has it proved possible to ascertain who was causing the 'unnecessary opposition' to the existing Guardians, and why. Had the performance of the five Guardians listed here proved unsatisfactory? Maybe some matter of contention had arisen. But there again, the protest may simply have been against the expense and the bother of holding an election at all. In 1840, the Guardians in all three parishes had been elected unopposed. According to a report in the local paper of 1837, should an election be necessary, 'the overseers are bound to deliver voting papers to each qualified rate-payer, and to call for them on a subsequent day. As ladies have the right of voting, they may exercise it without leaving their houses.' It was not until 1869 that unmarried women who were property owners could vote for councillors, a right extended to some married women in 1894.

Reading has many bridges. The charter granted by Queen Elizabeth I in 1560 mentioned 19 bridges, many of which were ruinous. The area where the Inner Distribution Road crosses Bridge Street near the bottom of Southampton Street was once known as Seven Bridges. Farther downstream, the present-day Blake's Bridge carries the IDR over the River Kennet, near the end of Chestnut Walk and the old gaol. This area is now being redeveloped, but was once the site of Huntley & Palmers factory and warehouses.

Keeping the bridges in repair was often problematic, since several parties would have to agree on the need for repair or rebuilding, and their liability to pay, before any action could be taken.

Blake's Bridge was a case in point. It stood on the site of the medieval Orts Bridge, which had belonged to Reading Abbey. It was near the East Gate, where orts, or scraps of food, were distributed to the poor. In the eighteenth century, it had become known as Blake's Bridge, after Robert Blake, the landowner who gave his name to a Wharf and a Lock in this area.

The notice under consideration, dating from 1849, says that at the Court of Quarter Sessions, held in the Guildhall, the Constables and Surveyors for the Parishes of St Lawrence and St Giles had declared that Blake's Bridge was dangerous and should be closed. The river at this point was the boundary between the two parishes. The Guildhall was what was commonly known as the Yield Hall, in Yield Hall Place near the High Bridge. The Recorder of Reading, Henry Alworth Merewether, ordered that Blake's Bridge be closed, and that 'the parties lawfully compellable to repair the same shall be duly indicted at the next ensuing Sessions'. The Recorder was the borough's legal officer, a forerunner of the Town Clerk.

The local paper shows that the matter was discussed by the court, the Borough Council and the local board of health, for the next few years without anyone coming to a decision as to who was liable, the bridge was closed and a temporary ferry-boat had to be laid on. In the end, a new iron bridge was opened in 1856, achieved 'without recourse to the law, and with the assistance of the gentlemen of the town, whose labours gratuitously given were highly praiseworthy.' George Palmer led the collection of subscriptions – he must have had to look at the dilapidated bridge more often than most, from the adjacent biscuit factory. In addition to subscriptions, the Court of Quarter Session paid £25 to release the county from any future liability towards the bridge, and the board of health paid £100, out of the total cost of around £300. The bridge became vested in the board, and then the Borough Council.

This bridge in turn was replaced by a new iron bridge, 1892–94, and replaced again by a concrete bridge with the coming of the Inner Distribution Road in the 1980s.

128. Reading Technical College, founded and funded by the Borough Council in 1948, opened its new building in 1955 and has had several changes of title since then.

Moving on to the provision of education, it was not until after the passing of the 1944 Education Act, the Borough Council took on responsibility for technical education, and began drawing up plans. This was much later than many towns, which had supported technical colleges since Victorian times, teaching practical subjects such as building, carpentry and engineering. In 1948, the technical college moved into the old St Giles' Girls' School, on the corner of London Road and Silver Street, with evening classes held in more than thirty centres around the town.

READING TECHNICAL COLLEGE

Order of Proceedings at the

OPENING CEREMONY

26 OCTOBER 1955 AT 2.45 P.M.

ONE

The National Anthem

TWO

The Right Worshipful the Mayor (Councillor A. E. Smith, J.P.) will welcome Her Majesty Queen Elizabeth the Queen Mother

THREE

OFFICIAL OPENING OF THE COLLEGE BY HER MAJESTY QUEEN ELIZABETH THE QUEEN MOTHER

FOUR

Vote of thanks by the Chairman of the Education Committee (Councillor A. Lockwood) supported by the Chairman of the Governors of the Reading Technical College (F. H. Lewis, Esq.)

FIVE

The Right Reverend the Lord Bishop Suffragan of Reading will offer dedicatory prayers

A section of the Reading Youth Orchestra will play before and after the ceremony

The new building for the college was on the site of Victoria Square, a development of elegant stone-faced houses set well back from Kings Road with lawns and trees in front, and designed by the architect John Billing in the 1840s. Over the next century, they must have gone down in the world, with the kind of wealthy people for whom they were built preferring to live out of town. They were replaced by the new college, which was described by Nikolaus Pevsner as 'Terrible, in the tamest squared-up Neo-Georgian of between the wars.' The building was intended to be extended eastwards in the same style in due course, but mercifully this never happened.

Movie film of the opening ceremony is held by the Wessex Film and Sound Archive in Winchester, and Reading Central Library has some photographs of the event. For the occasion, Huntley & Palmers had made an enormous cake, in the shape of the college building, and Queen Elizabeth, the Queen Mother, was photographed standing by it.

Over the years the college has undergone a number of changes in administration and changes of title. It was built for and initially run by the Borough Council. From the Technical College, it became Reading College of Technology. Then between 2004 and 2010 it was the Reading Campus of the Thames Valley University (now the University of West London), and currently it is Reading College and University Centre, one of a group of colleges called Activate Learning.

The Borough of Reading was also comparatively slow in adopting the Public Libraries Acts of 1850 and 1855. The first Central Library opened in 1882.

The 1850 Act allowed boroughs with a population of 10,000 or over to build and run public libraries, but they could only spend the product of a halfpenny rate on them. The 1855 Act allowed boroughs to spend the product of a penny rate on public libraries, but only if, at a meeting of ratepayers, two-thirds of those present agreed to do so. The purpose of this notice was to call such a meeting, in 1877.

It proved successful, but a further ratepayers' meeting had to be called two years later, to authorise the spending of a further £10,000 on the new building – which included a museum and a new town hall (now The Concert Hall) as well as the library. This was agreed. A reading room with an art gallery above was added in 1895.

129. Notice from 1877, calling for a meeting of the burgesses (i.e. ratepayers) to decide whether or not the Borough should open a public library.

Even so, the library was soon proving far too small for the demands made on it. To ease the pressure, reading rooms were opened in the evenings in schools in different parts of the town, and branch libraries were opened in the suburbs. The first branch library in Reading was the West Branch Library (now Battle Library) in Oxford Road, which opened in 1908. Caversham Library had opened the year before, but at the time belonged to Caversham Urban District Council in Oxfordshire. Eventually, the enlarged Reading borough was to have six branch libraries.

The old Municipal Buildings in the town centre were becoming increasingly inadequate and expensive to maintain, and in the 1960s plans were drawn up for a new Civic Centre, built just west of St Mary's Butts, between Castle Street and Oxford Road. An area of old housing, crossed by Lavender Street, Bosier's Square, Hope Street, Flint Street, Soho Street and Hosier Street was compulsorily purchased and demolished.

Besides the Civic Offices (opened 1976, closed 2014, demolished 2015–16) and The Hexagon (still standing), the development was to have included a Cultural Centre with a new library, museum and art gallery. The fact that no Cultural Centre was built was due in no small part to the local government changes of

BOROUGH OF READING.
THE PUBLIC LIBRARIES ACT, 1855

The following is a Copy of the Request in writing, of Ratepayers, referred to in the Notice convening the PUBLIC MEETING of the Burgesses of this Borough, to be held on Thursday, the 17th day of May, 1877.

(COPY REQUEST.)
BOROUGH OF READING.
THE PUBLIC LIBRARIES ACT, 1855.

To the Worshipful the Mayor of the Municipal Borough of Reading, in the County of Berks.
We, the undersigned, being Ratepayers, residing in the Municipal Borough of Reading, in the County of Berks, do hereby request you to convene a PUBLIC MEETING of the Burgesses of the said Borough, in order to determine whether the Public Libraries Act, 1855, shall be adopted for the said Municipal Borough of Reading.
Dated the Twenty-eight day of April, One Thousand Eight Hundred and Seventy-Seven.

NAME.	ADDRESS.	NAME.	ADDRESS.	NAME.	ADDRESS.
William Isaac Palmer	Kendrick road	Richard B. Burgis	Castle hill	Edward Townsend	72, Soho street
Thomas Rogers	The Forbury, Reading	Jacous Golder		William Albert Taylor	

130. The cover of one of several publications produced by the librarians in the Central Library in the 1970s.

1974, in which libraries were taken away from municipal and county boroughs, and given to county councils. Berkshire County Council opened the new Reading Central Library in 1985. Then in 1998, the County Council was abolished, and the responsibility for libraries was handed back to the Borough Council. In 2023, this council decided to build a new library near to the Civic Offices in Bridge Street – less than 40 years after the opening of the previous one.

When the present author came to work for Reading Public Libraries in 1969, the service was well regarded in the library world, despite its inadequate Central Library buildings. It now seems incredible that at the time, a librarian in a public library should be given the time to compile an annual booklet like the one illustrated here. It had over 400 entries, which had to be typed on a manual typewriter before being sent to the printer. The library also produced a monthly 'what's on' list, and a list of hotels and guest-houses in the area.

In the booklet the various organisations are arranged by subject, so, for example, there are 30 badminton clubs, 12 amateur dramatic societies, the Devon and Cornwall Association, the West Indian Women's Circle, the Winemakers' Circle, and even a Home Counties Magical Society. For each one, a contact name, postal address and telephone number is given.

The sheer amount of work involved in sending out the forms, collecting them back, and typing out the details accurately, then getting the entries into the correct order, was considerable. Of course, in the days before the Internet and websites, it was much more worthwhile than it would be now.

The booklet sold for 5p, the cost being kept low because the Borough Council had its own printer (and its own bookbinder) at the time.

The compilation was a task that in 1979 fell to the present author – I also designed the cover. I approached the job with some trepidation. My predecessor had once made a mistake, and the old Borough Librarian, who was something of a martinet, docked her salary the next month to pay for the cost of re-printing. Those were the days!

The first phase of the Municipal Buildings had been the Town Hall of 1788, now the Victoria Hall. The second came in the 1870s, designed by Alfred Waterhouse. It contained the council chamber, mayor's parlour and offices, and was dominated

READING CIVIC SOCIETY & OTHER AMENITY GROUPS

SAVE OUR TOWN HALL

OUR VICTORIAN HERITAGE THREATENED

DO YOU KNOW

that when the new municipal buildings and Assembly Hall are opened, our present Town Hall buildings will be in danger of demolition together with the famous Father Willis organ?

PUBLIC MEETING
IN THE
TOWN HALL
WEDNESDAY 17th JULY 1974
at 8 p.m.

Speakers of national & local repute. Short recital on the Father Willis organ.

EVERYONE WHO CARES MUST COME

131. The new 'Assembly Hall' referred to here is The Hexagon. It took another 26 years for the Town Hall (now Concert Hall) and its organ to be restored.

by the clock tower. As we have seen, less than ten years later came the third phase, extending the building northwards along Blagrave Street. Not only did it contain the public library, with the museum above it, but a much larger Town Hall, now called the Concert Hall. The fourth phase of the 1890s extended the buildings to the corner of Valpy Street, and contained a reading room downstairs, and the art gallery (now the Sir John Madejski Gallery) above.

There had been dissatisfaction with these Victorian buildings as early as the 1920s. In 1928, a grandiose group of buildings in the Forbury Gardens was proposed. There was considerable opposition, but the scheme was not formally rejected until 1937. After the war, the search for a suitable site continued, and as has been said, the Civic Offices, opening in 1976, and the Hexagon, opening in 1977 were built. The original plan was to sell the old buildings to a developer, to offset some of the cost of these new buildings, but as the Cultural Centre with a new library, museum and art gallery was not built, some of the Victorian buildings would have to remain, for the time being.

The worry for the Civic Society, music lovers and others in 1974 was the likely loss of the Concert Hall, and the 'Father' Willis organ which is now recognised as 'without question, one of the greatest of all Town Hall Organs.' (For the building and enlargement of the organ, see p. 154–5.)

The Civic Society, together with the Victorian Society and the Civic Trust made representations to the Department of the Environment, and the whole of the Town Hall complex was listed. The announcement of the listing was made at the 1974 public meeting advertised here. The old police station and magistrates' court in Valpy Street were not included, and were demolished and their site redeveloped.

The Municipal Buildings should then have been safe: the listing would have made them much less attractive to developers, but this meant that the Borough Council was still saddled with them. In the 1980s, a scheme was proposed which involved building a mezzanine floor across the Town Hall, which would have rendered the organ obsolete. There were protests once more, and in 1983, a meeting was called to which musical societies and anyone else interested was invited. At the meeting, no-one could be found to speak in favour of the 'mezzanine' scheme, and it was abandoned. During the 1990s the Hall was closed, and the organ gathered dust. Eventually a scheme was devised to refurbish the

Opposite page:
132. The Sunday afternoon walk failed to stop the building of the new houses.

hall and the organ, and with the help of the Heritage Lottery Fund, both were re-opened in 2000.

Today, the sorry saga of how the much-loved Concert Hall and its organ came close to destruction on several occasions seems incredible.

Town and Country Planning was another responsibility of the County Borough Council, and then as now, planning applications often resulted in objections, and occasionally protests. Bugs Bottom, otherwise known as Hemdean Bottom, is in Caversham, and part of a dry valley through the chalk, which starts somewhere near Nuney Green, crosses the Woodcote Road near the Pack Horse Inn, and runs more or less southwards. Lower down, it divides Caversham Heights, to the west, from Emmer Green, to the east, and towards the end, Hemdean Road (formerly Bottom Lane) follows the valley, which ends at the Thames, behind St Martin's shopping precinct.

According to local tradition, the area was once haunted by the 'bugs' or ghosts of people slain during a Civil War skirmish on Balmer's Field. The name of the field has given rise to Balmore House, Walk and Drive.

In the 1980s, plans to build houses over part of the land of Shipnell's Farm in the valley caused mass protests, with people living nearby fearing the loss of pleasant fields and an increase in motor traffic. This leaflet advertises a Sunday afternoon protest march in 1987.

An impasse was reached between the developers and the Borough Council, and in the end, the Environment Secretary in Mrs Thatcher's government, Nicholas Ridley, was asked to intervene. In 1990 he came down on the side of the developers, and the new houses were built.

The end result was not so bad as people had feared. Most of the vehicular access is from Kidmore Road, rather than Hemdean Road, and for pedestrians there is still the path running north from the end of Hemdean Road. From the path it's possible to reach Gravel Hill without seeing any houses at all. The Borough Council manages this Chiltern valley with not too heavy a hand, and the main path is shared between walkers, cyclists and equestrians.

133. This was Reading's first cemetery, set up by private enterprise in 1843, where the graves of many notable inhabitants can still be visited.

The burial of the dead had for centuries been the task of the church, but in Reading a new cemetery opened in 1843, which belonged to the Reading Cemetery Company until 1959, when it became the responsibility of Reading Corporation.

The table of charges and fees, part of which is reproduced here, is undated, and so may not be as old as 1843. Whenever it was, you could have purchased a family vault, to contain up to twelve coffins, for £7 10s., a 'brick grave' to contain up to six coffins for five guineas (£5.25), a private grave for three guineas, a compartment in a public vault for £3 13s. 6d., a 'common interment' in 'reserved ground' for £1, or a 'common interment' in 'open ground' for 5s. Some of these terms are not now self-explanatory. Vaults and 'brick graves' had brick bases and sides, and would have been covered by stone slabs or steel doors so that they could be re-opened for additional inhumations. The distinction between 'reserved ground' and 'open ground' is not obvious. It may be the difference between the part of the cemetery that was consecrated by the Bishop of Oxford for Anglican burials, and the other part that was not. Monuments were allowed at no additional charge, but were not allowed on 'common interments.'

This was what was known as a 'garden cemetery,' with paved pathways between the grave plots, two chapels (Anglican and Nonconformist), and was planted with trees and shrubs. Members of the public could wander round it on six days of the week, between 7 am and sunset. On Sundays, it was open only for funerals, and for visits from the families and friends of those interred there. Today, funerals are hardly ever held at weekends: at the time of this document, many people would probably have been reluctant or indeed forbidden to take the time off work on a weekday.

These 'garden cemeteries,' owned by private companies, were opened in many towns and cities around this time, because populations were increasing, and grave-space around the churches was already occupied. Human remains were being dug up and moved in the attempt to bury more recent corpses, there were bad smells and 'miasmas' hanging over graveyards, and there were concerns for public health. At Reading, the distance of a mile and more between the new cemetery and the town centre was seen as beneficial. But the Reading Cemetery Company seems not to have been popular in its early years. People liked tradition, they wanted to be buried with their families, and resented having to pay fees to a private company, so the initial uptake of graves was disappointing. Nevertheless, the cemetery eventually became the usual burial place in the town, and the cemetery gatehouse at Cemetery Junction, where the tramlines diverged between the London Road and the Wokingham Road, became a town landmark. As the 1843 cemetery began to become full, the Cemetery Company naturally lost its income, and the Borough Council took over the maintenance of the grounds in 1959. They are still a pleasant place to wander, with a gatehouse, old trees and interesting monuments, though the two mortuary chapels are now long since demolished.

1848 saw the introduction of Local Boards of Health, responsible for public health in their areas. They were a response to cholera epidemics which had first struck the country in the 1830s, and their work was directed by the General Board of Health in London. Though they met separately from town councils, the members of the local boards were nominated by the councillors. The council and the board remained as separate entities until 1873, when the two merged.

134. This petition of around 1852, or shortly afterwards, with the names of 282 ratepayers, asks for a new burial ground in Reading.

The printed petition appearing here, dating from around 1852, has the names of 282 Reading ratepayers. It asks the Board to delay the implementation of the recommendations of William Lee, in his *Report to the General Board of Health on an Inquiry respecting the Condition of the Burial Grounds in the District of the Borough of Reading*, published in that year. Mr Lee deplored the condition of most of the graveyards, which were 'in such a state as to be dangerous to the health of persons living in the neighbourhood thereof.' The decomposition of bodies gave rise to 'two deadly gases, to inhale which, even when largely diluted, is destructive to life,' and the report recommended that the existing burial grounds should be closed, except for those vaults and brick graves which were not already full. He also comments on the 'strong opinion entertained generally through the country that the burial of the dead ought not to be made a matter of trade.'

READING BURIAL GROUNDS.

TO THE GENERAL BOARD OF HEALTH, LONDON.

MY LORDS AND GENTLEMEN,

We, the undersigned Rated Inhabitants of the Borough of Reading, in the County of Berks, beg to represent to your Honorable Board, that we are anxious that a public Burial Ground shall be provided for the general use of the inhbaitants of this Borough, in which interments may be secured at reasonable rates and charges.

That we observed with satisfaction an announcement made by Lord John Manners, that it was the intention of the late Government to introduce a Bill into Parliament, to enable Local Boards of Health to provide additional Burial Grounds where a necessity for making such provision shall be found to exist, and from enquiries recently made in the House of Commons by Sir James Graham relative to such intended Bill, we have reason to hope that a similar Bill will be introduced by the present Government.

That if the recommendations contained in page 26 of the Report of WILLIAM LEE, Esq. to your Honorable Board, for closing the existing Burial Grounds in this Borough, with two exceptions only, shall be adopted, there will be no alternative for the inhabitants of this Borough except to avail themselves of the Ground belonging to the Reading Cemetery Company, and, inasmuch as that Company are not limited by either of their Acts of Parliament as to their scale of charges, we are apprehensive that if the existing Burial Grounds shall be closed the inhabitants of this Borough will be subject to much heavier charges for interment than are now required, as the present state of the affairs of the Reading Cemetery Company induce us to believe that such a result would of necessity follow.

That under these circumstances we respectfully request your Honorable Board will delay issuing your certificate as recommended by Mr. LEE, until the result of any Bill to be introduced by the Government into Parliament shall be known, as we think a Place for Public Interment should not be rendered a source of speculation or profit to any body of shareholders.

We have the honor to be,
My Lords and Gentlemen,
Your most obedient Servants,

Charles C. Bickham	John Maskell	James Greenway	William Phelp	J. D. Ruddock
D. S. Russell	S. Clayton	James Jones	Edward Pidgeon	John A. Taylor
J. W. Murray	Charles Sherwood	George A. L. Brain	J. W. Pidgeon	John Jenner
T. Crokine	Rupert Gurney	William Wilkins	William Paice	Gabriel Machin
John Turner	W. R. Buckridge	Henry Wheeler	E. Nixon	Robert Jenkins
Joseph Crapp	J. Goodwin Cooper	James Piercy	W. Munt	Robert Bradley
Joseph Leach	E. Keen	Daniel Reeves	Hoffman & Son	Richard Kimber
Francis Evans	Edward Lovegrove	William Gibbs	George Phillips	John Taylor
John Taylor	David Cook	Friend Clements	Alfred Thomson	John J. Tagg

The signatories were hoping for a new Act of Parliament which would enable the Reading Local Board of Health to provide a place of public interment. Their fear was that once the Reading Cemetery Company had a near monopoly on burials, they would increase their charges.

The petition appears to have been unsuccessful. Though an Act of 1857 allowed Local Burial Boards to be set up, it was only an enabling Act. Most of the old Reading burial grounds were closed. Land was found for extension graveyards in Tilehurst and Caversham, but in the town itself, the Cemetery Company had its near monopoly – until Reading Corporation opened the Reading Municipal Cemetery, in Caversham, in 1927.

On a more cheerful note, this chapter ends with two documents resulting from town twinning. In all, Reading has no fewer than 4 official twin towns. The idea of one town being officially twinned with one in another country became common following the Second World War. It was a matter of a town or city, through its mayor and corporation, holding out a hand of friendship to one which had been devastated by war, bringing about a measure of reconciliation between people in countries which had fought on the 'other side,' and fostering international relations, visits, culture and trade.

It was usual, in twinning arrangements, for the two towns or cities to have something in common, but the Reading-Düsseldorf twinning was different. Düsseldorf was a large industrial city which had been devastated by bombing, whereas Reading had escaped comparatively lightly. And Düsseldorf had more than three times the population of Reading.

The Reading-Düsseldorf Link was established by Phoebe Cusden in 1947, during her mayoral year. It was an informal arrangement which was made 'official' only in 1975. At the end of the Second World War, Düsseldorf was occupied by the Royal Berkshire Regiment, and Major-General Collins appealed for food and clothing to alleviate the suffering caused by bombing, homelessness and starvation. Mrs Cusden went to Düsseldorf to see for herself, and returned to organise the sending out of relief supplies, bringing six German children with her, to stay for a holiday. Return visits were arranged, and the movement grew from there – though naturally this did not please those in Reading for whom

Opposite page:
135. The Reading–Düsseldorf Link was first forged by Phoebe Cusden, one of Reading's most remarkable women.

136. The twinning between Reading and San Francisco Libre in 1988 was formalised in 1994.

Germany was still 'the enemy.' Mrs Cusden was an indefatigable campaigner for peace, women's rights, nursery education, and nuclear disarmament.

The booklet illustrated opposite contains the order of service in St Mary's Church to mark the 40th anniversary of the association. Worship began with the congregation standing for the arrival of the procession, headed by the Oberbürgermeister of Düsseldorf and the Mayor of Reading. The Rector and Vicar of the Minster Church, and the Bishop of Reading led the worship. The Chairman of the Reading and District Council of Churches and the Roman Catholic Dean of Reading read the lessons, the prayers were led by the President of the Reading Free Church Council, and Pastor Klaus Dedring gave the sermon.

Mrs Cusden is commemorated by a blue plaque on her former house in Castle Street, and the 30th anniversary of the forging of the Link was commemorated by a sculpture of a cartwheeling boy – the emblem of Düsseldorf. The sculpture stood by the Civic Offices until 2014, when they were demolished, and then stood by the hole in the ground, where the water feature once was, only to be itself demolished, by a storm in February 2022.

Since the 1947 Düsseldorf Link, in Reading there have been three further twinnings – with San Francisco Libre in Nicaragua in 1988, Clonmel in the Irish Republic in 1994, and Speightstown, Barbados, in 2003.

This San Francisco Libre Association leaflet explains its aims, and invites people to join it, or to request further information. The return address is the Reading International Support Centre (often referred to as RISC) in London Street. Whereas Düsseldorf now has a population of over 600,000, and Reading has a population of around 140,000, San Francisco Libre, together with surrounding areas, has only around 10,000 souls.

The Association was formed to support the small farming community in Nicaragua, and to work with the Mayor, Manuel Espinoza, and the Catholic priest, the extraordinarily-named Father Bismarck Antonio Castro Gomez. Their town had suffered greatly under the Samoza dictatorship, and although things had improved since the Sandinista Revolution, the country was still ravaged by war, hurricane and drought.

Money raised in Reading was used to pay for practical projects such as repairing a bridge and building a new classroom, and sponsoring a cultural exchange for young people. Youngsters here attended classes to learn about

THANKSGIVING SERVICE

For the 40th Anniversary
of the
READING-DÜSSELDORF LINK

Sunday, 26th April, 1987

at
THE MINSTER CHURCH
of
ST. MARY THE VIRGIN
in
READING

READING - SAN FRANCISCO LIBRE ASSOCIATION

Since 1988, Reading has been linked with San Francisco Libre n Nicaragua. This is a small town and surrounding districts with a population of 13,000 people.

The Reading-San Francisco Libre Association works to
- support projects in San Francisco Libre;
- to create in Reading, interest and awareness of SFL and Nicaragua generally

Nicaragua, to learn Spanish, and to learn how to ride a horse – and they had to raise some of the funding for themselves.

The Association was to be particularly active following a hurricane in 1998, when the Mayor of Reading, David Geary, led the fund-raising, and more than £13,000 was raised in less than two weeks. Initially, food was required, and then shelters, since many homes had been destroyed by flooding.

Opposite page:
137. This tract claims to have been written 'to un-deceive People from the lying reports raised by the Malignants'.

XVII. War and peace

This chapter looks at documents representing Reading's involvement in wars, and in the awarding of medals, peace celebrations, and war memorials, from the seventeenth century to the twentieth.

We begin by looking at the cover of a small, flimsy booklet which reported on the progress of the Civil War in 1643. Reading Central Library has a collection of over 30 of them, some issued by the Royalists and some by the Parliamentarians. They were written from several Berkshire towns – Abingdon, Newbury and Wallingford, as well as Reading. These Civil War Tracts were printed in London, carrying news with a strong element of propaganda.

Titles for the Parliamentary side include *Another Happy Victorie obtained by His Excellency the Earle of Essex, Decemb. 21, with 7,000 men … against 9,000 of the King's Army*, and *Good and True Intelligence from Reading, being a true relation of two late fights between the Parliament Forces and the Malignants*. (The population of Reading at the time was around 5,000.) From the Royalists we have: *A True Relation of the Taking of the Close at Lichfield by Prince Rupert … with the whole Proceedings of both Armies at Redding until the present Tuesday*.

In the example illustrated, the fortifications at Reading, 'as impregnable as Art can make them,' are described, together with the siege of April 1643.

Reading sat uneasily between the king's headquarters in Oxford, and Windsor which was held by the Parliamentarians. It changed hands four times during the conflict. Fortifications were erected round it, Caversham Bridge was partly demolished, and heavy artillery was set up on the fortifications and on Cawsam [Caversham] Hill. Each invading army demanded accommodation, food and money from the citizens, and they brought overcrowding and disease with them. Another tract, entitled *The Second Intelligence from Reading*, says: 'As for the town, we understand the state of it to be full of wants, both in provision and ammunition.'

Our next item dates from 1794, when the First Company of Reading Volunteers was formed, as a response to the threat of invasion from across the Channel during the French Revolutionary Wars and Napoleonic Wars. They were a part-time force, and must have been rather like the Home Guard in the Second World

Good and true Newes
FROM
REDDING,
BEING
An exact Relation of the proceedings of his Excellence the Earl of ESSEX, since he advanced from *Windsore*, the true estate of the Siege, what number of men slain, what Workes his Excellency hath gained from the Enemy, in what possibility he is of taking the town, faithfully related.

With a true Relation of the accesse of Forces to the Lord Generall, since his going before *Redding*.

Printed at the desires of many, to un-deceive the People, from the lying reports raised by Malignants.

LONDON
Printed for *J. G.* to be sold at the *Galley* in Corn-hill. 1643.

AT a *numerous Meeting* of the Volunteer Association of the Borough of *Reading*, held at the *Upper Ship* Inn, on *Tuesday*, the 16th instant, the following Resolutions were unanimously entered into:

RESOLVED, That this Meeting disapprove of any Persons being named to hold Commissions in the Volunteer Association of this Town, as premature, before this Corps was called together.

RESOLVED, That the Officers do consist of Gentlemen and principal Tradesmen above the Age of 30, and that no one holding a Commission in the Navy or in any Regiment, either Regulars or Militia, be recommended to his Majesty to hold a Commission in his Corps.

RESOLVED, That the Chairman do sign the above Resolutions in the Name of the Meeting.

Henry Smith.

R. Sare and Co. Printers, Reading.

Opposite page:
138. An intriguing scrap of paper: unfortunately, the *Reading Mercury* did not report on the meeting at the Upper Ship Inn.

War. Their task was to maintain peace and good order, in Reading and for six miles round the town. The first volunteers were gentlemen and the owners of businesses, who could afford their own uniforms and who were not tied to working for an employer. The later companies had their uniforms paid for by public subscription, and were paid two shillings a week by the government. We find the Reading Volunteers, together with the Woodley Volunteer Cavalry, assembled on Bulmershe Heath for training and inspection in 1798 and 1799.

The complete story behind this crumpled notice has proved hard to ascertain. There has obviously been a meeting of the Volunteer Association, at the Upper Ship Inn in Duke Street. (The Ibis Styles Hotel and Royal Tandoori Restaurant are now on the site.) It appears that the association is newly formed, and that recently-retired officers from the regular Army, the Militia and the Royal Navy have assumed that they have priority for the officers' posts in the volunteers, and the meeting has not welcomed them.

The document bears the name of Henry Smith, the Chairman of the Association, and someone has written what looks like 'St Mary 217' below. There was a Henry Smith, a clock and watchmaker, in Minster Street, in 1793.

On the back, 'The Revd. Wm. Marsh, Chaplain' is written in large letters, so he was probably the intended recipient of this copy of the notice, though a connection between a clergyman with this name and Reading has not been found around this time.

Then below are written six names in smaller handwriting, who are presumably among the members of the Association – John Valpy, B. Simonds, Wm. Stephens, Horace Man, John Biggs and Joseph Hawthorne. John Valpy was probably a relative of Dr. Richard Valpy, Headmaster of Reading School – though his son, Abraham John Valpy, was not born until 1786 and would have been too young in 1794 to have joined the Association. Similarly, Horace Man, the son of John Man the local historian, was born in 1782 and would also have been too young. Blackall Simonds (p. 109–10) and William Stephens were brewers at this time, John Biggs was a solicitor who died in 1840, and Joseph Hawthorne was described as a 'gentleman' when he joined the committee of the Reading Dispensary in 1826. So, for the time being, the exact significance of this notice, and the identities of the people named on the back, have proved elusive.

Opposite page:
139. It seems curious that the Mayor of Reading felt compelled to go to London in order to decide what action to take with regard to victory celebrations.

The main players in the Crimean War, 1854–56, were Russia, France, the United Kingdom and the Ottoman Empire, all with their own interests in the future of that Empire. Turkey had been nicknamed 'The Sick Man of Europe.' Russia wished to expand its territory southwards, and to control the Black Sea. In this country, people may at first have been enthusiastic about the war, but as time went on, and newspaper reports of disasters and incompetence (including the Charge of the Light Brigade) came in, the war became more and more unpopular. In 2023 it is interesting to see what happened to the Crimea subsequently.

Following the victory in 1856, the mayor made it his duty to ascertain the wishes of the citizens of Reading, and concluded that 'the wish appears to be very general that there should be an entire cessation of Business on the 29th; so as to make it, in reality, a general holiday in this Town.' The major employers had already agreed to give their workers the day off, and all tradesmen were now invited to close their shops, so that their employees could take the day off. The pages of the *Reading Mercury* show that in neighbouring towns, similar things happened.

Compared with the endings of the twentieth century World Wars, in Reading it seems likely that not many families would have experienced tragedy directly, and no elaborate celebrations were planned. As the mayor wrote at the end of this notice, the holiday was granted so that people could 'use the day in any way they may choose, for their own comfort and enjoyment.'

Nevertheless, meetings were hurriedly called, and subscriptions collected. On the day, there was a procession of school children and friendly societies, accompanied by three bands of musicians. There were some rustic sports, including bobbing for treacled rolls, and climbing the greasy pole for a leg of mutton, and at tea time, tables were set up in the Town Hall, the New Hall (in London Street), the Corn Exchange and the General Market (see p. 4–7), and around 4,000 people enjoyed tea and cake. The inmates of the workhouse were given a good dinner. As night fell, some of the buildings in the town centre were illuminated, and there was a firework display – though the fireworks were described as 'few and very far between.'

There was, however, to be a longer-lasting souvenir of this war: the town was presented with a Russian cannon, captured at the Siege of Sebastopol. It was

PEACE
CELEBRATION!

FELLOW TOWNSMEN,

Having felt desirous to ascertain accurately the intentions of the Government with reference to the 29th of May, I proceeded to London yesterday with this view, and, on enquiry at the Home Office, was informed that the Government do not contemplate taking any step to constitute the day in question *a holiday bylaw;* but prefer leaving the various Towns throughout the Kingdom to adopt their own course on the subject.

I have therefore made it my duty, this day, to ascertain, as f... ...inhabitants of this Borough, and, I am happy to say, that the wish appears to be very general that there should be an entire suspension of Business on the 29th; so as to make it, in reality, a general holiday in this Town.

Under these circumstances I do not hesitate to invite the Tradesmen of the Town to close their shops on the 29th inst. and the inhabitants gene-

140. Donations, by cheque or postal order, were to be sent to John Simonds, at the bank of J. & C. Simonds in King Street.

placed on Forbury Hill, and remained there until around 1941, when it was taken for scrap metal, to be used to fight another war.

The 'Maiwand Lion' in the Forbury Gardens, restored in 2023, has come to be a symbol of Reading. It commemorates the officers and men of the Royal Berkshire Regiment who had been killed at Maiwand during the Afghan Campaign of 1879–80. The 328 names were recorded on a terracotta plinth, which supported the monument itself, an enormous and very masculine lion of cast iron. The lion was the work of the sculptor George Blackall Simonds, a member of the Reading brewing family.

Legend has it that he was ridiculed because lions did not stand in that position, and had they done so, they would have fallen over. It was also said that the lion had no tongue, and that the distraught Mr Simonds had committed suicide as a result of the criticism. The legend seems to be at odds with the

---

ENGLEFIELD HOUSE, READING.
20th November, 1909.

DEAR SIR,

For some time past the pedestal of the Maiwand Memorial in the Forbury Gardens at Reading has been in an unsatisfactory condition.

As you may be aware this pedestal is faced with terra-cotta and owing to the action of the weather the names of the officers, non-commissioned officers and men recorded upon it are becoming obliterated. The perishable nature of terra-cotta renders it desirable that the pedestal should be cased in some more durable material and I therefore convened a meeting of a few of those specially interested in the matter for the purpose of considering what should be done in regard to it. At this meeting a Committee, consisting of myself, the Mayor of Reading, the Right Hon. G. W. Palmer, Col. Victor Van der Weyer, Col. Colebrooke Carter, Major Maurice, Mr. John Simonds, and Alderman Milsom (the Chairman of the Parks and Pleasure Grounds Committee of the Reading Town Council), was constituted for the purpose of raising a fund to carry out a scheme which Mr. G. W. Webb, F.R.I.B.A., of Reading, has prepared, at my request, for casing the pedestal in Portland stone and attaching to the stone either gun-metal or bronze panels bearing the names and inscriptions recorded on the present terra-cotta surface. The carrying out of this scheme will involve an expenditure of about £600, and I ask the people of Berkshire to provide this amount in order that the names of those who fell at Maiwand may be perpetuated in a suitable manner in the County Town.

truth: Mr Simonds had made a point of studying lions, their muscles and how they walked and stood, at London Zoo, and had gone on to win commissions for further monuments.

By 1909, the terracotta plinth had weathered badly, and the names of the fallen were flaking away. A Maiwand Memorial Restoration Fund was established, with the Lord Lieutenant of Berkshire, J. Herbert Benyon, of Englefield House, as its chairman. The local architect, George William Webb, had drawn up plans for the terracotta plinth to be encased in Portland stone, with metal plaques attached recording the 328 names of the fallen, at an estimated cost of £600. This was 'in order that the names of those who fell at Maiwand may be perpetuated in a suitable manner in the County Town.'

This letter, beginning 'Dear Sir,' was sent out by the Lord Lieutenant to elicit donations towards the restoration of the monument which had stood in the Forbury Gardens since 1886. The money was readily forthcoming, and the monument was re-dedicated in the following year, 1910.

Whilst the foreign wars in Victorian times gave rise to the monuments of high-ranking individuals, it is unusual to have a cenotaph to officers and men in a public space at this time. The lion, 31 feet in length, makes the memorial even more impressive. It is very different from the First World War memorial nearby (see p. 230–1).

The First World War spilled over from Europe and caused unprecedented devastation around the globe. The first document resulting from the conflict dates from the early days of the war, when the Christmas of 1914 found the 'E' Company of the 4th (Imperial Service) Battalion of the Royal Berkshire Regiment in barracks at Chelmsford in Essex. This was a battalion which remained in Britain during the First World War, supplying 'replacements' to the other Territorial battalions. Any one of the men was presumably likely to be sent to 'the front' whenever the need arose.

The Christmas dinner included 'turkeys, sausages, plumpuddings, mince-pies, and dessert.' Around the cartouche in which the bill of fare is listed are the names of places from which the men had been drawn – Aldermaston, Hungerford, Newbury and Reading. On either side of the cartouche, a soldier has been drawn. The man to the left is handsome and smart, but the man to

Opposite page:
141. Inside this cardboard cover is a sheet of paper with a list, in alphabetical order, of the 162 officers and men of 'E' Company.

the right is anything but smart, wearing a baggy greatcoat and nondescript, but hopefully warm, headgear, and is peering through field-glasses over the top of his trench. The names of the regiment and battalion are enclosed in seasonal holly wreaths, and at the top, below a crown, is the emblem of the regiment, a dragon, and the word 'China'.

The emblem had originally been awarded to the 49th (Hertfordshire) Regiment of Foot, for their part in the Chinese Opium Wars of 1840–42, now regarded as a shameful episode in British diplomatic and military history. The 49th Regiment was amalgamated with the 66th (Berkshire) Regiment of Foot, in 1881 as Princess Charlotte of Wales's Regiment, which was re-named the Royal Berkshire Regiment (Princess Charlotte of Wales's) in 1921. The Regimental Headquarters were at Brock Barracks in Oxford Road.

The Royal Berkshire Regiment passed out of existence in 1959, when it was merged with the Wiltshire Regiment as the Duke of Edinburgh's Royal Regiment. This was merged in 1994 with the Gloucestershire Regiment to form the Royal Gloucestershire, Berkshire and Wiltshire Regiment, which is now part of another regiment known as The Rifles.

The town's most celebrated soldier in the war was Trooper Frederick William Owen Potts, who was awarded the Victoria Cross in 1915. Shortly before the award was made, Reading Corporation presented him with an address, on parchment and in a casket, in the Council Chamber. The Mayor, Leonard Goodhart Sutton, presented the address on Friday 3 December. It was signed and sealed by the Mayor, and the Town Clerk, Mr W. S. Clutterbuck. The sheet of paper reproduced overleaf was probably given to the councillors and others present as a souvenir of the ceremony.

The Victoria Cross medal was presented by King George V at Buckingham Palace on Thursday 9 December, and Trooper Potts was married in St Giles's Church, Reading, on Wednesday 15 December.

Before the war, he was living with his parents in Edgehill Street, and working at the Pulsometer Works (see p. 83–4) on Oxford Road. He joined the Berkshire Yeomanry, and by August 1915 was involved in the Gallipoli Campaign.

He was awarded the V.C. for 'most conspicuous bravery and devotion to a wounded comrade.' Although wounded in the thigh himself, he managed to

TEXT OF THE CORPORATION'S ADDRESS

TO

Trooper F. W. O. Potts, V.C.

OF THE BERKSHIRE YEOMANRY.

To Trooper FREDERICK WILLIAM OWEN POTTS, V.C.,
OF THE BERKSHIRE YEOMANRY.

WE, the Mayor Aldermen and Burgesses of the Borough of Reading in the County of Berks, acting by the Council of the Borough, extend to you a cordial welcome on your return to this your native town.

We heartily congratulate you upon your recovery from the wounds which you received in fighting for your King and Country and upon His Majesty's gracious pleasure to award you the Victoria Cross for most conspicuous bravery and devotion to a wounded comrade in the Gallipoli peninsula.

It is a profound gratification to us that a fellow townsman should be the recipient of this coveted distinction: the heroism for which it has been awarded affords us even greater satisfaction.

We trust that you may long be spared to enjoy the distinction and we desire to convey to you our earnest wishes for your happiness and welfare.

GIVEN under our Common Seal this sixth day of December, 1915.

LEONARD SUTTON, *Mayor.*
W. S. CLUTTERBUCK, *Town Clerk.*

L.S.

drag a wounded comrade, Arthur Andrews, who was unable to move, some 600 yards back to the safety of the trench, using a shovel as a kind of sledge. It took more than two days to accomplish – progress could only be made under cover of darkness. The story of this heroic feat became better known as the centenary approached, when the Trooper Potts V.C. Memorial Trust was raising the money for a permanent monument to him and to the Berkshire Yeomanry. The life-size statue of Mr Potts and his comrade, unveiled on 4 October 2015, can now be seen on the edge of the Forbury Gardens, opposite the Roseate Hotel (formerly the Shire Hall and the Forbury Hotel).

In 1917 the government launched a war loans scheme to bring in the money needed to fight the war. The Mayor of Reading sent out letters announcing the opening of an information bureau, and appealing to the patriotism of the townspeople. 'The Chancellor of the Exchequer,' he wrote, 'in his speech delivered recently impressed upon all citizens of this great Empire the duty of lending money to the State to enable this Government to carry on the War to Victory. If everyone will do their bit, the triumphant success of the loan will be assured and our country preserved for its own people.' One of the mottoes of the time was 'If you can't enlist, invest.'

The bureau was opened by Reading Corporation at 6 Broad Street in January 1917, to give out information about the War Savings Certificates and War Loans, and to promote the formation of war savings associations in the borough.

The Savings Certificates were for the smaller investor, who could obtain a card, and special savings stamps, from banks and post offices. Each card had 31 spaces, and when each of the spaces had been filled with a sixpenny stamp, the card could be exchanged for a certificate, worth 15s. 6d. After five years, the certificate would be worth £1 – an increase of just over 5% a year.

Though fighting ceased in November 1918, the Treaty ending the war was not signed until 28 June of the following year. Saturday 19 July was declared a national holiday, and the booklet illustrated overleaf contains the programme of events in Reading for that day. It cost twopence.

Opposite page:
142. The Trooper Potts pub in Basingstoke Road opened in 2016, but was re-named The Victoria Cross three years later.

143. In 1917 the Information Bureau shared the building of the United Counties Bank. It has been rebuilt since then, and in 2024 was unoccupied.

144. Though the armistice was in November 1918, the day of national rejoicing was not celebrated until July the following year.

Rejoicing began at 9am with the ringing of the bells of the three parish churches in Reading, and those of St Peter's, Caversham, and St Michael's, Tilehurst. There were bowls competitions during the morning at Prospect Park and Palmer Park, and the Mayoress planted seedling oak trees, which had sprouted from acorns gathered from the battlefield of Verdun, in Prospect Park and the Forbury Gardens.

Midday brought a procession of men who had fought in the war, who assembled at the barracks in Oxford Road and at Yeomanry House on Castle Hill, and joined together to march through St Mary's Butts and Broad Street to the Town Hall. After taking the salute, they were 'entertained to lunch' in the Corn Exchange (see p. 4–6 for the Corn Exchange).

The afternoon brought children's festivals in Prospect Park and Palmer Park, and aquatic sports at the Thames Side Promenade. These sports included rowing races, some for men only, and others mixed, with novelty competitions such as the mop tournament and the dongola (i.e. punt) race. They were followed by a parade of decorated boats. Music was provided by the Reading Temperance Prize Band, and there was also a Pierrot Pavilion on the Prom, with performances by Mr George Smith's Concert Party, and the Lal Edwards Vaudeville Six. After that came dancing, till 9.30.

Meanwhile, in Forbury Gardens, there was music from the Band of the East Lancashire Fusiliers at 2.30, and again at 7.30pm. (One wonders why they weren't playing somewhere in East Lancashire.)

The evening concluded with illuminations at 10.15 – 'The Town will be Brilliantly Illuminated with Red, White and Blue Flares from the North, South, East and West. The Forbury Gardens and The Warren, Caversham, will also be illuminated.'

The memorial to those who fell in the war took even longer – it was not unveiled until 1932. The card illustrated here has the order of proceedings on Wednesday 27 July, the date chosen because not only was it the 52nd anniversary of the Battle of Maiwand (see p. 224–5), but also early closing day so that shop assistants could join the crowds who witnessed the event. The first hymn began:

> O Valiant Hearts, who to your glory came
> Through dust of conflict and through battle-flame:
> Tranquil you lie, your knightly virtue proved,
> Your memory hallowed in the land you loved.

Then followed the Lord's Prayer, and readings from The Wisdom of Solomon (one of the books of the Apocrypha) and the Epistle to the Romans. The Chairman of the Memorial Committee, Councillor Sainsbury, called on the Lord Lieutenant, Mr J. H. Benyon, to unveil the monument, and the Last Post was sounded, followed by a minute's silence. After the dedicatory prayers, the ceremony ended with the singing of *O God, our Help in Ages Past*.

Soon after the 1914–18 War, war memorials, great and small, sprang up across the country. Towns usually had a monument in a prominent public space, funded by public subscription, and county towns were expected to have a memorial to the men who had lost their lives, across the county.

A Berkshire War Memorial Committee was set up, but met with some opposition. The sudden return of so many men from the war had given rise to unemployment in Reading. The Mayor had set up a Relief Fund to help provide food for those in need. At the proceedings on the first Remembrance Day, in 1919, held in the Market Place, protesters carried a banner saying: 'The dead are remembered. The living are forgotten.'

The committee had planned for a monument similar to the cenotaph in Whitehall, London, with a statue on top, costing £8,000. Subscriptions, however, amounted to only around £1,000, and the disheartened committee disbanded. After almost a decade, the Mayor of Reading, Councillor Frederick G. Sainsbury, realising that Reading was one of only two county towns of England not to have a county memorial, re-formed the committee in April 1931. Despite further opposition, a local architect, Edward Leslie Gunston, was commissioned to design a smaller monument, a simple stone pillar bearing a cross and the words 'The Glorious Dead, 1914–1918. To the honoured memory of the men of Reading and Berkshire who gave their lives for King and Country during the Great War.' It was set on a stepped stone plinth into which were incorporated floodlights, provided free of charge by the Reading Electricity Supply Company. The sculptor was John Harvard Thomas, and the monument was erected by local builders, Collier and Catley.

145. Most war memorials were unveiled in the 1920s. In 1932, the Lord Lieutenant, after unveiling the pillar, referred to 'delays now regretted which can now be forgotten.'

READING TRADES COUNCIL & LABOUR PARTY

SPAIN

How did Reading respond to the Spanish Medical Aid Envelope Appeal?

COME TO

THE LABOUR HALL

ON

SUNDAY, MAY 2ND
at 7 p.m.

WHEN

Miss Margaret Bondfield
J.P., LL.D.

Will hand over, to a Representative of the Medical Aid Committee a Cheque representing the proceeds of the Appeal

Speakers will include :—

D. N. PRITT, K.C., M.P.

AND

A MEMBER OF THE INTERNATIONAL BRIGADE
On leave from the MADRID FRONT

COME AND BRING A FRIEND

Arrangements will be made for an overflow meeting

Secretary,
Spain Committee,
56 Minster Street

J. Cusden & Co., 55 & 57 Castle Street, Reading

Opposite page:
146. One wonders whether the 'overflow meeting' mentioned at the foot of the leaflet was actually necessary on the night.

War had broken out in Spain in July 1936, when right-wing troops attempted to overthrow the recently-elected Popular Front government, starting in Barcelona, and spreading across the land. The government in this country pursued a policy of non-intervention, but as the news of fighting and atrocities reached us, there was great sympathy for those who were suffering, and practical help was given. In the end, after bitter conflict, the coup was won, the civilian government overthrown, and Spain was governed by the military, under General Franco.

The book by Mike Cooper and Ray Parkes, *We Cannot Park on Both Sides*, explains some of the complexities of the conflict, and describes Reading's response. Twelve or thirteen individuals from the town actually went to Spain, some in a fighting capacity, and others to give medical aid. Volunteers from other countries arrived as well, and together they were known as the International Brigades. Three of those who went from Reading did not return, and are commemorated by a monument in Forbury Gardens.

Other practical help was forthcoming. Across Reading, money was raised, and food and clothes were collected by volunteers going from house to house. The supplies were taken to the Labour Party headquarters in Minster Street, and every Friday were collected by the Reading Co-operative Society's lorries and taken to the London docks, for onward transport to Spain. Some of the money raised went to support Spanish refugees in this country, and the Reading Co-op ran a 'Milk for Spain' scheme, involving the selling of sixpenny tokens in their shops and by their milkmen.

This handbill is an invitation to a Sunday evening meeting, organised by the Reading Trades Council and the Reading Labour Party, in the Labour Hall in Minster Street. The hall disappeared to make way for The Oracle shopping centre, and stood on the corner of Yield Hall Lane, opposite the side of the George Hotel.

At the Sunday evening meeting of 2 May there were to be speeches, including one from a member of the International Brigades who was on leave from the Madrid Front. The highlight of the meeting was to be the handing over of a cheque, the proceeds of the Spanish Medical Aid Appeal by Miss Margaret Bondfield, the prospective Labour Parliamentary Candidate. The amount collected was disappointing: 'Only £70 Collected for Medical Aid' was the headline in the local paper.

Opposite page:
147. It would be interesting to know quite what 'watermanship' comprised.

The Second World War had been anticipated for some years before it was sparked off by Germany's invasion of Poland in 1939. It involved civilians more than the 1914–18 war, and was more 'scientific,' with the bombing of towns and cities. Reading was considered as a comparatively safe place, and suffered only one bombing raid with fatal consequences, in 1943.

The document illustrated here is the Certificate of Proficiency awarded to Lieutenant-Corporal Edward George Terry in 1944. He lived at 195 Caversham Road, had received two training sessions, on 25 April and 30 May, and was now authorised to wear the Proficiency Badge.

The 12th Battalion of the Home Guard was the Upper Thames Patrol, on the certificate referred to as the U.T.P., which seems appropriate since he lived near Caversham Bridge. The patrol had the use of various vessels on the river itself, and guarded the bridges.

The subjects in which Mr Terry had been trained were general knowledge, the use of a rifle, a mortar grenade and a sten gun, watermanship and map-reading. The subjects in which he had not been trained, which are here crossed out, are signalling, battlecraft, coast artillery, heavy anti-aircraft battery work, 'Z' anti-aircraft battery work, bomb disposal, 'M.T.', field works and first aid. (A 'Z' battery was a group of rocket launchers which fired a mass of unguided projectiles at enemy aircraft.)

The Home Guard had begun in 1940 as the Local Defence Volunteers, in response to the invasion threat. In July of that year, the name had been changed to the Home Guard and by 1942 it was not so 'voluntary'. Men between the ages of 42 and 51 could be conscripted, in areas where the Home Guard was under strength. It is not obvious why Edward Terry was receiving training right at the end of the period when the Home Guard was active. In Reading, their final parade came in November 1944, shortly before they were stood down.

The war dragged on for more than five years. The declaration of Victory in Europe on 8 May, 1945, led to general rejoicing. Japan did not surrender until 15 August. Then in 1946, the government declared a day of national rejoicing on Saturday 8 June. The notice illustrated overleaf, signed by Mr G. F. Darlow, the Town Clerk, a month before the event, was to let citizens know about Reading's contribution to the day. All the arrangements were not yet in place. Band concerts were

— A.F.W. 4026 —

Certificate of Proficiency
HOME GUARD

On arrival at the Training Establishment, Primary Training Centre or Recruit Training Centre, the holder must produce this Certificate at once for the officer commanding, together with Certificate A if gained in the Junior Training Corps or Army Cadet Force.

PART I. I hereby certify that (Rank) L/Cpl. (Name and initials) TERRY.
of H.Q. ~~Battery~~ 12th Berks (UTP) ~~Regiment~~ HOME GUARD, has qualified
Company   Battalion
in the Proficiency Badge tests as laid down in the pamphlet "Qualifications for, and Conditions governing the Award of the Home Guard Proficiency Badges and Certificates" for the following subjects:—

	Subject	Date	Initials
1.	General knowledge (all candidates)	30.3.44.	a.ellg
2.	Rifle	25.4.44	a.ellg
3.	36 M Grenade	25.4.44	a.ellg
*4.	(a) Other weapon STEN	25.4.44	a.ellg
	(b) ~~Signalling~~		
*5.	(a) ~~Artillery~~ (b) ~~Coast Artillery~~ (c) ~~Heavy A.A.~~ (d) ~~Bty.~~ ~~(e) Bomb Disposal~~	30.5.44	Mat
	(f) Watermanship, (g) ~~M.T.~~		
*6.	(a) Map Reading, (b) ~~Fieldworks~~ ~~(c) First Aid.~~	30.3.44.	a.ellg

Date 30.3. 1944.   Signature a.ellgalm Capt
                              *President or Member of the Board.

Date 25.4. 1944.   Signature a.ellgalm Capt
                              *President or Member of the Board.

Date .... 194....   Signature ....
                              *President or Member of the Board.

Date .... 194....   Signature ....
                              *President or Member of the Board.

Date .... 194....   Signature ....
                              *President or Member of the Board.

PART II. I certify that (Rank) L/Cpl. (Name and initials) TERRY
of H.Q. ~~Battery~~ 12 Berks (UTP) ~~Regiment~~ HOME GUARD, having duly passed
       Company   Battalion
the Proficiency tests in the subjects detailed above in accordance with the pamphlet and is hereby authorized to wear the Proficiency Badge as laid down in Regulations for the Home Guard, Vol. 1, 1942, para 41d.

Date 6.6. 1944   Signature L.T. James
                             Commanding H.G.

PART III. If the holder joins H.M. Forces, his Company or equivalent Commander will record below any particulars which he considers useful in assessing the man's value on arrival at the T.E., P.T.C., R.T.C., e.g., service, rank, duties on which employed, power of leadership, etc.

COUNTY BOROUGH OF READING

VICTORY CELEBRATIONS
8th JUNE, 1946

The CORPORATION OF READING desire to give public notice of the following arrangements in respect of the Victory Celebrations on Saturday, 8th June next.

THAMES-SIDE PROMENADE.

AFTERNOON. From 3 p.m. until about 5-30 p.m.

Water Sports, consisting of mop-fighting in canoes, pillow fighting on a pole, dongola punt races (teams of eight), double sculling races, etc. Boats and dressing accommodation for both ladies and gentlemen will be provided. Bathing costumes *will be required for some events* and entries will be taken on the afternoon. There will also be races for fours from local rowing clubs.

Band concert.

EVENING. Public dancing.

FORBURY PLEASURE GROUNDS.

AFTERNOON. Band concert.

EVENING. Public dancing.

In the interval between the band concert and the dancing it is hoped to provide a variety concert. It is also proposed that there shall be flood lighting in the Forbury Pleasure Grounds.

PALMER PARK.

The Victory Day Celebrations will be preceded on Wednesday, 5th June by children's sports. On the 8th June a sports meeting has been arranged by the Reading Athletic Club. A motor cycle gymkhana will be given by the South Reading Motor Cycle Club. A band concert will also be given. Mr. J. Woolls' fair will be in attendance, and during the whole of the following week, until the 15th June.

TILEHURST AND WHITLEY.

Band concerts will be given in the afternoon and evening in a park at Tilehurst and in a park at Whitley.

DANCE IN THE LARGE TOWN HALL.

A dance will be held in the Large Town Hall on the evening of the 8th June from 8 p.m. to 12 midnight. Admission to the hall will be free, but the numbers to be admitted will be restricted to 600, and when this number have entered the hall, no others will be admitted.

ENTERTAINMENTS FOR OLD PEOPLE.

A film will be shown and a concert given at Battle Hospital at approximately 3-30 p.m. on the 7th June, and at approximately 6 p.m. the same day at Woodley Institution. It is hoped that band concerts will be given in the grounds of Battle and Park Hospitals on the 7th or 8th June.

Arrangements are being made for extras for tea for the inmates of Battle and Park Hospitals and Woodley Institution.

STREET AND OTHER DECORATIONS.

Arrangements are being made for decorating the Municipal Buildings and Reading and Caversham Bridges. The Victory Celebrations Committee request that business firms will decorate their premises. A competition will be held for the best decorated streets. Entries for this competition should be addressed to His Worship the Mayor, Town Hall, Reading. The competition will be closed on Thursday, 6th June, in order that the judges may inspect the streets on Friday, 7th June.

ENTERTAINMENTS TO BE FREE.

In all cases, except the amusement fair at Palmer Park, the entertainments to be provided for the public will be free and no charges for admission will be made.

REFRESHMENTS.

The public's attention is particularly drawn to the fact that no refreshments will be available for sale in the various parks on the 8th June, and persons attending are advised to bring their own.

BONFIRES IN STREETS.

Bonfires in public streets will not be permitted and the police have received special instructions to see that this decision is enforced.

On behalf of the Victory Celebrations Committee,

G. F. DARLOW,
Town Clerk.

Town Hall, Reading.
10th May, 1946.

Opposite page:
148. Compared with the celebrations of 1919, those of 1946 were less lavish, caused to some extent by food rationing which was still in force.

planned for 'a park in Tilehurst' and 'a park in Whitley,' as well as in the 'Forbury Pleasure Grounds,' Palmer Park, and the Thames Side Promenade. It was hoped that there would also be band concerts in the grounds of the Battle and (Prospect) Park Hospitals, and at the Woodley Institution, where a film (unspecified) was to be shown, and where there would be 'extras for tea.'

The usual water sports would take place at the Promenade, and those intending to take part were reminded that dressing accommodation for both ladies and gentlemen would be provided and that bathing costumes would be required for some events.

The Reading Athletic Club was holding a sports meeting in Palmer Park, to be followed by a motorcycle gymkhana staged by the Reading Motor Cycle Club. Mr J. Woolls' Fair was to be in the park from 8 June for a whole week.

The evening entertainments included dancing outdoors on the Thames Side Prom and in the Forbury Gardens, and an indoor dance at the Large Town Hall. Admission to all events was free, except for the rides at the Palmer Park fair. At the Town Hall, admission was limited to the first 600 to arrive.

The Municipal Buildings and the Reading and Caversham Bridges were to be decorated, and there was a competition for the best decorated streets.

Compared with the day of rejoicing at the end of the First World War, this one appears to be more restrained. No procession is mentioned. No refreshments would be provided in the parks, and persons attending were advised to bring their own. There were no fireworks or illuminations, and bonfires in the public streets were not allowed – the police had been given special instructions.

Soon after the end of the Second World War, Reading found itself with two uncomfortable neighbours – the High Explosive Research facility of the Ministry of Supply on the old airfield at Aldermaston in 1950, which became the Atomic Weapons Research Establishment two years later, and the Royal Ordnance Factory at Burghfield in 1954. In the 1980s they were joined, a little farther away, by the Cruise Missiles of the United States on the airfield at Greenham Common.

In the early days it was the A.W.R.E. site which attracted national attention, with the Aldermaston Marches taking place over Easter weekends between 1958 and 1963. The marchers, of course, passed through Reading on their way from London.

Opposite page:
149. A grim reminder of the 'Cold War' and how things stood in 1982.

This frightening leaflet claims to be 'Disarmament Bulletin No. 1,' but is the only one to have found its way into the Library's Collection. It was produced in 1982 by Nuclear Information (Berkshire), with address P.O. Box 163, Reading. Readers are asked to send for more information, to send for more of the leaflets which they can distribute themselves, and to send donations.

The front of the leaflet has this grim map showing 'what the Government thinks will happen to Berkshire in a Nuclear War,' and on the back is a list of nuclear hazards in peacetime.

The likely targets in a war are Heathrow Airport, Aldershot 'the Home of the British Army,' Aldermaston (Atomic Weapons Research Establishment), Greenham Common, and High Wycombe. The Royal Ordnance Factory isn't marked on the map, though it is mentioned on the back of the leaflet. At the time of publication, the Cruise Missiles hadn't yet arrived at Greenham, but the computer complex controlling them, we are told, was to be at High Wycombe.

Among the peacetime hazards on the back of the leaflet are:

- Nuclear waste from R.O.F. Burghfield was discharged into the River Kennet.
- Nuclear waste from A.W.R.E. Aldermaston was discharged into the River Thames.
- The discharges could cause cancer in humans.
- The Thames Water Authority stated that they had no control over discharges from defence establishments.

There is a worrying section towards the end, called 'Accidents Do Happen.'

With the ending of the Cold War, the Americans took their missiles away with them in 1992, leaving most of Greenham Common a nature reserve, open to the public. The Royal Ordnance Factory is now the Atomic Weapons Establishment, Burghfield, and the Atomic Weapons Research Establishment is now the Atomic Weapons Establishment, Aldermaston.

It isn't clear who was behind the issuing of our last item, a postcard which found its way into the Library's collection in January 1983. There is no address or telephone number, and no invitation to join anything, or to send money. The design on the front shows the R.O.F. Burghfield as a shadowy and threatening

WARNING

This is what the Government thinks will happen to Berkshire in a Nuclear War

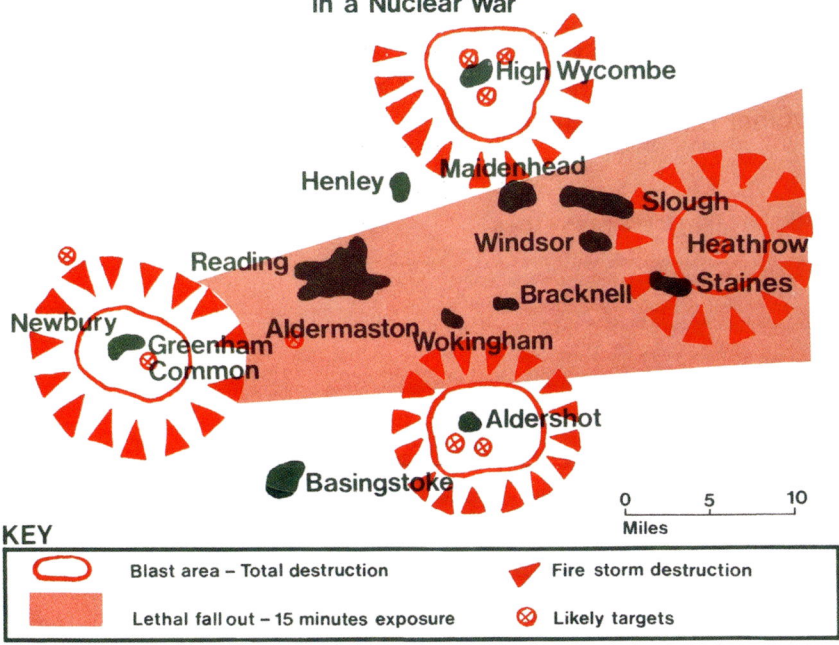

KEY

- ⬭ Blast area – Total destruction
- ▼ Fire storm destruction
- ▨ Lethal fall out – 15 minutes exposure
- ⊗ Likely targets

In Autumn 1980 the Government's widely reported 'Square Leg Exercise' aimed to test Defence Ministry plans in the wake of a nuclear attack on Britain.

The exercise considered only the most likely targets in any nuclear exchange, as based on official intelligence estimates. This gave a 'hit list' of 13 U.S. bases and key installations in the U.K. Berkshire would be hit by the following:

- Two airbursts over Greenham Common
- Three groundbursts on High Wycombe
- An airburst over Heathrow airport
- A groundburst on Newbury
- Two airbursts over Aldershot
- A groundburst on Heathrow

Each of these 'bursts' would deliver at least one megaton of explosive power. A megaton equals a million tons of TNT, about 65 times more powerful than the type of bomb dropped on Hiroshima.

* OUR DIAGRAM ILLUSTRATES THE EFFECTS

Greenham Common is the second most important target in the U.K. It will also be the site of the proposed Cruise Missiles in 1983. The computer complex to control the Cruise Missiles will be based at High Wycombe.

Berkshire is not without additional high risk targets such as Aldermaston and the Burghfield Royal Ordnance Factory. Hydrogen bombs are manufactured and stored at the Burghfield site which is within four miles of Reading town centre.

> QUOTE FROM ADMIRAL GENE LAROCQUE (Former strategic planner in the U.S. Pentagon):
> 'We fought World War I in Europe, we fought World War II in Europe, and if you dummies let us, we'll fight World War III in Europe'.

* The effects illustrated are those calculated by the Government in the official handbook 'Nuclear Weapons' published by the Home Office & Scottish Office Health Dept. available from Her Majesty's Stationery Office.

150. Though we may have become used to the 'Bomb Factory' at Burghfield, the nuclear threat still hangs over Reading, and, of course, the world.

place, its skyline punctuated by a crane and numerous chimneys. The back of the card tells us that in 1982, four members of the Burghfield Peace Camp were arrested for photographing and sketching the site, so perhaps the organisers of the Peace Camp produced the card. The lower part of the design appears to show a mushroom cloud above Reading, with burning buildings below.

Among the facts on the back of the card are:

- More than 600 people worked on the Burghfield site under heavy official secrecy.
- The site was removed from Ordnance Survey maps in 1980, and all road signs showing the location were removed.
- Heavily armoured convoys or lorries carrying radioactive materials and warheads regularly entered and left.
- An official statement of 1982 said: 'The function of the factory is the production and assembly of atomic weapons for the services.'
- In the event of a nuclear war it would be a prime target.

The R.O.F. Burghfield is now back on the Ordnance Survey maps, the road signs point the way to it, and it can be seen on satellite imagery.

Reading printers

Barcham and Beecroft
See p. 59–60

Edward Blackwell (later E. J. and F. Blackwell)
Edward Blackwell first appeared in the local papers as a bookseller at 31 London Street (now 64) in 1833, and in 1838 advertised his bookbinding service. By 1844, the business had moved down the hill, to No. 8 (now 20), where he was a printer, bookbinder, bookseller, stationer, and ran a circulating library. His sons, Edward John and Frederick Blackwell had joined the business by 1879. Around 1881 they opened a shop in the Market Place, trading as E. J. and F. Blackwell, while continuing to run the printing works in London Street. In 1899 they announced that the partnership was dissolved, with Edward John continuing the printing business in London Street, and his brother running the shop. The printing business last appeared in the local papers in 1901.

Samuel Bradley (later Bradley and Son)
Samuel Bradley set up his business in The Forbury in 1860. Three years later we find him, joined by his son, in the Market Place. Then, in 1920 the firm moved to Little Crown Yard, by the Little Crown Inn in Southampton Street. Little Crown Yard became Caxton Street. By the 1930s, they had come to specialise in high quality colour printing. With their take-over of Charles Elsbury and Sons and P. S. Lane in 1961, they could offer offset litho printing. The Elsburys were in Reading, at 25 Mill Lane. A move to larger premises was required, at first thwarted by the construction of the Inner Distribution Road, but around 1970 they acquired a new site, and were able to move into a new, purpose-built works in 1972. In 1976, Bradley and Son became a part of the Solicitors' Law Stationery Group, and they disappear from the Reading telephone directory between the 1984 and 1985 editions.

Castleden Press
At 57 Castle Street, this must have been the continuation of the business run by James and Albert Cusden (see below), after the retirement of Albert in 1952. It does not seem to have lasted long. In 1953 it was printing programmes for the Everyman Theatre, but the only mention of it in the local press is in an advertisement for the sale of a printing machine in 1954.

W. Clayton
William Charles Clayton was baptised in St Mary's Church in The Butts in 1823, the son of Charles Clayton, who was a printer at 24 Oxford Street. Charles died in 1841, and William can be found in local papers continuing the business in Oxford Street until 1851, when his address changed to 28 West Street. In 1852, he describes himself as a printer and music seller there, but disappears from the columns of the local papers after 1854.

Cowslade and Company (formerly A. M. Smart and T. Cowslade; later, H. and W. Cowslade)
The firm's main business was to edit and print the *Reading Mercury*, which had started in 1723. The ownership of the paper passed through many hands in its early years, and in 1762, it came to Anna Maria Smart, the wife of the poet, Christopher Smart. He had suffered bouts of mental illness, and at this time, was in a London asylum. Mrs Smart came

to Reading, and took an active role in editing the paper, while her brother, Thomas Carnan, looked after the printing. Following Carnan's death in 1785, Mrs Smart was joined by her son-in-law, Thomas Cowslade. On her death, in 1809, members of the Cowslade family ran the paper for the next hundred years or so. The H. and W. Cowslade, who printed the poster advertising the opening of the Corn Exchange in 1855 were Henry Hartley Cowslade and William Wallace Cowslade. Eventually, the paper was bought up by its rival, the *Berkshire Chronicle*, and both titles were published side-by-side for a number of years, until in 1987 the *Mercury* title was discontinued.

From the beginning, it was published from the Market Place, and there is evidence to suggest that the premises had previously been an inn called The Bible and Crown. They were rebuilt, in a grandiose Gothic style in 1874, a building which together with the equally grandiose Suttons Seeds building next door, was demolished around 1960. The office building with shops below, Soane Point, now covers the site.

James Cusden and Company

James Cusden was born in Reading in 1859, and attended the British School in Castle Street. He served as an apprentice printer with the Salvation Army Printing Works in London, then returned to Reading to set up his own business, the Victoria Press, 3 Queens Road. By 1917, J. Cusden and Company had moved the works to 55–57 Castle Street. After his retirement, the business was continued by his son, Albert Ernest Cusden.

Albert had married Phoebe Blackall, who as Phoebe Cusden became Mayor of Reading and established the town's connection with Düsseldorf (see p. 215–7). By 1930, he had opened up a stationery side to the business, and for a time he printed the Reading socialist newspaper, *The Reading Citizen*, which his wife edited. They lived in the same premises as the printing works. When Mr Cusden retired, in 1952, the company seems to have become the Castleden Press (see above).

William Drysdale

William Drysdale was one of the first proprietors of the *Berkshire Chronicle*, and also its printer. The paper was set up in 1825 as a Conservative newspaper in opposition to the Whig *Reading Mercury*. The offices were at 7 High Street – probably the same building as No. 7 today, listed and containing Perry's Caribbean Cuisine. His early departure from the *Chronicle* in 1826 may have been caused by two libel cases brought against the paper's proprietors. They had published a letter from a James Leach, the innkeeper of the Four Horseshoes at Whitley. His licence had been refused by the magistrates, and he made a scathing attack on them, and in particular on John Berkeley Monck, magistrate and Whig Member of Parliament for Reading. Drysdale and the other proprietors of the paper had to appear before the Court of King's Bench in London, where the case was dismissed, with no damages awarded to either side. Worse was to follow, as Drysdale and John Jackson Blandy, the remaining proprietors of the *Chronicle*, were prosecuted by a Captain Hall, a Whig supporter and churchwarden of St Mary's. Hall and a group of other men had helped following the overturning of a stage coach as it was turning from the Butts into Castle Street. The coach had been righted, the luggage had been rescued, and Captain Hall was given a sovereign, to be shared among those who had helped. Drysdale and Blandy had published a letter which suggested that the Captain had kept the sovereign for himself. The trial was held at the Newbury Assizes and damages of five pounds were awarded. Following the debacle, Drysdale left the *Chronicle* and set up as a printer, stationer and bookseller in Bridge Street. The last mention of him in local papers comes in 1830.

Charles Elsbury and Sons
See Samuel Bradley (see above)

Greenslade and Company
See p. 64

Knill and Sons
They took over the business of J. G. Wyly in Minster Street in 1883, and remained there until 1948, as printers, account book makers, bookbinders and wholesale stationers. Between around 1911 and 1949 they also had a retail stationery shop at 18 Duke Street, but the printing works was always at 38, 39 and 40 Minster Street, which must have been where Minster Court now stands – serviced apartments with shops below, opposite the back of the John Lewis store.

William Man
See Robert Snare and Company (see below)

Tom Morley
See p. 62–4

C. H. Nicholls and Company
See Petty and Sons Ltd. (see below)

Osco, Limited
When Philip Sizer retired as Chairman of Osco Ltd. in 1983, the local paper stated that the firm had been started by his father, and that his son, Simon Sizer, was to take over the firm from him. The printers and commercial stationers began at 47 London Street in 1932, where they were to remain for the next 57 years or so. In the dark days of the Second World War, they diversified, and were selling black-out paper, black-out felt, and anti-blast window netting, as well as writing-pads and envelopes, greaseproof paper and wrapping paper. By the end of the war, the emphasis was again on printing and commercial stationery, occasionally advertising in local papers when they needed to take on new staff. Then in 1989, Osco were advertising from Calleva Park, Aldermaston, and in 1993, they were in voluntary liquidation. Their London Street premises are now the offices of a firm of lawyers, N. C. Brothers and Company.

Parnell's the Printers
Parnell's started out, in 1900 or just before, in Mundesley Street, selling greaseproof paper and paper bags. This street still exists, though completely rebuilt in the twentieth century, leading off Southampton Street, just south of the Inner Distribution Road. In 1901 they moved to 34 London Street, where they advertised that their bags could be printed to meet purchasers' requirements. By 1907 they advertised themselves as printers, and continued as jobbing printers, producing tickets, handbills, letterheads, wedding stationery, etc., for the next 70-odd years. The 1976 newspaper obituary of Robert Parnell, master printer and Managing Director of Parnell's, stated that the firm had been started by George Bentley Parnell, Robert's father, and that it was now being run by his son. The closure of the firm, in 1983, could have been caused, at least in part, by the compulsory purchase of the premises, to allow the Inner Distribution Road to continue on its course from Southampton Street, cutting London Street into two.

Petty and Sons Ltd.

The firm had been established in Leeds in 1865 by John William Petty, and was opening works in different parts of the country around 1900. Two members of the family, Benjamin and J. P. Petty, opened a branch in Katesgrove Lane in Reading in 1895. Disaster struck in February 1900, when their premises burned down.

This was at a time when a buyer was being sought for the Queen's Hall, which occupied much of the northern side of Valpy Street. It was a large public entertainment hall, built by Robert Tompkins. With 750 seats, and a stage, in size it rivalled the Town Hall across the road. Tompkins' main claim to fame was his horse and carriage depository in Friar Street (see p.10–1).

After his death, in 1897, attempts to sell the hall as a going concern did not go well, and in 1900, Petty's bought it, and it became their 'Southern Printeries.' The premises in their turn were damaged by fire in 1920, but the business continued. It was taken over in 1936 by C. H. Nicholls and Company, but continued to trade as Petty's. In 1957, the decision was made to leave Reading, and transfer production to a recently extended works in Manchester. At the time the firm employed 120, some of whom moved to Manchester.

Most of the Queen's Hall was demolished in 1959, leaving one gabled section of the building standing, with the rest of the site being taken up by new Inland Revenue offices. The site of the offices has been redeveloped, but the gable still bears the initials of Robert Tompkins, the initials B.C., and the date 1770. Between the 1950s and 1980s, the building contained the offices of the Reading Newspaper Company, which published the *Mercury*, which started in 1723, and the *Chronicle*, which started in 1825. The 'B.C. 1770' harks back to a previous newspaper called the *Berkshire Chronicle* which had been founded in Wokingham in 1770 and closed in 1775. Petty and Sons continued in business in Yorkshire, until they became part of the British Printing Corporation in 1986.

E. Poynder and Son

See p. 60–2

John Read

The *Berkshire Telegraph* was announced in 1855, as 'a new Liberal journal for Berkshire.' Whether or not John Read was the first printer of this journal has not so far been ascertained. By 1870, he was printing the *Telegraph* from 8 Union Street. No copies of it seem to have survived locally: the British Library has copies from 1860 until 1873, when publication ceased. The title became merged with the *Reading Observer*, *Berkshire Telegraph*, and *Bucks, Hants and Surrey Paper*, with John Read as its printer. In 1875, the printing office of the *Observer* moved to 18 Kings Road. The paper closed in 1924, and a recent office block, The Carbon Building, occupies the site of the print works.

Reading Mercury Steam Press

See Cowslade and Company (see above)

Rusher and Johnson

James Rusher announced the opening of a bookselling, stationery and china and glass business in Castle Street in 1794. By 1796 he had moved to King Street, next to the George Inn and opposite the post office, and no longer sold china and glass. He opened a circulating library, and became a printer and publisher. From 1801, he became well known for his annual publication, *Rusher's Reading Guide and Berkshire Directory*, and was also a print-seller.

In 1823 he published the well-known *Twelve Views of the Town of Reading and its Vicinity*, by W. H. Timms, which have been re-published and appeared in books many times since.

He was joined in the business by James Johnson around 1827, and in 1833, Johnson married Rusher's daughter. After the death of James Rusher in 1837, Johnson continued the business until his death, in 1861, still trading as Rusher and Johnson. The last edition of *Rusher's Reading Guide* was published in 1856, the 1857 edition.

Anna Maria Smart

See Cowslade and Company (see above)

Robert Snare and Company

Robert Snare started in business around 1790, as a bookseller, bookbinder and stationer. He was living 'over the shop' at 16 Minster Street, but eventually was able to move to a house in Castle Street. He took William Man into apprenticeship in 1807. William was the son of John Man, schoolmaster, bargemaster and author. Snare and Man printed the two major books by William's father, *The Stranger in Reading* (1810), and *The History and Antiquities … of Reading* (1816).

Robert Snare also had an interest in politics, supporting the Whig cause, and was also an advocate for Parliamentary reform, printing election posters and pamphlets, some of them satirical.

At some stage, William Man left to set up on his own in Butcher Row in Broad Street. *The Epitome of the Benevolence of the late Edward Simeon* of 1812 (see p. 128–31) was printed by Man in Butcher Row, but *The Stranger in Reading* was published by Snare and Man from Seven Bridges. This was the area between Southampton Street and Bridge Street, where the Kennet and Holy Brook flow. He announced his retirement as a printer, stationer and bookseller, at 119 Broad Street, in 1831.

Around 1834, Robert Snare took his nephew, John Snare, into partnership, and they traded as Snare and Nephew, and then as R. and J. Snare. John continued the business after the death of his uncle in 1837, but his main interests lay elsewhere, and the firm closed down in 1849, when his printing equipment was sold off. A fuller history of the firm is given in an article by Diana Mackarill (see Sources, overleaf).

Richard Welch

When in 1837 he bought up the *Berkshire Chronicle* newspaper, he moved the offices from 7 King Street to 16 Duke Street, which had been the shop of a Mr Wrake, bookseller, stationer, printer, and circulating library. In 1844 he moved once more, this time 12 Market Place, the site now occupied by Stevenson's, school outfitters, which was very close to the offices of his arch-rival, the *Reading Mercury*. The *Chronicle* office remained there until the time of Mr Welch's death, in 1863. It was later to move to Valpy Street.

Sources

Airs and Places: People and Music in Berkshire. Reading: Corridor Press, 1999

Amyce, Roger. *Survey of the Borough of Reading*, 1552. Original document is in The National Archives, Misc. Bks. Land Rev. vol. 187, ff. 314–347. The local studies collection, Reading Central Library, has a transcription, and a hand-drawn map based on the Survey

Benham, Daniel. *Excursion to Reading, 1843 …* Manuscript, Local Studies Collection, Reading Central Library

Bowcock, Philip and Marr, Peter. *The Organ in Reading Town Hall*. Reading: Berkshire Organists' Association, 2000.

Burton, K. G. *The Early Newspaper Press in Berkshire*. Reading: the author, 1954

Childs, William McBride. *The Town of Reading during the Early Part of the Nineteenth Century*. Reading: Reading University College, 1910

Clark, Gillian. *Down by the River: the Thames and Kennet in Reading*. Reading: Two Rivers Press, 2009

Cliffe, David. *Picture Palace to Penny Plunge: Reading's Cinemas*. Reading: Two Rivers Press for The History of Reading Society, 2017

Cooper, Mike and Parkes, Ray. *We Cannot Park on Both Sides: Reading Volunteers in the Spanish Civil War, 1936–39*. Reading: Reading International Brigades Memorial Committee, 2000

Corley, T. A. B. *Quaker Enterprise in Biscuits: Huntley and Palmers of Reading, 1822–1972*. London: Hutchinson, 1972

Darter, William Silver. *Reminiscences of an Octogenarian*. Reading: printed at the Blagrave Street Steam Printing Works, 1889

Dearing, John, Cliffe, David, and Williams, Evelyn. *Abbot Cook to Zero Degrees: an A to Z of Reading's Pubs and Breweries*. Reading: The History of Reading Society, 2021

Dils, Joan. *Reading: a History*. Lancaster: Carnegie Publishing, 2019

Dils, Joan (editor). *Reading St Laurence Churchwardens' Accounts, 1498–1536*. Reading: Berkshire Record Society, 2013

Doran, John. *The History and Antiquities of the Town and Borough of Reading in Berkshire*. Reading: Charles Ingall, 1835

Earley Local History Group. *Sutton's Seeds: a History, 1806–2006*. Earley: Earley Local History Group, 2006

A Gentleman of Reading. *A Reply to the Dissenters on their Attacks on the Established Church: Addressed to the People of England*. Reading: printed by R. and J. Snare, 1835

Gold, Sidney M. *A Biographical Dictionary of Architects at Reading*. Reading: the author, 1999

Green, Roy, Brown, Jonathan, and Corley, Tony. *Barratt, Exall and Andrewes: The Reading Iron Works: the Firm and its Products*. Andover: The Road Locomotive Society, 2010

Hands of Friendship: the Story of Reading's Twinning Links. Reading: Corridor Press [c.2000]

Harman, Leslie. *The Parish of St Giles-in-Reading*. Reading: the Vicar and P.C.C. of St Giles-in-Reading, 1946

Hop Leaf Gazette: the Monthly Journal of H. and G. Simonds, Ltd. Reading: H. & G. Simonds, 1926–1960

Lacey, Paul. *Smith's Coaches of Reading, 1922 to 1979*. Wokingham: Paul Lacey, 2018

Lee, William. *Report to the General Board of Health on an Inquiry respecting the Condition of the Burial-Grounds in the District of the Borough of Reading*. London: Eyre and Spottiswoode, 1852

Macey, Thomas. *Jackson's: E. Jackson and Sons Ltd.: the Story of Reading's Oldest Family-Owned Department Store*. Reading: Thomas Macey, 2009

Mackarill, Diana. *Early Nineteenth-century Printers in Reading*, in *Berkshire Old and New* No. 25. Reading: Berkshire Local History Association, 2008

Mackarill, Diana. *A Reading Calendar*. Unpublished typescript, Reading Central Library

Man, John. *The Stranger in Reading*. Reading: printed by Snare and Man, 1810

Pevsner, Nikolaus. *Berkshire*. [The Buildings of England] Harmondsworth: Penguin Books, 1966

Phillips, Daphne. *Reading Theatres, Cinemas and Other Entertainments*. Reading: Reading Libraries, 1978

Phillips, Daphne. *The Story of Reading*. Newbury: Countryside Books, 1980

Piller, Caroline. *The Life and Times of Oliver Dixon; a Reading Horseman Remembered*. Reading: Vikenzo Books, 2020.

Rees, Norman S. *Reading College of Technology: a Brief Historical Introduction*. Reading: Reading College of Technology, c.1970.

Smart, James (editor). *London Street Described: a Reading Historical Record*. Reading: London Street Research Group, 2007

Smart, Pat. *Corn for Sale! The Markets and Corn Exchanges in Reading and Wokingham*, in *Berkshire Old and New*, No. 30. Reading: Berkshire Local History Association, 2013

Smart, Pat. *Reading Cemetery: a Private Enterprise*, in *Berkshire Old and New*, No. 5. Reading: Berkshire Local History Association, 1988

Smith, Sidney and Bott, Michael. *One Hundred Years of University Education in Reading: a Pictorial History*. Reading: the University of Reading, 1992

Stout, Adam. *A Bigness of Heart: Phoebe Cusden of Reading*. Reading: Reading-Düsseldorf Association, 1997

Summers, Malcolm. *Signs of the Times: Reading's Memorials*. Reading: Two Rivers Press, 2019

Sutcliffe Nigel. *Reading: a Horse-Racing Town*. Reading: Two Rivers Press, 2010

Tyack, Geoffrey, Bradley, Simon, and Pevsner, Nikolaus. *Berkshire [The Buildings of England]*. New Haven and London: Yale University Press, 2010

Vincent's: the First Hundred Years, 1867–1967. [Reading: Vincent's, 1967]

Waugh, Ellen M. *Lawrence Herbert Beecroft: an Entertaining Artist*. Randwick. New South Wales: Randwick and District Historical Society, 1997

Wilder, William C. *The Wilder Family*. London: Research Publishing Company, 1962

Online sources

www.berkshirehistory.com
David Nash Ford's Royal Berkshire History

www.reading.gov.uk/libraries
for the library catalogue which can be used to search the collection of local illustrations

Illustrations

RBL   Reading Borough Libraries

CES   Centre for Ephemera Studies
      Lettering, Printing and Graphic Design Collections
      Department of Typography & Graphic Communication
      University of Reading

1. 11¼ in × 8½ in. RBL
   Printed at the *Reading Mercury* Steam Press
2. 13½ in × 8¾ in. RBL
   Printed by H. and W. Cowslade, Market Place, Reading
3. 5 in × 8 in. RBL
4. 8¼ in × 5¾ in, 9 pages. RBL
5. The whole document measures 20 in × 11 in. RBL
   Printed by Bradley & Son, Market Place, Reading
6. 6¾ in × 4½ in. RBL
7. 6 in × 4 in. CES
8. 10 in × 8 in. RBL
9. Each stamp approx. ¾ in × ½ in. RBL
10. 7 in × 4¾ in. CES
11. 6½ in × 6 in. Author's collection
12. 10 in × 8 in. RBL
13. 11 in × 4¼ in. RBL
    Printed by Knill and Sons, Minster Street, Reading
14. 10½ in × 8½ in. Lent by a friend to the author
15. 5¼ in × 6½ in. RBL
16. 5¾ in × 3 in, 8 pages. RBL
17. 6 in × 7¾ in. RBL
18. 10¼ in × 8 in. RBL
19. 2 in × 3 in. CES
20. 4½ in × 2¾ in . CES
21. 14¼ in × 10¼ in. CES
22. 5¼ in × 8 in. CES
23. 7½ in × 7 in. CES
24. 8 in × 8 in. RBL
25. 8½ in × 5 in. RBL
26. Scan supplied by Thomas Macey
27. 8½ in × 4½ in. RBL
    Printed by Lamson Paragon, London
28. 4½ in × 6¾ in. RBL
29. approx. 4 in × 7 in . CES
30. 10½ in × 8¼ in. CES
31. 10¼ in × 8¼ in. RBL
32. 8½ in × 5¼ in. CES
33. 5½ in × 7½ in, folded leaflet. RBL
34. 10¼ in × 4¾ in. RBL
35. 8¼ in × 5½ in, 4 pages. Norman Wicks Collection, courtesy of the History of Reading Society
36. 7 in × 8 in. CES
37. Remaining portion of this calendar, 11 in × 12 in. RBL
    Printed by Barcham and Beecroft, and designed by Herbert Beecroft
38. 8 in × 5 in. RBL
39. 7 in × 4¾ in, card. CES
40. 7 in × 8 in. RBL
41. 7½ in × 5 in. CES
42. 5½ in × 6½ in. CES
43. 6¾ in × 8 in. RBL
44. 8¼ in × 6 in . CES
45. 10 in × 8 in. RBL
46. 10 in × 7½ in. RBL
47. 4 in × 4 in. RBL
48. 10¼ in × 8¼ in. RBL
49. 10 in × 8 in. RBL
50. 9½ in × 7¼ in, 28 pages. RBL
51. 9¾ in × 7¼ in, page from a catalogue. RBL
52. approx. 7 in × 5½ in. CES
53. 5 in × 4 in, folded pamphlet. RBL
54. 8¼ in × 4 in, folded leaflet. Author's collection
55. 3 in × 4½ in. RBL
    Printed by Cowslade and Company
56. 2 in × 2¾ in. RBL
57. 9¾ in × 7½ in. RBL
58. 13 in × 8½ in. RBL
59. 4½ in × 3 in, 128 pages. RBL
    Printed by Bradley, Reading
60. 5½ in × 2½ in. RBL
61. Scan from Gerry Westall's collection
    Printed by Bradley and Son, Reading
62. 8¼ in × 5¾ in, folded sheet. Author's collection
63. Scan from Gerry Westall's collection
64. 8¼ in × 5¾ in, folded leaflet. Author's collection
65. 8 in × 4¾ in. RBL
66. 4 in × 3 in, card. RBL
67. 6 in × 4 in. RBL

68. Scan of matchbox cover from Alan Bosher's collection
69. 3¾ in × 4½ in. RBL
70. 7½ in (diameter). CES
71. 9 in × 5½ in. CES
    Printed by R. & J. Snare
72. 7½ in × 5½ in. RBL
73. 8½ in × 5½ in. CES
    Printed by Parnell's the Printers Ltd.
74. 8 in × 5 in, folded card. RBL
75. 13¼ in × 8¼ in, folded sheet. RBL
    Printed by J. Read, *Berks Telegraph* Office
76. 7 in × 4½ in, folded card. RBL
77. 7 in × 4½ in, folded sheet. RBL
78. 10½ in × 8¼ in. RBL
79. 10 in × 8 in, folded sheet. RBL
80. The whole broadside measures 8 × 13½ in. RBL
    Printed and sold by J. Davenport, 6 St George's Court, St John's Lane, West Smithfield, London, where may be had the greatest variety of slips, collections, patters, etc.
81. 7¼ in × 5¼ in. RBL
    Printed by W. Man, Butcher Row, Reading
82. 8¼ in × 6½ in, folded leaflet. CES
83. 9½ in × 8 in. RBL
    Printed on watered silk at the *Reading Mercury* office
84. 15 in × 10 in. RBL
85. 10¼ in × 8 in, folded sheet. RBL
86. 11½ in × 9 in. RBL
    Printed by Petty & Sons Ltd., Reading
87. 8½ in × 5½ in. RBL
88. 8 in × 5 in. CES
    Printed by Cusden, Reading
89. 8¾ in × 5½ in. RBL
    Printed by the Castleden Press, 57 Castle Street, Reading
90. 4½ in × 5½ in, folded card. RBL
91. 8 in × 5 in, 12 pages. RBL
92. 9½ in × 6¼ in, folded card. Author's collection
93. 6¼ in × 8¼ in, folded card. Author's collection
94. 9¾ in × 7¼ in, 5 pages. Author's collection
95. Scan of item from John Whitehead's collection
96. 8½ in × 5¼ in, folded leaflet. Author's collection
97. 8 in × 4 in, folded leaflet. RBL
    Designed by Howard Bull Advertising, of Reading
98. 3½ in × 4½ in, folded card. RBL
99. 8½ in × 5½ in, 6 pages. Author's collection
100. 9½ in × 7½ in, 8 pages. RBL
101. 8¼ in × 5¾ in, 4 pages. Author's collection
102. 8¼ in × 4 in, folded sheet. RBL
103. 8 in × 4 in, folded sheet. RBL
104. Photograph of the original. RBL
105. 10 in × 6 in. CES
106. 3¾ in × 2¾ in. CES
107. 8½ in × 5½ in. CES
     Printed by Osco, Reading
108. 9 in × 8¼ in. CES
109. 7¾ in × 6¼ in. RBL
110. The whole poster measures 15 in × 10 in. RBL
     Printed by S. Bradley, Market Place, Reading
111. 10½ in × 8¼ in, 7 pages. RBL
     Cover designed by W. Blackwell, and the programme printed and sold by E. J. and F. Blackwell, Market Place
112. 4¾ in × 8 in. CES
     Printed by Greenslade and Company
113. 9½ in × 7 in, 16 pages. RBL
     Designed and printed by Petty and Sons
114. 9¼ in × 7 in, 16 pages. RBL
     Designed by Austin Knight, and printed by Bradley and Son
115. 7½ in × 4¼ in, folded card. RBL
116. 7½ in × 5½ in, 23 pages. Author's collection
     Printed at Petty's Press by C. H. Nicholls and Company
117. 9¾ in × 7¼ in, 48 pages. Author's collection
     Printed by Bradley's, Caxton Street, Reading
118. 8¼ in × 5¾ in, 20 pages. Author's collection
119. 8¼ in × 5¾ in, 24 pages. Author's collection
120. 8½ in × 5½ in, 48 pages. Author's collection
121. 10 in × 7½ in. RBL
122. 9¾ in × 7½ in. RBL
     Printed by Cowslade and Co.
123. 11½ in × 7½ in. RBL
124. 10½ in × 8¾ in. CES
     Printed by Drysdale, Reading
125. 9 in × 11½ in. RBL
     Printed by W. Clayton, printer and music seller, 28 West Street, Reading

126. 11¼ in × 9 in. RBL
    Printed by Rusher and Johnson
127. 13½ in × 8½ in. RBL
    Printed by R. Welch, Market Place, Reading
128. 9½ in × 7¼ in. RBL
129. 17½ in × 11¼ in. RBL
130. 8¼ in × 5¾ in, 34 pages. Author's collection
131. 8 in × 5 in. RBL
132. 11½ in × 8¼ in. CES
133. The whole sheet measures 8¼ in × 13½ in. RBL
    Printed by R. Welch, Reading
134. The whole document measures 17¾ in × 11 in. RBL
    Printed by Blackwell, London Street, Reading
135. 8¼ in × 5¾ in, folded card cover, 4 pages. RBL
136. 8¼ in × 5¾ in, folded leaflet. RBL
137. 7½ in × 5½ in, 5 pages. RBL
138. 8½ in × 7 in. RBL
    Printed by R. Snare and Company
139. The whole poster measures 15¼ in × 9½ in. RBL
    Printed by Blackwell, 8 London Street, Reading
140. 10¼ in × 8¼ in, folded card. RBL
141. 8 in × 6 in, folded card with a single sheet of paper inside. RBL
142. 10 in × 8 in. RBL
143. 13¼ in × 8¼ in. RBL
144. 8½ in × 5½ in, 16 pages. RBL
    Printed by Bradley & Son
145. 8½ in × 5½ in, folded card. RBL
146. 8½ in × 5½ in. RBL
    Printed by J. Cusden & Co., 55–57 Castle Street.
147. The whole document is 10¾ in × 7½ in. RBL
148. The whole poster measures 17½ in × 11¼ in. RBL
    Printed by Parnell's the Printers
149. 11¾ in × 8¼ in. RBL
150. 4 in × 5¾ in. RBL

Two Rivers Press has been publishing in and about Reading since 1994. Founded by the artist Peter Hay (1951–2003), the press continues to delight readers, local and further afield, with its varied list of individually designed, thought-provoking books.